MEMORY, EMPIRE, AND POSTCOLONIALISM

After the Empire:
The Francophone World and
Postcolonial France

Series Editor

Valérie Orlando, Illinois Wesleyan University

Advisory Board

Robert Bernasconi, Memphis University; Alec Hargreaves, Florida State University; Chima Korieh, Rowan University; Françoise Lionnet, UCLA; Obioma Nnaemeka, Indiana University; Kamal Salhi, University of Leeds; Tracy D. Sharpley-Whiting, Hamilton College; Frank Ukadike, Tulane University

*See www.lexingtonbooks.com/series for the series description and
a complete list of published titles.*

Recent and Forthcoming Titles

French Civilization and Its Discontents: Nationalism, Colonialism, Race,
edited by Tyler Stovall and Georges Van Den Abbeele

*After the Deluge: New Perspectives on Postwar French Intellectual and Cultural
History,* edited by Julian Bourg, afterword by François Dosse

Remnants of Empire in Algeria and Vietnam: Women, Words, and War,
by Pamela A. Pears

*Packaging Post/Coloniality: The Manufacture of Literary Identity in the
Francophone World,* by Richard Watts

The Production of the Muslim Woman: Negotiating Text, History, and Ideology,
by Lamia Ben Youssef Zayzafoon

France and "Indochina": Cultural Representations, edited by Kathryn Robson and
Jennifer Yee

Against the Postcolonial: "Francophone" Writers at the Ends of French Empire,
by Richard Serrano

Youth Mobilization in Vichy Indochina and Its Legacies, 1940 to 1970,
by Anne Raffin

Afrique sur Seine: A New Generation of African Writers in Paris, by Odile
Cazenave

Memory, Empire, and Postcolonialism: Legacies of French Colonialism,
edited by Alec G. Hargreaves

Ouregano: A Novel, by Paule Constant, translated and annotated
by Margot Miller, and introduced by Claudine Fisher

Contents

Part III: Postcolonial Migration

MEMORY, EMPIRE, AND POSTCOLONIALISM

Legacies of French Colonialism

Edited by
Alec G. Hargreaves

LEXINGTON BOOKS

A Divison of
ROWMAN & LITTLEFIELD PUBLISHERS, INC.
Lanham • Boulder • New York • Toronto • Oxford

LEXINGTON BOOKS

A division of Rowman & Littlefield Publishers, Inc.
A wholly owned subsidary of The Rowman & Littlefield Publishing Group, Inc.
4501 Forbes Boulevard, Suite 200
Lanham, MD 20706

PO Box 317
Oxford
OX2 9RU, UK

British Library Cataloguing in Publication Information Available

Library of Congress Cataloging-in-Publication Data

Memory, empire, and postcolonialism : legacies of French colonialism / edited by
  Alec G. Hargreaves.
    p. cm. — (After the empire)
  Includes bibliographical references and index.
  ISBN 0-7391-0820-4 (cloth : alk. paper) — ISBN 0-7391-0821-2 (pbk. : alk. paper)
    1. French literature—French-speaking countries—History and criticism. 2.
Postcolonialism—French-speaking countries. 3. Postcolonialism in literature. 4.
France—Colonies—History. I. Hargreaves, Alec G. II. Series.
  PQ3897.M46 2005
  840.9'358—dc22   2005009044

Printed in the United States of America

♾™ The paper used in this publication meets the minimum requirements of American
National Standard for Information Sciences—Permanence of Paper for Printed Library
Materials, ANSI/NISO Z39.48-1992.

List of Figures

Introduction

Alec G. Hargreaves

ON THE EVE OF THE SECOND WORLD WAR, France stood at the head of a colonial empire that was second in size only to that of Great Britain, the largest the world had ever seen. Little more than twenty years later, both empires had been almost completely dismantled. The death knell of the French empire was sounded by the bitterly fought Algerian war of independence, which ended in 1962. Almost overnight, centuries of overseas expansion and rule seemed to disappear from public consciousness in France. Public institutions and buildings which had previously trumpeted the nation's overseas possessions were renamed so as to airbrush out any explicit reference to the colonial past. Paris's *Jardin colonial* (Colonial Gardens) became the *Jardin tropical* (Tropical Gardens); the *Musée des colonies et de la France extérieure* (Colonial and Overseas France Museum) became the *Musée des Arts d'Afrique et d'Océanie* (Museum of African and Oceanic Arts); the *Académie des sciences coloniales* (Academy of Colonial Sciences) became the *Académie des sciences d'outre-mer* (Academy of Overseas Sciences); and the former *Ministère des Colonies* (Colonial Ministry), already transformed into the *Ministère de la France d'outre-mer* (Ministry for Overseas France), became the *Ministère de la Coopération* (Ministry for Cooperation).[1] The marginalization of French colonialism in institutionalized forms of historical knowledge such as school textbooks and academic research programs was exemplified in the almost complete absence of any discussion of the overseas empire in Pierre Nora's highly influential exploration of *Les Lieux de mémoire* (Realms of Memory), the seven volumes of which were published between 1984 and 1992.[2] When, in the late 1980s and early 1990s, postcolonial studies became a major field of scholarly enquiry in the English-speaking

world, the terminology and problematics of postcolonialism (generally understood to span the colonial period as well as its aftermath) were largely shunned
in France.[3]

Two main sets of reasons may be advanced to account for this apparent amnesia. Firstly, it has often been observed that public awareness of the overseas
empire was never as deep in France as it was in Britain. Where Britain experienced an almost uninterrupted expansion and celebration of her overseas
possessions from the late sixteenth century to the early twentieth century,
France lost most of her first overseas empire before or during the Napoleonic
wars. The conquest of Algeria, starting in 1830, marked the beginning of
France's second colonial empire, most of which was acquired during the Third
Republic (1870-1940). There were deep divisions during the late nineteenth
century between those who felt the nation should focus its energies on recov-
ering the northeastern parts of France lost in the Franco-Prussian war of 1870
and those who believed colonial expansion could help compensate for the territories lost at home. Most historians agree that it was not until the interwar
period that the overseas empire ingrained itself to a significant degree on popular consciousness in France, most notably with the celebrations in 1930
marking the centenary of the conquest of Algeria and above all with the much
visited Colonial Exhibition of 1931.[4] By this time, a rising tide of nationalism
was already beginning to weaken the colonial edifice, which scarcely thirty
years later would end in the ruins of the Algerian débâcle.

If the shorter and more fragmentary nature of the colonial experience generated less extensive memories of empire in France than in Britain, a second
factor contributing to public forgetfulness lay in the unhappy manner in
which France was severed from her overseas possessions. While Britain di-
vested herself more or less voluntarily of her empire, beginning with the jewel
in the crown, India, in 1947, France engaged in a series of bloody and ultimately futile military campaigns, most notably in Indochina and then in Algeria, in unsuccessful attempts to resist decolonization. This made the loss of
empire all the more painful and humiliating, and by the same token engendered a widespread desire to positively repress memories of the colonial experience.[5]

If recent years have witnessed "the opening of the floodgates of memory
from the Algerian conflict"[6] and in a more general sense from the colonial period as a whole, at least three sets of factors appear to have contributed to this.
Firstly, while the initial instinct of many in France was to cast off or bury reminders of the overseas adventures which had foundered so traumatically,
France's continuing relations with former colonies inevitably kept memories
of empire alive even if these were not explicitly verbalized. It became a truism
to say that behind new forms of nomenclature such as *coopération* (coopera-

tion) and *francophonie* (the global community of speakers of French and efforts to unite them) lay the historical experience of empire, transmuted during the postcolonial period into a pattern of international relations which many have described as neocolonial in nature. Moreover, the new states built on the ruins of empire in Africa, Oceania, and elsewhere continued to base their claims to legitimacy on reminders of the dark days of colonialism and emphasized the fundamental importance of the struggle for independence in setting the terms for postcolonial nation-building. Thus if the "c" word was largely removed from French discourse, its semantic field nevertheless continued to reverberate in other ways.

The passage of time was a second factor contributing to the reemergence of the colonial past. Far from fading, memories of empire seemed to strengthen as the generations who had experienced the colonial venture advanced in age. This has been especially true of participants in the Algerian war, in the course of which almost three million young Frenchmen were mobilized and a comparable number of Algerians were displaced, while around half a million lost their lives.[7] Today, those who fought in the war are nearing old age and a growing number have become anxious to unburden themselves of secrets which they have kept for almost half a century. An early example of this was the 1992 documentary film *La Guerre sans nom* (The War Without a Name), in which Patrick Rotman and Bertrand Tavernier interviewed French conscripts, many of whom for the first time spoke openly of the use of torture during the Algerian war. In 2000, another major taboo was broken when an Algerian woman, Louisette Ighilahriz, spoke of the way French soldiers had systematically raped her and other women during the conflict.[8] Her testimony sparked off a vast outpouring of further testimony by leading participants in the war such as Generals Jacques Massu and Paul Aussaresses[9] and was followed by the publication of historical research documenting for the first time the widespread use of torture and other human rights abuses in France's unsuccessful attempts to keep Algeria under colonial rule.[10]

At about the same time, after decades of denial the French state at last began to publicly commemorate the Algerian war and the wider legacy of empire. In 1999, Parliament voted a law that for the first time publicly designated the Algerian conflict as a war (previously it had officially been referred to under the euphemism of "*opérations de maintien de l'ordre*" [operations for the maintenance of order]—hence its nickname as "the war without a name"). In 2001 the Socialist Mayor of Paris, Bertrand Delanoë, unveiled a plaque on the Pont Saint-Michel in memory of an unknown number of Algerians killed by French police during a pro-independence demonstration on 17 October 1961, the details of which had until recently been largely suppressed by the French state.[11] The following year, a national memorial to the Algerian war and the fighting which had preceded independence in the neighboring North African colonies of Morocco and Tunisia was inaugurated by President Jacques Chirac on the Quai Branly, close to the Eiffel Tower. The government also committed itself to support a *Mémorial national de la France d'outre-mer* (National Memorial to France Overseas) due to be inaugurated in Marseilles in 2007.[12]

A government decision to turn 5 December, the date on which Chirac had inaugurated the Quai Branly memorial, into an annual commemoration of those who had died fighting for France in North Africa reignited fierce disagreements among competing groups—French veterans' associations, *pieds-noirs*, also known as *rapatriés* (former European settlers), *harkis* (Algerian Muslims who had fought on the side of the French against independence) and others—concerning the most appropriate date for officially commemorating the Algerian war.[13] Another group of Algerian origin in France—economic migrants—had played a key role in keeping alive memories of the police killings of Algerian demonstrators in 1961. Those migrants had been the principal source of funding for the Algerian nationalist movement. Their children, popularly known as *Beurs*, helped to bring memories of the 1961 events back into public view through novels, films, and other public discourses produced as early as the mid-1980s.[14] The *Beurs* are the most visible part of a wider phenomenon that constitutes a third reason for the resurfacing of memories of empire in recent years. When the French quit Algeria in 1962, the last thing they expected was an influx of former colonial subjects following them to France. But that is precisely what happened, with economic migration from former colonies leading to the rise of now permanently settled postcolonial minorities originating in North and West Africa, the Caribbean, Indochina, and other regions formerly ruled by France.[15] These minorities—especially those of Muslim heritage—have become ever more visible reminders of France's colonial past. Significantly, when the government announced in 2004 that the historical importance of immigration—until recently another *non-lieu de mémoire* in dominant constructions of French history[16]—would at last be recognized with the opening in 2007 of a *Cité nationale de l'histoire de l' immigration* (National Center for Immigration History), the premises chosen to house the new institution were none other than those previously occupied by the *Musée National des Arts d'Afrique et d'Océanie*, formerly known as the *Musée des colonies et de la France extérieure*.[17]

Part of the thinking behind this venture was the hope that it might help to dampen public distrust of immigrant minorities, especially those originating in former French North Africa. Typical of the controversies that have surrounded these minorities have been the periodic eruptions of the Islamic headscarf affair, first in 1989, then in 1994 and most recently in 2003-04. Sometimes subliminally and at other times quite consciously, animosities directed against these minorities have been informed by still-unhealed wounds arising from the trauma of decolonization.[18] Thus, if, as has recently been suggested by leading historians of the Algerian war, it is now safe to say that the amnesia surrounding it has been overcome,[19] it is also the case that divisive memories of the conflict continue to fuel antagonisms between different groups now living in France.

The same is true of the wider field of French colonialism, where divisions between former colonizers and colonized continue to frame the memories of the now aging actors who participated personally in the last days of empire as well as the work of younger historians, writers, filmmakers, and others originating on different sides of the (post-)colonial divide. It is on the complexities of the memory work generated by French colonialism and its aftermath, and especially on the interface between political and cultural dynamics, that the present volume focuses. The book is based on a selection of papers delivered at an international conference on "Cultural Memory in France: Margins and Centers" hosted by Florida State University's Winthrop-King Institute for Contemporary French and Francophone Studies in 2003. Drawing on recent and current research, contributors show how the politics of memory in the colonial field are inflected by the cultural forms in which the past is represented and reworked.

The three parts into which the book is divided broadly reflect the chronological and geographical spread of the French colonial enterprise. Part I examines memories of the French presence in North America and the Caribbean. Sugar plantations and the slave labor on which they depended made Haiti, then known as Saint Domingue, the richest territory in France's first colonial empire until a slave revolt led initially by Toussaint l'Ouverture resulted in the creation of the world's first Black republic in 1804. The bicentenary of this event in 2004 typified the divisions that continue to mark commemorations of French colonialism and resistance to it in the Caribbean. Similar tensions had been apparent in 1998 during commemorations of the 150th anniversary of the abolition of slavery in France's overseas empire. Divisions of this kind are examined by Catherine Reinhardt and Nick Nesbitt in sculptural, pictorial, scholarly, and media representations of the struggle against slavery while Nicole Simek shows how Caribbean writers such as Maryse Condé are beginning to look beyond the binary division between former colonizer and colonized to embrace new horizons in a globalized world. Jean-Luc Desalvo, who highlights the profound sense of historical injustice felt by Acadian writers descended from French colonists expelled from Canada by the British in the mid-eighteenth century and who now consider their heritage to be marginalized as much by Anglophone Canadians as by metropolitan France, addresses France's faded legacy on the North American mainland. The case of the Acadians, like that of the *rapatriés* (repatriated European settlers) who fled Algeria in 1962, shows how certain colonizers, and not just the colonized, may come to be regarded as victims of colonial history.

Part II focuses on France's second colonial empire, the largest parts of which were in Africa and Indochina. Alison Levine shows how early twentieth-century cinematic representations of Africa lingered well after formal decolonization, enabling those who felt nostalgic for the colonial period to bask in the warm glow of sanitized images insulated from more problematic aspects of the colonial system. Hee Ko and Marie-Pierre Ulloa discuss the ways in which memories of the Second World War were deployed in support of their causes by different and sometimes opposing camps during the French-Indochina War of 1945-1954 and the Algerian War of 1954-1962. Joshua Cole and Sylvie Durmelat examine the ways in which torture and other human rights abuses have continued to weigh heavily upon memory work among historians and participants in the Algerian conflict, while Florence Martin and Mireille Rosello focus on recent literary representations of memories relating to the colonial period.

Part III examines the role of postcolonial migration in bringing memories of the colonized into the heartland of the former colonial power. Dayna Oscherwitz shows how these memories have helped to inform major debates over multiculturalism and the future of French national identity, while Susan Ireland and Janice Gross discuss recent works by writers of Algerian origin that have attempted to bridge some of the gaps which still divide the postcolonial world. The writers studied by Gross fled Algeria during the civil war that erupted there between Islamist insurgents and the army-backed government in the 1990s. Linguistic and other links inherited from the colonial period made it natural for them to seek refuge in France. By the same token, they constitute yet another reminder of a colonial past which shows no sign of fading from memory.

Notes

1. On public monuments in France relating to the colonial period see Robert Aldrich, *Vestiges of the Overseas Empire in France: Colonial Monuments, Colonial Memories* (Houndmills, U.K.: Palgrave, 2005).

2. Pierre Nora, ed., *Les Lieux de mémoire*, 7 vols (Paris: Gallimard, 1984-1992). The only chapter in this multi-volume work devoted to France's colonial past is that of Charles-André Ageron, "L'Exposition coloniale de 1931: Mythe républicain ou mythe impérial?" in vol. 1, *La République* (Paris: Gallimard, 1984), pp. 561-591.

3. Alec G. Hargreaves, "Ships Passing in the Night? France, Postcolonialism and the Globalization of Literature," in *Francophone Postcolonial Studies* 1, no. 2 (Autumn-Winter 2003), pp. 64-69.

4. Raoul Girardet, *L'Idée coloniale en France 1871-1962* (Paris: La Table Ronde, 1972); Charles-Robert Ageron, *L'Anticolonialisme de 1871 à 1914* (Paris: Presses Universitaires de France, 1973); Tony Chafer and Amanda Sackur, eds., *Promoting the Colonial Idea: Propaganda and Visions of Empire in France* (Houndmills: Palgrave, 2001).

5. Benjamin Stora, *La Gangrène et l'oubli: La mémoire de la guerre d'Algérie* (Paris: La Découverte, 1991).

6. Eric T. Jennings, "Remembering 'Other' Losses: The *Temple du Souvenir Indochinois* of Nogent-sur-Marne," in *History and Memory* 15, no. 1 (Summer 2003), p. 7.

7. On the complex and controversial question of the numbers killed during the Algerian war, see Guy Pervillé, "La Guerre d'Algérie: Combien de morts?" in *La Guerre d'Algérie 1954-2004: La fin de l'amnésie*, ed. Mohammed Harbi and Benjamin Stora (Paris: Robert Laffont, 2004), pp. 477-494.

8. Florence Beaugé, "Torturée par l'armée française en Algérie, Lila recherche l'homme qui l'a sauvée," *Le Monde*, 20 June 2000; Louisette Ighilahriz, *Algérienne*, récit recueilli par Anne Nivat (Paris: Fayard/Calmann-Lévy, 2001).

9. Florence Beaugé, "Le Général Massu exprime ses regrets pour la torture en Algérie," *Le Monde*, 22 June 2000; Général Aussaresses, *Services spéciaux en Algérie 1955-1957* (Paris: Perrin, 2001).

10. Raphaëlle Branche, *La Torture et l'armée pendant la guerre d'Algérie, 1954-1962* (Paris: Gallimard, 2001).

11. The events of 17 October 1961 have now generated a substantial body of scholarly and other literature. For an overview, see Joshua Cole, "Remembering the Battle of Paris: 17 October 1961 in French and Algerian Memory," *French Politics, Culture and Society* 21, no. 3 (Fall 2003), pp. 21-50.

12. "Un Mémorial pour 'Nous les Africains qui revenons de loin . . . ,'" *Le Monde*, 28 October 2004.

13. Philippe Bernard, "Le 5 décembre devient journée nationale d'hommage aux morts d'Afrique du Nord," *Le Monde*, 19 September 2003; Sylvia Zappi, "Polémique à Paris autour de la 'place du 19-Mars-1962' dédiée au morts d'Algérie," *Le Monde*, 22 April 2004. Cf Frédéric Rouyard, "La Bataille du 19 mars," in *La Guerre d'Algérie et les Français*, ed. Jean-Pierre Rioux (Paris: Fayard, 1990), pp. 545-552.

14. On the role of second-generation Algerians in constructing and transmitting memories of the Algerian presence in France, see Alec G. Hargreaves, "Generating Migrant Memories," in *Algeria and France from the Colonial to the Present: Identity, Memory and Nostalgia*, ed. Patricia M. Lorcin (Syracuse, N.Y.: Syracuse University Press, forthcoming).

15. Pascal Blanchard and Nicolas Bancel, *De l'indigène à l'immigré* (Paris: Gallimard, 1998); Eric Savarèse, *Histoire coloniale et immigration: Une invention de l'étranger* (Paris: Séguier, 2000).

16. Gérard Noiriel, *Le Creuset français: histoire de l'immigration: Histoire de l'immigration xixe-xxe siècles* (Paris: Seuil, 1988), pp. 13-67.

17. "Lancement de la Cité nationale de l'histoire de l'immigration. Discours du premier ministre, 8 juillet 2004, Palais de la Porte Dorée," supplement to *ADRI Info*, no. 275, 20 July 2004. On the relationship between history, memory, and immigration

see "Vers un lieu de mémoire de l'immigration," themed number of *Hommes et migrations* 1247 (January-February 2004), and "Mythe(s), mémoire(s), identité(s)," themed number of *Migrations société*, vol. 14, no. 84, November-December 2002. The role of second- and third-generation members of postcolonial minorities in pressing for more inclusive memories of French national history is typified by "Mémoires d'une France métissée," themed number of *Respect magazine*, no. 4, 2004.

18. Benjamin Stora, *Le Transfert d'une mémoire: De l' "Algérie française" au racisme anti-arabe* (Paris: La Découverte, 1999).

19. Mohammed Harbi and Benjamin Stora, eds., *La Guerre d'Algérie, 1954-2004, la fin de l'amnésie* (Paris: Laffont, 2004).

I

NORTH AMERICA AND
THE CARIBBEAN

1

Slavery and Commemoration

Remembering the French Abolitionary Decree 150 Years Later

Catherine Reinhardt

THE 150TH ANNIVERSARY OF THE ABOLITION of slavery in France's overseas colonies was extensively commemorated in 1998 both in France and in the overseas *départements* of Guadeloupe, Martinique, Guyana, and Reunion. For the first time since the abolition of slavery in 1848, the French government publicly addressed its slave past. Despite this breakthrough, a heated debate was provoked by the anniversary celebrations. In articles of major French and French Caribbean newspapers such as *Le Monde, Libération, Le Figaro,* and *France-Antilles,* French and Caribbean writers, historians, politicians, and journalists took position both for and against the celebrations organized by the government. Who and what should be commemorated? The 1848 decree declaring the emancipation of black slaves in France's colonies? The French men, most importantly Victor Schoelcher, who made the signing of this decree possible? The three centuries of slave trade and plantation slavery that ended in 1848? The daily resistance and countless rebellions of blacks that continually destabilized the system of exploitation, rendering it unfeasible and thus ultimately contributing to its demise? The heroes who led their people in these struggles for freedom: Makendal, Boukman, and Toussaint Louverture from Saint Domingue, Louis Delgrès from Martinique, Ignace and Mulâtresse Solitude from Guadeloupe, to name a few?

The debate provoked by the 150th anniversary turned the commemoration into an unprecedented cultural moment for France and for her remaining overseas domains. It brought into focus the most controversial aspects of the past that continue to haunt the memory of slavery today. French historian Pierre Nora calls moments, places, people, or objects that symbolize a community's memorial heritage *lieux de mémoire*[1] ("realms of memory"). These realms of memory are characterized by an overwhelming presence of the past.[2] Submerging the present with conflicting memories of the nation's slave past, the 1998 commemoration became a realm of memory *par excellence.* It brought to light the discord between France's universalist interpretation of the abolitionary decree and the Caribbean's historical specificity, marginalized yet one more time. Silenced for centuries by France's assimilatory practices, the people of the Caribbean struggled to make their voice heard in 1998. Parallel to France's celebration of the abolitionary decree itself, Guadeloupeans and Martinicans expressed their share in the history of slavery through memorials, sculptures, and murals. Their artistic renditions focus on aspects of the past that continue to be left out of France's centralizing historical narrative.

From the official perspective of the government, the abolitionary decree was commemorated as a founding moment of the much-vaunted principles of equality, fraternity, and liberty. In his speech opening the celebrations of the 150th anniversary of the abolition of slavery in France's colonies, President Jacques Chirac presented the abolitionary decree as a building block of the nation: In this optic, the abolitionary process was undertaken in a spirit of integration, helping to strengthen the unity of the nation. Emancipated, the former slaves became members of the nation that had formerly enslaved them. The freedom bestowed upon them further strengthened the principles upon which the nation's unity was constructed: "By ending an iniquitous situation, the promoters of the abolition of slavery did not only act in the name of humanity. They reinforced the foundations of democracy and of the Republic."[3] The long historical period preceding 1848—three centuries of slavery—did not disrupt the unitary vision that emerged from Chirac's remarks. Abolition became an unproblematic moment of France's history that was part of the legacy of universal freedom.

Trumpeting the abolition of slavery as a symbol of France's commitment to freedom and democracy, the commemoration primarily celebrated the memory of French individuals who contributed to this achievement. One of the earliest French figures to be remembered during the commemoration was the historian and philosopher Abbé Raynal. His polemical work *Histoire philosophique et politique des établissements et du commerce des Européens dans les deux Indes,* published during the last decades of the eighteenth century, presents European colonial expansion in a critical light. Certain inflammatory passages of this work are believed to have fueled slave revolts in the French Caribbean. "The slaves revolted as they brandished his work," wrote a journalist in an article of *Le Figaro.* This provocative work, she held, "concentrates all the subversive seeds that could be found in the terrain of the Enlightenment."[4] The author of this article portrays Raynal and the Enlightenment's alleged subversiveness as the source of Caribbean slave revolts. However, the Enlightenment and the French Revolution are not points in a continuum, symbolizing France's linear progression toward fraternal nationhood. According to Nora, France's vision of its rooted past must be replaced by an experience of history in terms of its discontinuity.[5] In line with this, we should beware of viewing the slaves' struggle for freedom as a direct consequence of Montesquieu's, Diderot's, or Raynal's denunciations of the slave regime. Instead of seeing that struggle as a mechanical outgrowth of French thought, we should be mindful of the fact that "history is nourished by a plurality of memories, a plurality of archives and a diversity of documents."[6]

Countless colloquia organized by various organizations based in Martinique, Guadeloupe, and French Guyana on the occasion of the 150th anniversary of the abolitionary decree reveal the same feeling of unease with regard to the way France chose to commemorate this event. Martinican writer Patrick Chamoiseau laments France's "self-glorification" through the exclusive celebration of the abolitionary moment.[7] 1848 became a moment of victory for the French, the victory of humanitarian ideology over a horrific system of human exploitation. In their reactions to the 1998 commemoration, people from the French Caribbean primarily emphasized the importance of remembering their slave heritage. In particular, they brought into focus the power of the slaves' struggle that made abolition inevitable. Alfred Marie-Jeanne, the president of the Martinican Independentist Party and of the Regional Council of Martinique, clearly distinguished the celebrations on his island from those organized in France: "We do not celebrate the abolition of slavery! We commemorate the antislavery insurrection. There is a difference. The Negroes did not wait for a divine liberator from metropolitan France to lead the revolt. The slaves conquered their freedom on their own."[8] Similarly, Guadeloupean historian Oruno Lara underlined the importance of placing the abolition of slavery in a Caribbean context: "[the] start of a process of destruction of the system of slavery that propagates itself progressively throughout the Caribbean area" can be found in this geo-historical region as early as 1760.[9] The 1998 commemoration sidestepped the powerful influence of Caribbean liberation movements by focusing exclusively on the legacy of the Enlightenment and the French Revolution.

A "layer of silence" has obstructed the memory of slavery throughout the centuries.[10] With the abolition of slavery in 1848, the French Republic compelled the new citizens to forget their former enslavement.[11] Despite the numerous traces of slavery in their daily lives and in their mental makeup, the people had to forget a past replete with painful memories.[12] This systematic "silencing" of history, Martinican writer Edouard Glissant repeatedly points out in his *Discours antillais,* has erased the people's collective memory.[13]

French sociologist Maurice Halbwachs pioneered the concept of memory as a collective faculty. A group within a given society can reconstruct its past at any given moment by relying on the social memory of the group at large. However, a national society can only survive if there is sufficient unity among the different groups and individuals that comprise it. In order to achieve this unity, society erases from its memory those recollections that might separate groups and individuals too far from one another.[14] In his *Imagined Communities*, Benedict Anderson similarly discusses the importance of forgetting in the process of community building. Like Halbwachs, Anderson maintains that all must tacitly forget those events in a nation that set communities against one another, for instance fratricidal wars. Even so, this implicit agreement between the communities guarantees that on the occasion of a commemoration, for example, the forgotten events need only be recalled for the communities to share a common knowledge of this divided past.[15]

In the case of slavery, this unspoken acknowledgment never took place. Despite the nation's purported ideals of equality, the assimilated new citizens were never on an equal footing with the French. Deemed problematic by the State, their entire history was replaced by that of the French nation. As a result, the foundation for a collective memory shared by both the metropolitan French and descendants from slavery alike was never laid. Reconstructing the past is the function of social memory, according to Halbwachs. However, since the West Indians' collective memory has always been silenced, it must somehow be conjured up before it can point the way to the past. Nora calls such summoned memories realms of memory that emerge as "moments of history are plucked out of the flow of history, then returned to it—no longer quite alive but not yet entirely dead, like shells left on the shore when the sea of living memory has receded."[16] The experience of slavery is plucked out of the historical consciousness of West Indians and becomes, to use Chamoiseau's expression, an "obscure memory." In order to mobilize this painful past, to turn it into a realm of memory, to make it available for the collective memory of the people, slavery must become a part of "conscious memory."[17]

How have Martinicans and Guadeloupeans tried to turn this past into "conscious memory?" How have they artistically expressed the marginalized history of their slave ancestors? On the occasion of the yearly commemorations, most notably since 1998, they have erected memorials. Through their own personal vision and understanding, they have sought to bring to their compatriots' attention aspects of the past that can no longer be ignored. Some memorials are artistically influenced while others are primarily historical markers. Some focus on events, others on heroes. Others again use the Caribbean land- and seascape as their primary inspiration. All tell fascinating stories of the past that reveal the vivid spark of memory still alive in the imagination of French West Indians today.

The memorials erected during the past decade in Guadeloupe and Martinique depict slaves as dignified human beings, standing up to their fate and freeing themselves by their own voluntary doing. This constitutes a profound break with the cultural construction of slavery in European and North American art. Blacks are continually stripped of their power whether they are visually represented during the middle passage, as runaways, or as tortured slaves.[18] Through artistic representations of their slave ancestors, Martinicans and Guadeloupeans bring to light the profoundly Caribbean dimension of their historical experience. Rooted in the land- and seascape of the islands, in the longstanding resistance of maroons, and finally in the heroism of individuals who fought against oppression, this artwork reclaims the West Indians' rightful share in the destruction of the slave regime. The artists disregard the emblematic abolitionary decree of 1848, focusing their message instead on different aspects of the slave experience.

The memorial at Anse Caffard is the sculpture most powerfully rooted in the Caribbean, drawing the forcefulness of its message from its geographic location atop a cliff, overhanging the ocean on the southernmost tip of Martinique. The city of Diamant initiated the creation of this memorial in 1998. Sculpted by Laurent Valère, the fifteen statues, 2.5 meters high and each weighing four tons, are made of cement. They are arranged in a triangle facing the ocean to symbolize the triangular trade between Europe, Africa, and the Americas (Figures 1.1 & 1.2).

The white color of the statues is the traditional color of sepulture in the Caribbean. It draws attention to the funerary dimension of the site, which, beyond the shipwreck of a slave ship on 8 April 1830 that led to the death of nearly 300 enchained slaves, also commemorates all the unknown victims of the slave trade. It is for this reason that the statues face the Gulf of Guinea at a 110-degree angle. The memorial's motto, "Memory and Fraternity"—inscribed on the first statue—highlights its primary purpose: to remember the victims of the slave trade in a spirit of fraternity between human beings.

Anse Caffard is perhaps one of the most remarkable memorials erected in the memory of slavery and the slave trade during the past ten years in the French West Indies. The communication between the fifteen giant white statues and the vast expanse of water below the cliff creates a reverential quality about the memorial that is quite uncanny. The statues are slightly bowed, their posture solemn and reflective as though in prayer before the collective grave of their brothers (Figure 1.3). They express the first stanza of "The Sea Is History" by St. Lucian poet Derek Walcott: "Where are your monuments, your battles, martyrs? / Where is your tribal memory? Sirs, / in that grey vault. The

Figure 1.1. The statues of the memorial at Anse Caffard.

Figure 1.2. The triangular group of statues at Anse Caffard facing the Caribbean Sea.

Figure 1.3.   The statues are slightly bowed,
their posture solemn and reflective as though
in prayer before the collective grave of their
brothers.

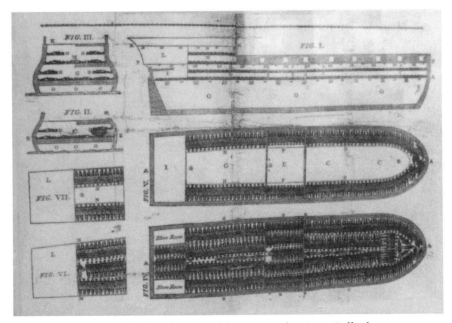

Figure 1.4.   The *Description of a Slave Ship* on a panel at Anse Caffard.

Mémorial
de l'Anse Caffard

Bienvenue.

Voici l'histoire de ces lieux :

e 8 avril 1830, vers midi, un bateau effectue d'étranges manœuvres
au large du Diamant, et vers cinq heures de l'après-midi,
jette l'ancre, ici même, dans les **parages dangereux de l'Anse Caffard.**
Un habitant du quartier, François **Dizac, Géreur de l'Habitation**
Plage du Diamant, propriété du **Comte de Latournelle,**
se rend compte du danger couru par le navire, mais une houle
très forte l'empêche de mettre une pirogue à la mer pour prévenir
le capitaine du péril imminent qu'il courait d'être jeté sur la côte.
Il doit se borner à faire des signaux que le capitaine ne voit pas
ou ne veut pas voir.
A 23 heures, des cris et des craquements sinistres déchirent la nuit.

Dizac et un groupe d'esclaves de l'Habitation, se rendent
immédiatement sur les lieux pour découvrir une vision d'horreur :
le bateau disloqué sur les rochers, avec ses passagers, pris dans
la terrible furie de la mer déchaînée.
es sauveteurs virent alors le mât de misaine, surchargé d'individus affolés
e briser et entraîner définitivement dans l'écume et les rochers
a grand nombre de personnes.

Figure 1.5.   A scene from Biard's painting *L'Abolition de l'esclavage* on another panel.

Figure 1.6.   Statue of a maroon in Diamant, Martinique, sculpted in 1998.

Figure 1.7. Sculpture of maroon holding a dying child in Fort-de-France, Martinique.

Figure 1.8.   Memorial to the maroon in Saint Esprit, Martinique, sculpted in 2000.

Figure 1.9. Memorial to the maroon in Saint Esprit.

Figure 1.10. Painting of the middle passage on the base of the memorial in Saint Esprit.

Figure 1.11. Painting of tortured slaves on the base of the memorial in Saint Esprit.

Figure 1.12. The statue of Ignace erected on 27 May 1998 in Pointe-à-Pitre, Guadeloupe.

Figure 1.13.   The statue of Mulâtresse Solitude erected on 27 May 1999.

Figure 1.14.   The statue of Louis Delgrès erected on 27 May 2001.

Figure 1.15. Ignace and Delgrès painted on the mural in 1998 in Pointe-à-Pitre, Guadeloupe.

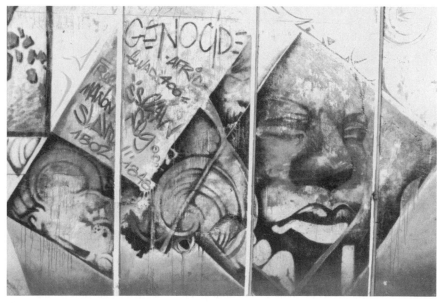

Figure 1.16. Representations of slavery painted on the mural in Pointe-à-Pitre, Guadeloupe.

Figure 1.17. The *Description of a Slave Ship* and the embracing man and woman from Biard's *The Abolition of Slavery* painted on the mural next to Ignace and Delgrès.

sea. The sea / has locked them up. The sea is History."[19] The ocean surrounding the islands is replete with history, a history that is almost palpable, ready to spill out into the consciousness of the people at any time. The imposing white sculptures powerfully convey the message of this past by taking the spectators back in time in their imagination, guiding them in their vision of the middle passage.

The persuasiveness of Anse Caffard lies not only in the communion between the sculptures and the geographic surroundings, but also in the detailed historical description of the site provided on panels in both French and English. As opposed to most memorials that present only minimal or no information about the artwork, these explanatory panels provide a detailed account of the shipwreck commemorated by the memorial, historical facts about the slave trade accompanied by illustrations, as well as the background and meaning of the memorial itself.

One illustration on the panels is particularly significant. It is the famous copper engraving, *Description of a Slave Ship*, commissioned by the London Society for the Abolition of the Slave Trade in April 1789 (Figure 1.4). In *Blind Memory: Visual Representations of Slavery in England and America*, Marcus Wood wonders if this image, used over and over again across the centuries, has not in a sense become a monument to the middle passage.[20] This heritage, however, is not unproblematic. It is based on an image popularized by abolitionists who portrayed slaves as totally passive and helpless victims.[21] The "cultural void" created around the slave in this Western visualization of the middle passage was obtained by focusing on the economically efficient packing of the slave cargo. The striking contrast between the black bodies and the white spaces accentuates the stillness of the slaves, completely subdued by Western commercial venture. The depiction of the black as "cultural absentee," argues Wood, was essential for the abolitionist polemic to successfully stimulate guilt and culpability in European audiences.[22]

It is interesting to examine some of these arguments in the context of the Memorial at Anse Caffard. The *Description of the Slave Ship*, along with the other illustrations and maps on the panels alongside the statues, firmly root the memorial in the Western tradition of visual representation of slavery and the slave trade. Notable in this regard is also the image of the slave man and woman embracing each other with opened chains in their hands (Figure 1.5). This scene is taken from the famous painting by Auguste-François Biard entitled *L'Abolition de l'esclavage dans les colonies françaises en 1848* (*The Abolition of Slavery in the French Colonies in 1848*) painted in 1849. Similarly to the *Description of the Slave Ship*, this painting has come to symbolize slavery in the Western—and more specifically in the French—imagination. It is used in many textbooks and on the covers of novels.[23] The emancipated slaves are depicted as joyful beneficiaries of France's generosity. No longer helpless victims, they nonetheless remain passive recipients of Western humanitarianism and "cultural absentees" who are inscribed like a blank page.

What is striking about the memorial is the contrast between the Western narrative found on the panels and the completely non-Western atmosphere exuded by the scene of the fifteen statues. Their imposing stature gives everything but an impression of passivity. Facing the vast body of water in the direction of the Gulf of Guinea, the statues embody the memory of the West Indians' ancestors: their origin, their violent uprooting, and the middle passage ending for many in the ocean's "grey vault." Although the memory is tragic, nothing about the scene evokes the pity commonly elicited by Western representations of slavery and the slave trade. On the contrary, the statues inspire reverence before their dignified bearing and the devotional atmosphere of the scene.

The sculptures of maroons, particularly abundant in Martinique, command the same respectful gaze as the statues at Anse Caffard. Unlike Anse Caffard, however, the maroons do not draw their powerful message directly from the Caribbean land- and seascape but from the people's imagination. Maroons are the most complete and vivid embodiment of popular memory in the Caribbean today. In fact, Glissant considers them the only true popular heroes of the West Indies.[24] Having left imaginary traces in the forested mountain regions of the islands, maroons are very much tied to the Caribbean landscape. However, the ephemeral quality of these traces has turned the figure of the maroon into a myth both in the literary and popular imagination. Guyanese critic Lydie Ho-Fong-Choy Choucoutou considers literary representations of the maroon as a way of reappropriating history by turning blacks into agents of their own destiny. The figure of the literary maroon thus denounces the "decorative role" often attributed to blacks who are considered unsuited for freedom.[25] Haunting the West Indians' imagination,[26] the maroon dismantles Western representations of the slave as a passive victim who will tend to run away rather than fight the oppressor.[27]

Particularly dominating in Martinique, the iconography of the maroon breaking his own chains with a machete in his hands symbolizes the diatribe between Enlightenment ideology and the impact of slave rebellions. To what extent was the abolitionary decree a generous donation from France and to what extent did the slaves liberate themselves by making the abolition of slavery ineluctable? In the context of the anniversary celebrations of the abolition of slavery, French Caribbean artists have brought slave resistance as a major historical agent into center stage.[28] Their sculptures typically focus on the independent will of the maroon, determined to fight for freedom with his own physical strength and through violent means.

Sculpted in 1998 by Hector Charpentier, the statue of the maroon in the city of Diamant, Martinique embodies strength, pride and dignity (Figure 1.6). The physical and mental weight of the maroon is directed toward the fist that has just broken the chains of slavery. The act of self-liberation lends an air of assurance and nobility to his facial expression. He holds his head high, gazing intently into the distance over his fist as though focusing and concentrating his energies. Though assuredly ready to fight for his freedom, his muscular body is graced with a dignified posture that ennobles his physical and mental power. He draws the source of his energy from the symbols of his Afro-American heritage: the *lambi* shell in his right hand and the drum lying between his feet. Not only does this symbolism root the maroon's actions in a decidedly non-European tradition, it also shows that he is part of a larger group to whom he communicates through the *lambi* shell and the drum. Actively engaged in his destiny as a free man, the maroon of Diamant stands in contrast to traditional Western representations of slaves as passive recipients of European benevolence. This is particularly striking on the seal of the London Society for the Abolition of the Slave Trade. Made by Josiah Wedgwood in 1788, the seal represents a kneeling, enchained Negro pleading, "Am I not a man and a brother?" The submissiveness of the man on the seal focuses on his total dependency on potential European benefactors. The maroon of Diamant undoes this posture as he literally and figuratively stands up for his inherent rights.

Violence is an important element of the maroons' fight for freedom. The sculpture by Coco René Corail in the neighborhood of Trénelle in Fort-de-France, Martinique illustrates this facet of rebellion very poignantly. Sculpted out of wrought iron, the maroon holds what appears to be a dead or dying child in his left arm while raising a machete up above his head in his right hand in an attacking gesture (Figure 1.7). He is ready to violently avenge his child's death. Below the sculpture a plaque is inscribed with the following words: "Square of 22 May 1848. Martinican remember!" Commemorated here is not the abolition of slavery but the slave rebellion of 22 May forcing Rostoland, the governor of Martinique, to decree the abolition of slavery on 23 May before the arrival of the official decree from France. It is the violence of the 22 May events that is symbolized by the sculpture and that Martinicans are admonished to remember. Bringing this violent episode of Martinican history to the forefront counterbalances the oppressive weight of French paternalism embodied by the abolitionary decree. There is a refusal here to bow down submissively before France's proclaimed benevolence. Instead, the maroon of Trénelle captures the violence of the slave past and the endless human suffering it caused. The effectiveness of this sculpture as a representation of slavery in the popular imagination was born out by an unusual incident. Fixed to a

stone wall, the sculpture is located in the middle of a working-class neighborhood surrounded by public-sector housing. At one time it was supposed to be
lent to the city of Fort-de-France. However, afraid that the sculpture would
not be returned, the youth of the neighborhood attached it with pikes thereby
managing to keep it in place.[29] The youth's desire to protect the sculpture
shows the extent to which they were able to identify with its message. Making
the past come alive, the maroon of Trénelle imprints itself on the youth's present reality, thus creating a meaningful link between the slave past and contemporary Martinican society.

The memorial to the maroon in Saint Esprit, Martinique, sculpted and
painted by Michel Glondu in February 2000, combines elements of the maroons of Diamant and Trénelle with traditional Western representations of
slavery. Sculpted out of wrought iron, a maroon brandishes his machete high
up in the air in an exalted gesture with broken chains hanging from his wrists
(Figures 1.8-9). He is standing on a drum with a *lambi* shell attached to its
side. The drum is on top of a cone-shaped structure that is decorated with objects of torture, masks of skeleton faces, bones, and blood. On the large square
cement base below the sculpture are four naïve paintings of the slave trade and
plantation slavery in the Caribbean.

Similarly to the maroon of Diamant, the maroon of Saint Esprit has also liberated himself with his own strength symbolized by the machete, the drum,
and the *lambi* shell. This sculpture—like the one in Trénelle—also embodies
the violent aspect of self-liberation although the maroon of Saint Esprit has a
far less aggressive stance. What is interesting about this memorial is the contrast between the portrayal of rebellion and Afro-American symbolism
through the sculpture and the representation of Western ideology through the
paintings on the base. Particularly noteworthy is the painting of the middle
passage inspired by M. W. Turner's *Slavers Throwing Overboard the Dead and
Dying, Typhoon Coming On* painted in 1840 (Figure 1.10). Sharks eat drown-
ing slaves who have just been thrown overboard a slave ship. Although Gondu's
painting does not share the artistic qualities of Turner's, the allusion to this
well-known and controversial English painting is striking.[30] This reference to
Western depictions of the middle passage adds a dimension of defiance to the
rejoicing maroon on top of his African drum. The painting of tortured slaves
has a similar effect (Figure 1.11). In particular the figure inspired by William
Blakes's 1798 copper engraving *A Negro Hung Alive by the Ribs to a Gallows*
from John Stedman's *Narrative of a Five Years' Expedition Against the Revolted
Negroes of Surinam* clearly links these images to Western representations of
slavery. Again, the maroon with his broken chains who has clearly freed himself by his own means stands in sharp contrast to the plight of tortured and
dying slaves generally focused upon in Western art. Glondu's maroon has risen

above oppression to defy not only the Europeans' tyranny but also their representations of blacks as helpless and submissive victims. He is clearly not a victim and despite torture and death—symbolized by the objects attached to the cone-like structure—has been able to triumph over injustice. His machete triumphantly raised, the maroon proclaims his freedom not only from slavery but also from European thought: he owes his freedom to nobody but himself.

While Martinicans have expressed their memory of slavery through sculptures of the maroon, Guadeloupeans have instead focused on specific heroes of their history. The first abolition of slavery in 1794, followed by the antislavery revolution against its violent reinstatement by Napoleon in 1802, gave rise to such important historical figures as Delgrès, Ignace, and Mulâtresse Solitude. Mulâtresse Solitude is remembered for her tireless fight against the French troops. Although she was pregnant she never ceased to abandon the cause of freedom until her capture and hanging. Ignace was one of the leading figures of the revolution. He died in combat on 25 May 1802. The military leader Louis Delgrès has become the principal symbol of the antislavery revolution because of the extraordinary mass suicide he committed with several hundred of his companions once it was clear they had lost the war and slavery would be reestablished in Guadeloupe. Delgrès lived the revolutionaries' rallying cry until the very end: "Vivre libres ou mourir!" (To live in freedom or to die!)

Statues were erected in memory of each one of these emblematic figures on the Boulevard des Héros in Pointe-à-Pitre, Guadeloupe, in 1998, 1999, and 2001 (Figures 1.12–14). Particularly noteworthy about Mulâtresse Solitude and Ignace is their proud and insubordinate stance. The statue of Delgrès, consisting in disconnected body parts, symbolizes the suicidal explosion. Delgrès' head rests in the palm of his hand as he pensively looks at the book lying before him entitled "1789—Human Rights." He is surrounded by the men and women who died with him. Plaques below the statues explain the purpose of these memorials and provide a brief biography of the heroes. The most interesting inscription below all three statues is the following: "Gwadloupéyen sonjé Milatres Solitid (Ignace/Delgrès) en me 1802" (Guadeloupeans remember Mulâtresse Solitude (Ignace/Delgrès) in May 1802). Though erected on the anniversary date of the abolition of slavery, the memory evoked by these memorials is not of the ending of servitude but of the people's resistance and fight against the restoration of slavery in 1802. The heroes are given an active role in the fashioning of Guadeloupean identity. In order to reclaim their own Caribbean identity, West Indians distance themselves from the overpowering narrative of the French abolitionist movement led by Victor Schœlcher. Instead, they remember and honor their ancestors' engagement in the historical process. The plaque on the statue of Ignace suggests as much: "Honor and Respect to all the Negro maroons, to all Guadeloupean freedom fighters who preferred death in Baimbridge, on the heights of Matouba and everywhere else to the humiliation of a return to slavery." The heroes of the antislavery revolution are key to reclaiming Guadeloupean history, thereby constructing an identity that reflects the people's unique social and geographic realities.

Painted in May 1998 by Guadeloupean high school artists, the mural in front of Baimbridge High School in the urban area of Pointe-à-Pitre is perhaps the most accomplished expression of popular memory to be found in Guadeloupe. Ignace and Delgrès are principal figures on the mural along with images from Africa, the middle passage, and the abolition of slavery (Figures 1.15-17). Guadeloupean youth have made these historical images their own, turning them into realms of memory for their generation. With the following words painted on the mural, high school student Valérie Mylène poetically impels the past into her present-day reality:

> Born from the blood shed by our enslaved fathers.
> Today you exist.
> I want you and I experience you.
> I cry out your name.
> Liberty . . .

The past has come to life under the stroke of these young people. Similarly to the sculptors of the memorials, they have depicted symbols of their Caribbean heritage alongside Western visualizations of slavery and liberation. Ignace and Delgrès are painted right next to the *Description of a Slave Ship* and the famous scene from Biard's *The Abolition of Slavery*, in which the recently emancipated man and woman embrace one another with chains still hanging from their wrists (Figure 1.17). The juxtaposition of Caribbean and Western images symbolizes the West Indians' double heritage: uniquely tied to the geography and history of their islands, they also have to continually negotiate their relationship to France, both historically and in the present. With one out of four persons born in the French Caribbean residing in France today, the acknowledgement of this double heritage has become paramount.[31] Amidst the bustling city life of Pointe-à-Pitre, the mural of Baimbridge High School is reckoning with past, present, and future. It is rooting an experience in the collective consciousness of the people, thereby turning the past into an identity-forging process for the future: "We are coming out of the shadow, we had no rights and we had no glory, that is precisely why we are speaking up and starting to tell our history."[32]

Notes

1. Pierre Nora, *Realms of Memory,* vol. 1 of *Conflicts and Divisions,* trans. Arthur Goldhammer (New York: Columbia University Press, 1996), xvii.

2. Nora, *Realms of Memory*, 16.

3. "L'Humanisme est aussi une politique," *Le Figaro* (Paris), 24 April 1998.

4. Vézianne de Vezins, "Les Brûlots de l'abbé Raynal," *Le Figaro* (Paris), April 1998, 25-26.

5. Nora, *Realms of Memory*, 12-13.

6. Elisabeth Landi, "La Construction d'un événement historique," *France-Antilles: Supplément-Édition* (Guadeloupe), 25 May 1998.

7. Patrick Chamoiseau, "De la mémoire obscure à la mémoire consciente," in *De l'esclavage aux réparations*, eds. Serge Chalons et al. (Paris: Karthala, 2000), 112.

8. Annick Cojean, "En Martinique, la commémoration de l'abolition est d'abord celle de la révolte des esclaves," *Le Monde* (Paris), 25 April 1998.

9. Oruno Lara, "Histoire et abolition," *France-Antilles: Supplément-Édition* (Guadeloupe), 25 May 1998.

10. Annick Cojean, "En Guadeloupe, des voix demandent à la France de reconnaître son passé esclavagiste," *Le Monde* (Paris) 26-27 April 1998.

11. Cojean, "En Martinique."

12. René Bélénus, "René Bélénus: 'Un non-évènement en Guadeloupe,'" *France-Antilles: Supplément-Édition* (Guadeloupe), 25 May 1998.

13. Edouard Glissant, *Le Discours antillais* (Paris: Gallimard, 1997), 88, 131, 278.

14. Maurice Halbwachs, *On Collective Memory* (Chicago: University of Chicago Press, 1992), 182-183, 188.

15. Benedict Anderson, *Imagined Communities: Reflections on the Origin and Spread of Nationalism* (London: Verso, 1991), 199-201.

16. Nora, *Realms of Memory*, 7.

17. Patrick Chamoiseau, "La Mémoire obscure de l'esclavage," *Le Figaro* (Paris), 24 April 1998.

18. Marcus Wood, *Blind Memory: Visual representations of Slavery in England and America 1780-1865* (London: Routledge, 2000).

19. Derek Walcott, "The Sea is History," from *The Star-Apple Kingdom*, in *Collected Poems 1948-1984* (London: Faber and Faber, 1992), 364.

20. Wood, *Blind Memory*, 36.

21. Wood, *Blind Memory*, 19.

22. Wood, *Blind Memory*, 23.

23. Delas, "Commémorer/Manipuler," 271.

24. Glissant, *Le Discours antillais*, 104.

25. Lydie Ho-Fong-Choy Choucoutou, "Littérature et esclavage," in *De l'esclavage aux réparations*, eds. Serge Chalons et al. (Paris: Karthala, 2000), 20-23.

26. Richard D. E. Burton, *Le Roman marron: Études sur la littérature martiniquaise contemporaine* (Paris: L'Harmattan, 1997), 10.

27. Wood, *Blind Memory*, 97, 113, 218.

28. Marie-Christine Rochmann, "Introduction," in *Esclavages et abolitions*, ed. Marie-Christine Rochmann (Paris: Karthala, 2000), 7.

29. The author was told this story by an artist living in that part of Fort-de-France.

30. For more information on Turner's painting see Wood's excellent analysis in *Blind Memory*, 41-68.

31. *INSEE Ile-de-France à la page*, no. 207 (January 2002): 1. These numbers are based on the 1999 census. They cover persons born in the French Caribbean now residing in France. When people born in France of migrant parents originating in the Caribbean are added, the population of Caribbean origin living in metropolitan France is significantly larger.

32. Michel Foucault, *"Il faut défendre la société": Cours au Collège de France (1975-1976)*, (Paris: Gallimard-Seuil, 1997), 62.

2

A Singular Revolution

Nick Nesbitt

IF HISTORICAL AWARENESS of the Haitian Revolution has amounted, in the words of the January 2004 Debray report[1] to the French government, to a "singular absence," the task of any remmemoration of the events of 1791-1804 would be to bear witness to this revolutionary sequence: briefly put, the Haitian Revolution overthrew for the first time the world of the plantation and slavery that dominated the economy of the Age of Enlightenment, it invented both decolonization and neocolonialism, and instantiated for the first time in world history the universal rights of all humans to freedom from slavery. And yet, the Haitian Revolution does not exist, as one of the handful of books published on Haiti in the year of its bicentennial of independence puts it.[2] Haiti has only ever been perceived in Western Modernity as a lack, as pure negativity: as violence, destruction, poverty, political dysfunction, dictatorship, and (let us stop there, though we could go on and on) exploitation. One wonders who could have conceived such a perfect dumping ground for our disavowed imperfections and failings, as though these things only existed in this Dark Continent of the New World. The task of any remembrance of the Haitian Revolution must surely be to bring into question this perfect scenario, one that leaves those outside Haiti miraculously cleansed of the dirt and grime of any guilt.

Compared with its glorious cousin in France, we know little of the Haitian Revolution, despite the fact that it has never receded from public consciousness throughout the African Diaspora.[3] It has remained actively "silenced" and largely "unthinkable" in Western discourse, as Michel-Rolph Trouillot has argued, a scandal since the moment it began to unfold in 1791.[4] A search of the

Cornell library database on the historiography of the French Revolution reveals over three hundred and fifty Library of Congress subject headings alone, and well over 7,000 individual volumes. A similar search for Haiti reveals twelve subject headings and a grand total of 235 volumes (many of them duplicates) on the events of 1791-1804.

In France, this lack of knowledge is even more striking. Walking from bookstore to bookstore on the Rue des Écoles a month before the Bicentennial of Haitian Independence, I could find not a single work on the Haitian Revolution in any of the famous stores that line that street (Gibert, Compagnie, etc.) until I reached the niche bookseller L'Harmattan, where I finally found three dusty volumes: one from 1960 (Césaire), and the other two reprints from the nineteenth century (Schoelcher, Lacroix).[5] What are the causes of the Revolution and how did it proceed? Compared with the plethora of written documents that have driven French Revolutionary scholarship for two centuries, much of this period will remain forever unknown to scholars.[6]

What can it mean for us, today, to remember the bicentennial of the end of the Haitian Revolution and the Declaration of Independence in 1804 of the first decolonized society in the modern world? It might first of all mean something like an injunction to remember the losers of history, those sacrificed in the triumphant march of history. In the case of Haiti, this might mean not so much remembering a failed attempt at global colonization as to recall as best we can all those who found themselves caught up in the grinding machinery of the Napoleonic war machine, the victims of an arbitrary and subjective decision to make war, a decision taken by a leader who came to power in a bureaucratic coup d'état. It might mean remembering those who enlisted in his army in a combination of economic necessity and patriotic fervor to defend the universal democratic ideals of the French Republic, only to find that hope betrayed, to find themselves sent overseas as cannon fodder in a unilateral and offensive war to reassert the global hegemony of a colonizing empire. The Haitian Revolution was preeminently an offensive war of empire; it was Haitian sugar that oiled the French economy in the age of Enlightenment, providing two-thirds of France's foreign trade in 1789.

If the Haitian Revolution were only, as we often read, "the only successful modern slave revolt" it would hardly be of more than passing historical interest. In fact, two of the processes that came to distinguish the twentieth century were invented in Haiti: decolonization and neocolonialism. Haiti was the first of the European colonies successfully to demonstrate that the colonized can take hold of their own historical destiny and enter the stage of world history as autonomous actors, and not merely passive, enslaved subjects. Newly independent Haiti also demonstrated to the world the first instance of what we now call neocolonialism, as ruling elites (both mulatto and black) united with the military and a merchant class to create an unstable balance of power. This depended upon the skimming of surplus profits from tertiary imports and a corresponding systematic underdevelopment of local productive forces, all at the expense of the excluded majority, a process that Fanon would first identify in *Les Damnés de la terre* and that Michel-Rolph Trouillot has brilliantly analyzed in *Haiti: State Against Nation.*[7] Both the unfinished project of decolonization and the actuality of neocolonial imperialism imply that attention to the Haitian revolution and its aftermath is of most pressing concern if we are to understand the origins and classic forms of these problems that continue to confront our twenty-first century.

To remember the Haitian Revolution in its singularity is to reorient our thought away from a defense of localized, communitarian politics to questions of universal truth, to singular events, and to what Alain Badiou terms a "politics of emancipation."[8] But if the Haitian Revolution constitutes a singular event in human history, it was not a miraculous epiphany, an undetermined break with the ontology of the slave-holding world. Granted, historians will never be able to totalize our knowledge of the causes of the Haitian Revolution; as a phenomenon of a largely oral culture, most of its traces vanished at the moment they occurred, to an incomparably greater extent than the French or American Revolutions. But that does not mean the truth of the Haitian Revolution was an absolute and undetermined rupture with historical being. Its singularity can only become clear in mediated relation with everything it denied. In 1797 Toussaint Louverture declared to the Directory, "we renew [our oath] to bury ourselves under the ruins of a country revived by liberty rather than suffer the return of slavery . . . Do [you] think that [those] who have been able to enjoy the blessing of liberty will calmly see it snatched away? . . . [I renew my oath to defend] the rights . . . of humanity, for the triumph of liberty and equality."[9] Toussaint constructed this universal imperative, this politics of emancipation, not from divine inspiration, but from diverse elements like a personal knowledge of the dehumanization of slavery and an interrogation of the 1789 *Déclaration des droits de l'homme et du citoyen.* The difficulty of interpreting the Haitian Revolution is to grasp the coexistence of these two dimensions, of a determinate relation with other historical factors and the explosive appearance of the new within the continuity of human experience.

Has there been any progress in implementing universal human rights since 1789? A whole tradition of critique says no, from Edmund Burke's *Reflections on the French Revolution* (1790), through Heidegger ("the they") and Carl Schmitt (*Crisis of Parliamentary Democracy*).[10] These critics point to events such as the degeneration of the ethical idealism announced in 1789 into the Terror of 1793 and the guillotine.[11] In Haiti, both the Napoleonic French army and the rebel slaves resorted to terrorization through ultra-violence and every form of torture imaginable to them to a much greater degree than ever occurred in the French Revolution. Among its many distinctions, the Haitian Revolution was also the first modern case of unlimited warfare through the means of mass terrorization. From the hamstrung and economically desolate nation that resulted from the Haitian Revolution to the impotence of the United Nations and its Declaration of Human Rights, powerless to stop the Rwandan genocide, war in Iraq, or the subjection of millions of stateless, rightless refugees around the globe, it remains an open question whether there has been any progress.

Given the suffering it engendered and its historical aftereffects in an (economically and juridically) impoverished country, does the Haitian Revolution demonstrate historical progress in social justice? Immanuel Kant asked the same question about the French Revolution in his 1798 text "Contest of the Faculties," and responded that it was precisely not the contingent violence and incompletion of the Terror, all the failings and shortcomings of such an event that in fact pale in light of the total violence of Saint-Domingue, that should retain our attention. Rather, Kant claimed, the progress brought about by the French Revolution lies in its construction of a universal idea of freedom, an idea that negated the local, communitarian politics of race, ethnicity, and nation to interpellate all those innately endowed with the capacity to understand its logic.[12] Kant asks the question "Is the human race continually improving?" and in offering a positive answer to this question, Kant presumes precisely what remains first to be demonstrated: that humanity actually exists as an immanent totality. Instead, Haiti and the case of slavery as an attempt at radical *de*-humanization posit humanity as no more than an immanent *possibility* to be conquered: amid the violence and destruction of enslavement and war, humanity remains only an idea of which we can conceive, and thus produce historically (we can become human).[13]

To remember the Haitian Revolution is to witness the flash of a revolutionary event, an event that escapes the linear temporal sequence of labor (work from sunup to sundown), that flees the linear tracing of the triangular slave trade and its destruction of human singularity. When, in his letter of 25 August 1793, Toussaint Louverture moves beyond mere local revolt to pose the concept "*liberté générale*" as defining the revolutionary sequence in St. Domingue, the point is not that he was till then a royalist who had not previously allied himself with the idea of universal emancipation, though this is true.[14] In this moment, Toussaint suddenly brings contingent, local, historical events into relation with their foundation, the eternity of a singular truth, in the attempt precisely to make that eternity realize itself *in time*, that is to say, historically.[15] While it is quite right to observe that the Haitian Revolution and

Toussaint himself never lived up to the truth of those concepts, indeed, that he betrayed them when he forced people back to the plantations, we can only recognize this failure because a truth had been posed in its transcendence of historical time. To point to such a relation to the universal would be absurd in the case of a mere local revolt, because its only ideal would have been, say, to obtain a garden plot behind one's shack, or to have Saturdays off from slave labor. Instead, the guiding concept of general emancipation that Toussaint put forward in 1793 illuminates his subsequent failure to implement this truth historically. In both posing it and failing to live up to it, Toussaint gives general emancipation an afterlife in which it can live on, as Žižek says, "to haunt the emancipatory imaginary as a dream waiting to be realized."[16]

A Singular Enlightenment

If the idea of a general, universal emancipation from enslavement is the founding and determinant idea of the Haitian Revolution, we should not conclude that it characterized the events in Saint Domingue uniformly from the first revolt of 1791 to the final declaration of independence by Dessalines on 1 January 1804. Rather, the idea of general emancipation gradually came to predominate the revolutionary events in their many twists and turns over thirteen long years. French officials received demands for freedom from slavery as early as 1791, but it was not in fact until the declarations of Toussaint Louverture and Sonthonax in August 1793 that there occurred an unambiguous call for a general and universal end to slavery.[17] Toussaint, himself free and a land and slave owner since the mid-1770s, never supported general emancipation of the slaves in first two years of the revolt (1791-93).[18] It was only on 23 August 1793 that Toussaint publicly expressed his unequivocal support for general emancipation, and on 25 August that he made his famous declaration: "I am Toussaint Louverture. . . . I want liberty and equality to reign in Saint Domingue."[19]

The idea of general emancipation gradually came to determine the Haitian Revolution in a temporal process of *singularization*, in which the specificity of the events in Saint Domingue arose from a complex historical matrix, including news of the French and American Revolutions and their Declarations of Independence and the Rights of Man, the brutal experience of New World slavery, and Afro-American religious experience (Vodou). This process of singularization implies that in its relation to the Age of Enlightenment, Saint Domingue was neither a mere subordinate tributary and backwater where European ideas of the Rights of Man took on a "tropical" flavor, nor entirely isolated from European ideas and history. Instead, the Enlightenment idea of a universal and natural right of humans to freedom adopted an unforeseen character in Saint Domingue when slaves, who had previously been excluded and excepted from this vision, claimed those rights as their own in an event at once singular in its localized destruction of the plantation regime and universal in its address to all human beings.

The Haitian Revolution offers perhaps the most compelling argument that the intellectual and historical climate of the second half of the eighteenth century must be understood as a variegated complex of multiple "Enlightenments," which nonetheless share a common concern for the universal problem of human freedom. The Haitian Revolution serves to disprove both the notion that there was any single "Enlightenment project" (slavery was actively excluded from discussions of freedom in Paris, but not in Saint Domingue) as well as the current received wisdom that a putatively monological "Enlightenment" thought erased the singularity of individual cultures and people beneath abstract universal moral principles (in theory, this is contradicted in the moral philosophy of Kant, while in practice, Saint Domingue sustains the singularity of the experience of slavery in its relation to a universal moral imperative).[20] "Prevalent accounts of what is called 'the Enlightenment' or 'the Enlightenment project,'" writes Sankar Muthu, "make a series of generalizations that very often egregiously misrepresent, blur, or hide from view entire strands of thought, some of which (were it not for the distorting lens through which they are viewed) might have been understood to be nuanced and intellectually productive contributions not only to debates of the long eighteenth century, but also to a range of still debated principles, intellectual tendencies, and institutions."[21] The events in Haiti from 1791 to 1804 demonstrate that debate over the complementary notions of human freedom, universals, singularity and multiplicity, and political autonomy extended far beyond the geographical limits of Western Europe, and with singular and dramatic consequences for the very content of that debate.

To understand the events of the Haitian Revolution as a *singularization* of the Enlightenment implies that it be understood not merely in its *difference from* the French and American Revolutions, but rather in both its *singularity* and *commonality* with other revolutionary moments in the Age of Enlightenment. These events must be understood not as a subordinate negation of 1789; no less did they find their transcendental foundation in The Rights of Man. Rather, the challenge confronting any contemporary interpretation of the Haitian Revolution is to grasp how these events came to construct their singularity in relation to 1776 and 1789: their internal difference taken as a historical project and not a purely internal and unrelated ontological difference. Singularization is to be understood not as a purely non-relational essence (singularity), but rather as a developing process occurring in relation to other events (1789).

The Haitian Revolution demonstrates not only the falsity of any monological understanding of the Enlightenment, but also, paradoxically, its truth. The specificity of Saint Domingue in the eighteenth century is utterly determined by the universalist and globalizing structure of capital that expanded beyond Europe to create sugar production facilities that incorporated humans into its machinic assemblages. There is no way to understand the Haitian striving for a singularization of political subjectivity except as a dialectical negation of slavery, violence, and global capital. As Haitians strove for a political singularization of their experience, they could not simply pull themselves up from this world by their bootstraps. Like all of us, only more so, Haitians have never been free to fashion their identities in any way they wanted, in abstraction from either the global plantation-slavery complex or the global politico-military-capital machine of death and devastation that has worked to isolate and actively destroy Haitian independence from 1804 to the present day. The process of Haitian singularization is only comprehensible as existing in tension with the determinate conditions that impelled and governed its emergence. To claim univocally that the Enlightenment was not one but multiple, indeed to claim that any singularity exists without external relation "with another thing [. . . that is] all that it is not," is to ignore and cover up the monological universalism of modern capital, to remain only on the surface of its diverse implementations and effects.[22] The violent *erasure* of difference that was slavery and the plantation accompanied, or rather, dialectically compelled the attempt in the late eighteenth century to recover a realm for free human action within this world of terrible necessity.

Haitians did not simply *reproduce* the 1789 *Déclaration* by transplanting this foreign bird to tropical climes; they demonstrated human freedom precisely in their unique transformation of this empirical object. The violent experience of enslavement allowed Haitians to transform the immanent meaning of the universal declaration of 1789, and it was their singular experience that made the Haitian Revolution the greatest political event of the Age of Enlightenment. While the American and French revolutionaries, following John Locke, spoke endlessly of "slavery," few understood their critique to apply unequivocally to all citizens. The American revolutionaries in particular were often more concerned with enlightenment as a passage from "barbarism" to "civility" and mastery of gentlemanly social behavior than with the problem of (positive) freedom.[23] The American Revolution was primarily a revolution for equality (of non-slaves) (232-33), where liberty meant merely the negative freedom from unjust taxation and military conscription.

If the English, French, and American bourgeois revolutions all served to create the structural conditions for the protection of individual liberties of economic choice, the particularity of the Haitian Revolution was to redress the imbalance they had introduced between equality and liberty, in favor of the latter. The Haitian constitutions of 1801 and 1804 invented the concept of a post-racial society, a step motivated by the absolute imperative of universal human autonomy. Though Article 4 of the 1793 Revolutionary Constitution granted citizenship to any adult foreigner who resided in Metropolitan France for a year,[24] the French Revolution had instituted an assimilationist version of nationalism that predicated social unity upon the erasure (rather than tolerance) of communitarian difference and only banned slavery under duress in 1794. On the other hand, the American Revolution could only base its pluralist conception of social totality upon the continuing enslavement of a portion of its population.

The Haitian Revolution, informed as it was by the direct experience of slavery, could not simply take over unchanged the liberal model of society imported from England and North America: not simply because of the formal emphasis placed upon individual (negative) liberties at the expense of universal freedom, but because the liberal model further *presupposes* individuals as free autonomous subjects who merely need to be left alone to go about their business, a view that Marx would later critique as the self-serving ideology of a dominant social class. The former slaves who drove the Haitian Revolution to its culmination in a novel constitution and state knew from experience that all humans are *not* free; they took human autonomy not as an *a priori* given, but strove to enact it as a social, human accomplishment, an ongoing construction that was itself only instantiated in the process of giving form to an emancipated society. The simple exigencies of experience led them to the same conclusions Marx would theorize a half-century later: human autonomy can only be conquered by a community as an inter-subjective process; by herself, an individual can only return to a state of nature (marooning).

In the attempt to place the Haitian Revolution within the flow of linear, journalistic time, historical experience and understanding disappears. Though few major media sites noted the Haitian Bicentennial on 1 January 2004, amid the increase in violence there in the following months, even the slightest attempt to place these events in historical perspective magically disappeared. Instead, the evocation of some nature-based, eternally recurring Haitian cycle of violence, ever-renewed, ever the same, became a magic incantation in American and French media seemingly intent on the active "otherization" of Haitian violence, convincing us that such things only happen there, in what was endlessly labeled as the "poorest country in the Western Hemisphere." When an article actually attempted to provide some sort of explanation, its impoverished thinking was palpable, and the lack of any desire even to try to understand was paraded as insight. On 24 February 2004, I read with astonishment this sentence in a *New York Times* editorial: "Abrupt and violent changes of government have been a regular feature of Haitian politics over the years and are among the main reasons that Haiti has never developed stable democratic institutions." Through the magical incantations of first world pundits, effect miraculously becomes historical causation, and Haiti is returned safely to its eternal, natural state as the land of "abrupt and violent changes," that is to say a place where the realm of human control over our social destiny, our political existence, is mere nature, where violence can erupt at any moment like the hurricanes, earthquakes, and volcanic eruptions that mark the Caribbean submission to natural time. As though the United States bore no particular burden in Haiti's two-century-old political dysfunction, as though we hadn't actively supported the French imposition of a 150-million-franc ransom to recognize its independence in 1826, a ransom that left the country by 1880 paying 80 percent of its gross national product to finance the loan it took from France itself to pay the ransom. As though the U.S. Marines had left things better than when they found them after occupying Haiti twice in the last century to "democratize" this country.

To remember Haiti in the year of its bicentennial is to bear witness to its testimony; a testimony not, as the Debray report would have it, to an imminent threat of Haiti contaminating other countries (as a consequence of poverty and political dysfunction).[25] No, the scandalous singularity of the Haitian Revolution stands before us as if to demand from us a call akin to that of Zola's "J'accuse!" It reminds us precisely of a world of total violence and terrorization, where torture was the daily coin of existence. It reminds us that Haitians were the first in world history to demonstrate that torture and slavery are never the isolated "mistake" of "a few . . . who dishonored our country and disregarded our values."[26] Slavery and torture are *systems* that are themselves predicated upon a global system that enables them, that encourages them, that founds its daily function upon their incessant recapitulation. Torture does not only happen over there, across an ocean or Gulf while we continue on in our splendid ignorance and superiority, having found a dumping ground for the rotting core of our society. There are more slave laborers in the world today—at least 27 million—than at any other moment in human history.[27] Many of these slaves are laboring today in the United States of America. The Haitian Revolution demands that we bring into question the system of our daily existence that enables slavery to occur, to interrogate our lives as a constant enabling of this torture insofar as we reconfirm, over and over, a regime that bases itself upon violence, torture, and a culture of terrorization and fear. To undertake this remmemoration and questioning successfully, even to begin to remain faithful to the singular event that was Haiti in 1804, is precisely to come to grasp, as did the slaves of Saint Domingue, that we live in such a culture of torture and violence, and that it is right here with us, not far off in some postmodern Congo. This culture of violence and fear resides in our culture of ubiquitous citizen surveillance, a culture that eats away at our rights and freedoms on a daily basis; this culture is just down the side road off a country highway or behind a brick enclosure in the middle of downtown, in our houses of torture and devastation that we call prisons.

A decade ago, amid the turmoil of the coup led by Raoul Cedras that overthrew Aristide, Haiti's first democratically elected president in two centuries, the Brazilian musicians Caetano Veloso and Gilberto Gil wrote a song entitled "Haiti" for their album *Tropicália 25*. The album marked the twenty-fifth anniversary of the counterculture movement that the two had led in 1968 to protest a Brazil of ever-increasing political dysfunction, torture, and dissolution of the rule of law by successive military regimes since 1964.[28] The song's refrain gives us an answer to the question of Haiti's "singular absence" in the form of a Zen koan: "O Haiti é aqui. O Haiti não é aqui" [Haiti is here. Haiti is not here]. "Think of Haiti, pray for Haiti" Caetano and Gil tell us, and this thinking must take the form of an active confrontation with the impossibility of our situation, from wherever we find ourselves in the world: "Haiti is not here. Haiti is here."

Rather than describing any events in Haiti, the Brazilian rap that Caetano wrote represents the violence and despair he witnesses in Brazil. It describes police beating blacks at a concert he went to by the afrocentric, black-pride group Olodum on the very site where slaves were whipped in colonial Salvador: the neighborhood of Pelourinho (literally translated, the "whipping post"). It condemns the massacre of 111 prisoners in a São Paulo prison and the omnipresent violence of a Brazilian racism that dares call itself a "racial paradise." If we think Haiti is a small island far from us in the Caribbean, a site where we can download violence and misery to assure ourselves that we live in the land of peace and prosperity, or as the Brazilian flag would have it, the land of "Ordem e progresso" [Order and Progress], we should think again, because what we think of as Haiti is right here around us every day. In Brazil, and here in the United States, as we all know. The United States, where, as Barry Maxwell reminded me, the incarcerated population has now reached the highest levels in both absolute and proportional terms in human history, higher than the USSR of Stalin's Gulag, the United States where the Patriot Act undertakes the deformalization of the rule of law and the installation of a perpetual rule of the state of emergency, a United States pursuing the destruction of universal human rights at home and in Guantanamo, in its scandalous attempt to destroy the World Criminal Court, and on and on. To think of Haiti, to remember its violence from a distance, our distance, is to refuse to reduce it to the bestialized space of the eternal return of natural violence. It is to represent instead to ourselves the degree to which that Haiti is right here with us.

At the same time, it is to renew Haiti's struggle for the universalization of human singularity, as freedom, as beauty, as pleasure, as desire, as understanding, as the freedom to create and communicate, a freedom and beauty that marks Haiti, with Brazil perhaps its only rival, as the greatest, freest, and most humane creative culture in the Western hemisphere.

Notes

1. The report of the committee headed by Régis Debray to Dominique de Villepin, *Haïti et la France*, presents an overview of Franco-Haitian relations since 1804, and offers a series of recommendations to the French government. The report calls attention to France's slave-holding past, asking: "How many French know that the Declaration of the Rights of Man and Citizen was *initiated* in Paris, but instantiated [*accomplie*] in Saint-Domingue, where human rights became, almost [sic] against our wishes, truly universal?" (18). Released in the months before France led the invasion to overthrow Aristide by force, the report paternalistically calls upon Haitians to "assume their share of responsibilities in the incredible degeneration . . . of the richest colony in the world . . . to an African [*sahélien*] level of malediction" (20). It then goes on to reduce the question of the repayment of Haiti's 90-million-franc payment to France for recognition of its independence, extorted from the country in 1825 and perhaps the single greatest cause of its economic underdevelopment, to a "propaganda campaign . . . without juridical foundation" (21, 23). Could it be that current transnational juridical norms are not fully developed? Such a simple question eludes the authors of the report, for whom the question remains a terrifying (in its rightful claims on French responsibility?) "Pandora's box" (25). The report hypocritically goes on to describe the seemingly unlimited "goodwill" of French aid projects in the face of Haitian "failures," "waste," and "egoism" (28-9), and laments over the "painful . . . trauma" of Dessaline's massacre of the last French planters in Haiti (32). Régis Debray, *Haïti et la France: Rapport à Dominique de Villepin* (Paris: La Table Ronde, 2004).

2. Christophe Wargny, *Haïti n'existe pas. 1804-2004: Deux cents ans de solitude* (Paris: Éditions Autrement, 2004). The bicentennial of Haitian Independence has seen relatively few studies published, compared with the outpouring that accompanied the coming of the bicentennial of the French Revolution in 1989. Exceptions include Laurent Dubois's study of the Revolution and the volume edited by Jacques de Cauna. Laurent Dubois, *Avengers of the New World: The Story of the Haitian Revolution* (Cambridge: Harvard University Press, 2004). Jacques de Cauna, ed., *Toussaint Louverture et l'indépendance de l'Haïti* (Paris: Karthala, 2004).

3. The articles collected by David Geggus in the volume *The Impact of the Haitian Revolution in the Atlantic World* chart the spreading awareness of the events of the Haitian Revolution throughout the Black Atlantic world in the decades following 1804. David Geggus, ed., *The Impact of the Haitian Revolution in the Atlantic World* (Columbia, S.C.: University of South Carolina Press, 2001). In the twentieth century, the Trinidadian C. L. R. James's *Black Jacobins* (1938) and the Martinican Aimé Césaire's

Toussaint Louverture (1960) remain the quintessential statements of the founding role of 1804 in Pan-African self-consciousness and the drive toward decolonization and autonomy. C. L. R. James, *The Black Jacobins: Toussaint Louverture and the San Domingo Revolution* (New York: Vintage, 1989). Aimé Césaire, *Toussaint Louverture: La Révolution française et le problème colonial*, (Paris: Présence africaine, 1960).

4. Michel-Rolph Trouillot, *Silencing the Past: Power and the Production of History* (Boston: Beacon, 1995).

5. Peter Hallward points out that "Saint-Domingue isn't even mentioned in Simon Schama's best-selling *Citizens* (1989) or Keith Baker's *Inventing the French Revolution* (1990), while François Furet and Mona Ozouf were unable to find room in their 1100 page *Critical Dictionary of the French Revolution* (1989) for an entry on Toussaint L'Ouverture; the entry on 'Slavery' in their index refers only to America's revolution, not Haiti's." Peter Hallward, "Option Zero in Haiti," in *New Left Review* 27 (May-June 2004), 23-47.

6. However, David Geggus's incredibly useful study *Haitian Revolutionary Studies* is a watershed that reveals how many archives still remain unexplored, pointing to years of future research. David Geggus, *Haitian Revolutionary Studies* (Bloomington: Indiana University Press, 2002).

7. Michel-Rolph Trouillot, *Haiti: State Against Nation; The Origins and Legacy of Duvalierism* (New York: Monthly Review Press, 1990).

8. Alain Badiou, *Abrégé de métapolitique* (Paris: Seuil, 1998).

9. Cited in Césaire, *Toussaint Louverture*, 197.

10. It is important not to conflate Heidegger's insightful and original (Jameson calls it "thrilling") critique of modern subjectivity as *Vorstellung*, as representation, with his critique of technological modernity. In the former, Heidegger shows how objects are made available *for* (*Vor-*) a subject, a subject that itself only comes into existence, finds an opening for its existence, in this arranging of an object world. Fredric Jameson, *A Singular Modernity* (New York: Verso, 2002), 45-48. In Heidegger's critique of technological modernity, however, from *Being and Time* through later essays such as "The Question Concerning Technology," he extends this insight only to make a crude and naïve (which is not to say incorrect) condemnation of (what the Frankfurt School will call) "instrumental reason," of the creation of a world in which every object exists merely in its use value *for* the autonomous subject (a forest becomes timber, a river hydroelectric power). Even cruder is his reactionary solution to this dilemma; thanks to his refusal to engage with the complexities of modern society, he can only withdraw into the *Heimat* of the Black Forest, philosophically stylized as the turn from beings to Being. Carl Schmitt, *The Crisis of Parliamentary Democracy* (Cambridge, Mass.: MIT Press, 1986); Martin Heidegger, *Being and Time: A Translation of Sein und Zeit*, Trans. Joan Stambaugh (Albany: State University of New York Press, 1996); and David Farrell Krell, ed., *Basic Writings* (New York: Harper & Row, 1977).

11. The locus classicus of this critique is found in the work of François Furet. Caroline Weber offers a striking analysis of the Jacobin attempt to destroy all differential dissent in *Terror and its Discontents: Suspect Words in Revolutionary France* (Minneapolis: University of Minnesota Press, 2003). François Furet, *Interpreting the French Revolution* (Cambridge, U.K.: Cambridge University Press, 1981).

12. Deleuze makes a similar point in *Negotiations*, arguing that to "say revolutions turn out badly [. . . confuses] two different things, the way revolutions turn out historically and people's revolutionary becoming." Cited in Slavov Žižek, *Organs Without Bodies: Deleuze and Consequences* (New York: Routledge, 2004), 12. In Deleuze's complex understanding of the relation between becoming and history, the former indicates the break with the past, the event that allows the emergence of the New.

13. Immanuel Kant, *Political Writings*, ed. Hans Reiss (Cambridge, U.K.: Cambridge University Press, 1970).

14. Geggus, *Haitian Revolutionary Studies*, 127.

15. "In the revolutionary explosion as an Event," says Žižek of the French Revolution, "another utopian dimension shines through, the dimension of universal emancipation, which, precisely, is the excess betrayed by the market reality that takes over 'the day after'—as such, this excess is not simply abolished, dismissed as irrelevant, but, as it were, *transposed into the virtual state*, continuing to haunt the emancipatory imaginary as a dream waiting to be realized" (*Organs Without Bodies*: 31).

16. Žižek, *Organs Without Bodies*, 31.

17. Robin Blackburn, "Of Human Bondage," in *The Nation* (4 October 2004, 26-32). See also Blackburn's *The Overthrow of Colonial Slavery: 1776-1848* (New York: Verso, 1988).

18. Geggus, *Haitian Revolutionary Studies*, 125. Thomas Madiou claimed that the idea of general emancipation "was not completely formed in the minds of either the blacks or the men of color" in this early period (cited in *Haitian Revolutionary Studies*, 126).

19. Cited in Geggus, *Haitian Revolutionary Studies*, 127.

20. Sankar Muthu offers a brilliant critique of this intellectual *doxa* in the concluding chapter of *Enlightenment Against Empire*, while recent revisionist descriptions of the multiple, often contradictory "Enlightenments" can be found in Baker and Reill, Jacob, Porter, and Teichs, and Israel. I develop these claims—particularly those regarding Kantian moral philosophy and Haiti—more fully in my forthcoming study of the Haitian Revolution and the Enlightenment. Sankar Muthu, *Enlightenment Against Empire* (Princeton, N.J.: Princeton University Press, 2003). Keith Michael Baker and Peter Hanns Reill, eds., *What's Left of Enlightenment?* (Stanford, Calif.: Stanford University Press, 2001). Margaret C. Jacob, *The Radical Enlightenment: Pantheists, Freemasons, and Republicans* (London: Allen & Unwin, 1981). Ray Porter and Mikulás Teich, eds., *The Enlightenment in National Context* (Cambridge, U.K.: Cambridge University Press, 1981). Jonathan I. Israel, *Radical Enlightenment: Philosophy and the Making of Modernity, 1650-1750* (Oxford, N.Y.: Oxford University Press, 2001).

21. Muthu, *Enlightenment Against Empire*, 263.

22. Gilles Deleuze, *L'Île déserte et autres textes* (Paris: Les Éditions de Minuit, 2002), 33. See also Jameson, *A Singular Modernity*, and Žižek, *Organs Without Bodies*, 186.

23. Gordon S. Wood, *The Radicalism of the American Revolution* (New York: Vintage Books, 1991), 192-98. Wood points out, however, that if the patrician American revolutionaries failed to abolish slavery, their egalitarianism created the social conditions in which it immediately became a glaring and impossible to ignore contradiction that led inexorably to the civil war and Abolition (186). See chapter 7 of David Brion

Davis's *The Problem of Slavery in the Age of Revolution, 1770-1823* (Ithaca, N.Y.: Cornell University Press, 1975) on the complex and contradictory forces at work in the long process leading to American Abolition.

24. Jurgen Habermas, *Between Facts and Norms: Contributions to a Discourse Theory of Law and Democracy*, trans. William Rehg (Cambridge, Mass.: MIT Press, 1998), 509.

25. Debray, *Haïti et la France*, 16.

26. George W. Bush, cited in Mark Danner, "Abu Ghraib: The Hidden Story," in *New York Review of Books* 51, no. 15, 7 October 2004.

27. For more information, see *Hidden Slaves: Forced Labor in the United States*, available online at: freetheslaves.net/home.php. See also Anti-Slavery International at www.antislavery.org/index.htm (26 Nov. 2004).

28. Caetano Veloso, *Verdade Tropical* (São Paulo: Companhia das letras, 1997). Christopher Dunn, *Brutality Garden: Tropicália and the Emergence of a Brazilian Counterculture* (Chapel Hill: University of North Carolina Press, 2001).

3

The Past Is *passé*

Time and Memory in Maryse Condé's *La Belle Créole*

Nicole J. Simek

IN HER SUGGESTIVE ARTICLE "O Brave New World," Maryse Condé envisions how fundamental changes in memory and community might be brought about through globalization: "Globalization can not only be controlled but used to our benefit. It may become the creation of a universe where the notions of race, nationality, and language, which for so long have divided us, are re-examined and find new expressions; where the notions of hybridity, *métissage*, multiculturalism are fully redefined."[1] Linking globalization mainly to migration, she points out that rather than viewing all migrant communities as "dysfunctional [. . .], having no roots and no means of expressing a confused identity," we should recognize that such communities, under the proper conditions, can become—and already have been—the "seat of an extraordinary creativity" and new, hybrid forms of cultural production.[2]

Such a forward-looking stance might seem to coincide with claims by some globalization theorists that history, and by extension postcolonial theory (with its emphasis on deconstructing and rereading narratives about the past), is no longer pertinent to the analysis of current global conditions—or even that a concern for history is counterproductive, retarding the development of a society built on a postidentitarian conception of subjectivity (a conception of the subject as fluid, constructed, and deterritorialized, as, in other words, beyond the confines of fixed, originary identity).[3] Fredric Jameson and Arif Dirlik both refer to such a trend in summarizing globalization debate, the former pointing to those who equate globalization with postmodernism and observe in both the theory of "the disappearance of History as the fundamental element in which human beings exist,"[4] and the latter highlighting one of the "paradoxes" of "our age," namely our "preoccupation with history at a time when history seems to be increasingly irrelevant to understanding the present."[5] "Worked over by postmodernism, among other things," Dirlik continues, "the past itself seems to be up for grabs, as though it can be made to say anything we want it to say."[6] The global subject is one who no longer exists in history, for whom the past no longer has meaning or relevance to the present. Naming the structure that produces such global subjects "Empire," Michael Hardt and Antonio Negri describe it as a "new regime," a "new notion of right, or rather, a new inscription of authority and a new design of the production of norms and legal instruments of coercion," brought about by the "radical transformation" of key concepts and characterized by its "lack of boundaries."[7] These fluctuating boundaries include not only spatial frontiers, but temporal distinctions as well, since "the concept of Empire presents itself not as a historical regime originating in conquest, but rather as an order that effectively suspends history and thereby fixes the existing state of affairs for eternity."[8]

Set against the dismal background of a civil servants' and workers' strike in 1999 Guadeloupe, Maryse Condé's 2001 novel *La Belle Créole* is resolutely anchored in the present, and explicitly concerned with the questions of time and memory central to debates over globalizing forces and structures currently at work in the world.[9] How is one to interpret today, the text asks, the relation of the past to the present and future, history to memory, individual to collective experience? Interrogating the use of (re)reading and (re)writing historical paradigms in order to understand the present, Condé's text also raises the question of the extent to which the perceived disappearance of history in the new global order can be distinguished from the absence of collective memory that Edouard Glissant and others identify as symptomatic of the Antillean postcolonial condition.[10] Is globalization in this respect the generalization of the Caribbean experience? If so, one may wonder whether globalization is an emancipatory force, or contains within it the potential for liberation. Does the disappearance of historical memory free one from the past? Should it be viewed rather as an effect of trauma or violence to be rectified through the reconstitution of history or memory?

Relating the events of the last night of Dieudonné, a young man charged with murdering his *békée*[11] employer and lover, Loraine, the action of *La Belle Créole* unfolds over the course of only twenty-four hours. The specificity of the present is evoked from the start of the novel: the opening pages describe in detail the exceptionally hard times on which Guadeloupe has fallen as crime rates rise, city services disappear, and an unprecedented heat wave— "pire que celle du carême des vingt dernières années se plaignaient ceux qui avaient la force de garder mémoire" (13) [worse than any dry season of the last twenty years, complained those with the strength to remember][12]—grips the country. The arrival of a seemingly new and ominous state of affairs is summed up and framed by the book's epigraph as well: "Voici le temps des assassins" [This is the time of the assassins]. Yet this epigraph, a line excerpted from Arthur Rimbaud's "Matinée d'ivresse,"[13] [Morning of Drunkenness] not only reflects the attitude of a population fed up with "cette jeunesse qui ne savait que tuer, braquer, violer, incendier, cette jeunesse dont les rêves avaient la démesure des effets spéciaux des films" [this youth that only knew how to kill, steal, rape, and set fires, this youth whose dreams were as excessive as the special effects of movies], but also renders such a reading of the present's specificity problematic. Rimbaud's verse, once it is freed of its original interpretive context, identifies "le temps des assassins" as exemplary of "this" era: the time of the assassins is no longer a specific time of day (morning), but "now" more generally, and the current moment is distinct because it belongs to assassins. Yet the invocation of a sentence written over 100 years before, if taken as useful for elucidating the story that follows, also raises doubts about any claim that the present is significantly new or radically Other, rather than a perpetuation of the Same. This temporal ambiguity is doubled by a referential one, further throwing doubt on the epigraph's hermeneutical function. Rimbaud's line, we recall, plays on the etymological sense of the word assassin, which in the nineteenth century was thought to have originally meant "hashish-eaters." While Dieudonné will be labeled an "assassin" at one point in the book, and will also internalize this label, his status as a murderer, like the identity of Rimbaud's assassins, remains unclear, and must be continually reassessed and reconfigured as the novel progresses. The ambiguity of the phrase is mirrored not only by the uncertainty of Dieudonné's guilt (we will learn that he killed Loraine accidentally, in self-defense), but also by the uncertain extent to which he exemplifies a plural collective. *Who* the assassins are (Dieudonné and his generation? Loraine and the *béké* class? Society? History?) is debatable, especially in the light of Dieudonné's death at the end of the book. This referential ambiguity resembles that of the book's title itself: although *La Belle Créole* could be taken to refer to Loraine or her class, or to represent a personified Guadeloupe, it is primarily the exotic name of a boat on which Dieudonné takes refuge, a boat adored by its owners yet abandoned when they return to Europe, and the boat on which Dieudonné will die.

The question of the past's explanatory value remains central to the novel, as various characters attempt to reconstruct and decipher Dieudonné's actions and their meaning. If the defense given by his lawyer during the trial appears old-fashioned and overly simplistic to many of the characters—the lawyer unproblematically assimilates racial discrimination and class struggle motifs in portraying Dieudonné as a mistreated slave who has killed his oppressive white employer in revolt—most of them are still sympathetic to this portrait. Local artists view Loraine's patronage as a resource to be exploited and discarded, with the reasoning that she was only paying "une partie de la dette considérable, accumulée vis-à-vis de la Race" (219-20) [a part of the considerable debt to the Race accumulated over the years]. Others view Dieudonné's love for Loraine as either a mark of alienation or a calculated strategy of social ascension. Dieudonné, for his part, refuses to view himself as in any way exemplary of his race and its specific history in Guadeloupe: "Benjy et Boris [leaders of the independence movement] l'ennuyaient avec leurs discours. Toujours à lui seriner qu'il appartenait à la classe des opprimés. Opprimé par qui? Par quoi? Il était né dans un mauvais berceau, manque de chance! La chance, cela ne se discute pas. C'est affaire de hasard" (75) [Benjy and Boris bored him with their speeches. Always drumming into him that he belonged to the class of the oppressed. Oppressed by who? By what? He was born in an unfortunate cradle, hard luck! You can't question luck. It's a matter of chance]. While the past is not completely unknown to Dieudonné, its authoritative status is flatly denied. In his view the past has little bearing on the present:

> Quand il voyait d'autres noirs, africains ou américains, au cinéma, à la télévision, il n'ignorait pas qu'une parenté singulière les unissait. Il n'ignorait pas que dans le temps-longtemps, ils avaient été frères et sœurs, sortis du même ventre avant qu'une force cruelle ne les disperse aux quatre coins du monde. Comment cela s'était-il produit exactement? Il l'ignorait et ne s'en préoccupait guère. Ce passé-là ne valait pas le présent qu'il vivait avec ses affres et ses manques. (220)

> When he saw other African or American blacks, in the movies or on television, he was not unaware that a unique heritage united them. He was not unaware that long ago they had been brothers and sisters, fruits of the same womb before a cruel force dispersed them across the four corners of the world. How had that happened exactly? He didn't know and hardly cared about it. That past was worth nothing compared to the present he was living with its torments and deprivations.

Refusing to grant any privileged hermeneutic status to the past, Dieudonné suggests that his mode of being is more or less self-explanatory: his miserable condition needs no abstraction or theorization since it is simply lived. Yet if the past does not matter, neither, it seems, does time itself. Even the here and now is cast into doubt in a moment of transcendence that takes place, significantly, on New Year's Eve (at once a temporally uncertain, transitional time between end and beginning, and the most explicit and celebrated marker of time's progression): "[Dieudonné] cessa d'avoir conscience du temps, de l'endroit où il se trouvait. Il ne fut plus qu'un patchwork d'impressions, de sensations. Des éclairs de lumière l'aveuglaient, des sons, des éclats de voix, de rire l'assourdissaient. Ce goût âpre dans la bouche était celui du bonheur" (215) [[Dieudonné's] consciousness of time, of where he was at ceased. He was nothing but a patchwork of impressions and sensations anymore. Bolts of light blinded him, bursts of laughter and voices deafened him. This bitter taste in his mouth was the taste of happiness].

On one level this passage may be read as a simple cliché, a passing sentiment of blissful atemporality. Yet the dissolution of both temporal boundaries and the contours of fixed, monadic identity that takes place in these two moments should not simply be dismissed, but taken into account in an analysis of how time can or should be experienced today. Indeed, Dieudonné seems to exemplify at these moments a postidentitarian subject, one for whom time is no longer a "fundamental element" of existence.[14] How such an experience should be understood, whether it is emblematic of Guadeloupeans as a collectivity, and whether it should be prescribed remains debatable throughout *La Belle Créole*. The novel is framed by questions of interpretation, and frustrates attempts to construct explanatory models relating the present to the past. Opening in a courtroom, at the moment a jury is rendering its verdict on Dieudonné's case, the novel similarly closes with a debate over how to interpret another of Dieudonné's acts, this time his apparent suicide. Competing interpretations of his life and death circulate throughout the rest of the text. Notably, historical memory appears less and less viable as an interpretive paradigm for understanding Dieudonné's plight as the novel progresses: the characters who invoke Guadeloupe's history of slavery and racial tension as the unique determining force in his life are unable to recognize the specificity of Dieudonné's personality, nor the distinction between past and present relations of power. History is increasingly displaced by literature and film as points of reference for many of the characters. Their tendency to read reality through the lens of fiction, to rely on prior fictive examples in conceptualizing events presently occurring around them, and, conversely, to appreciate fiction for its resemblance to reality is striking. Dieudonné's affair with Loraine elicits numerous comparisons to fictional plots. The German-American student Ana views their story as "une version tropicale des amours de Lady Chatterley" [a tropical version of Lady Chatterley's love affair], while another young girl compares Loraine to Glenn Close, but more specifically to Glenn Close in *Fatal Attraction* (1987), that is, to a role or persona. More generally, reality itself has become transfigured for one character, who likens the streets of Port-Mahault to the set of an action movie or science fiction film. How are we to interpret this recourse to art? Is it a sign of historical amnesia, an absence of historical knowledge from which to draw comparisons and contrasts with the present? Is it rather a response to the radical newness of this present, which appears so irreducible to the past as to only be comparable to fantasy or invention? Moreover, how are we as readers to take the fictional work at hand? Does the novel function as a vehicle for memory, lending itself to appropriation, or does it affect a rupture with the very process of appropriating, of interpreting contemporary events through artistic or fictional precedents?

On the one hand, *La Belle Créole* as a work appears to privilege art for its ability to accommodate ambiguity and multiplicity, and for its ability to break with the past. The first qualities are apparent in Dieudonné's own aesthetic preferences, as evidenced by the only two paintings he likes among all those that Loraine has displayed in her house:

> Il faisait une exception pour deux tableaux. L'un petit, tout dans les tons de brun. Qu'est-ce qu'il représentait? Il croyait reconnaître un poisson d'argent. Ou était-ce un croissant de lune? Le moutonnement de la mer. Ou étaient-ce des nuages? L'autre, plus grand, très grand, représentait une feuille d'arbre. Une feuille de bananier géant. Ou était-ce un visage, ses nervures symbolisant des traits, un nez, une bouche? (58)

> He made an exception for two paintings. The first one, small, was all done in shades of brown. What did it represent? He thought he recognized a silverfish. Or was it a moon crescent? The foam of the sea. Or was it clouds? The other, larger, very large, represented a leaf. A giant banana tree leaf. Or was it a face, its veins symbolizing features, a nose, a mouth?

Other characters turn to literary and cinematic models to inform their interpretation of Dieudonné out of dissatisfaction with what they view as a reductive and outdated historical narrative, what one thinks of as an "équation manichéiste" (122) [Manichean equation]: "Maîtresse, esclave, c'était du passé," reflects another. "La société avait changé et, en pleine vingtième siècle, personne ne croyait plus à ces bêtises-là" (193) [Mistress, slave, that was all in the past now. Society had changed, and at the height of the twentieth century nobody believed in that nonsense any more]. Yet characters' reliance on the media—on television in general, and on the newspapers *France-Caraïbe* and *France-Antilles* in particular, which cover all the details of Dieudonné's "crime passionnel" (202) ["crime of passion"]—also seems to reflect what Arjun Appadurai has described as the "new role for the imagination in social life" today, "something critical and new in global cultural processes: *the imagination as social practice* . . . a form of negotiation between sites of agency (individuals) and globally defined fields of possibility."[15] The new role of the imaginary in the global world, Appadurai contends, has significant implications for the way in which the past is experienced:

The past is now not a land to return to in a simple politics of memory. It has become a synchronic warehouse of cultural scenarios, a kind of temporal central casting, to which recourse can be taken as appropriate, depending on the movie to be made, the scene to be enacted, the hostages to be rescued.[16]

Yet rather than simply prescribing art as the most useful paradigm for reading the present, the *mise-en-abyme* of the reading or interpretive process at work in *La Belle Créole* also draws attention to the problems inherent in such an interpretive move, namely to the problems inherent in reducing two disparate cases to instantiations of the same. Going back to the comparison of Dieudonné's story to *Lady Chatterley's Lover*, we can begin to see how this problematic is highlighted. While the book jacket picks up on this quote and presents *La Belle Créole* as a loose adaptation of D. H. Lawrence's text, the details of the plot diverge considerably. *Lady Chatterley's Lover* emphasizes love across class divisions, but ends happily, with Connie Chatterley acting on her principles and leaving her husband for the lower-class man she loves. A more appropriate intertext, and one that Condé introduces obliquely, is another English work, Shakespeare's *Othello*. The play, which underscores racial tensions and violence, is mentioned in passing through another of the novel's key characters, Boris, a poet and union leader, who, we learn, "affectionnait tout particulièrement *Othello or the Moor of Venice*, la tragédie d'un homme qui avait eu le courage de tuer celle qui le trompait" (35) [was particularly fond of *Othello or the Moor of Venice*, the tragedy of a man who had had the courage to kill the woman who deceived him]. Moreover, *La Belle Créole*'s Caribbean setting recalls *Othello*'s emphasis on Cyprus as a backdrop for the play's action, while its theme of Venetian mercantilism and interest in material wealth is paralleled by *La Belle Créole*'s exposition of Guadeloupean consumerism. The intertextual reference to *Othello* could be seen then as a critique of or supplement to Ana's model, providing the reader with a framework for understanding both Dieudonné's story and that of his society.

Yet what is striking in this reference is Boris's questionable reading, or misreading, of the play, which highlights Othello's courage, but elides his tragic mistake. The reference then takes on a second function, becoming a *mise-en-garde* against uncritically assimilating Dieudonné to Othello, or Loraine to Desdemona. As the novel advances Condé multiplies and complicates intertextual references, and *Othello* becomes one of a series of disparate examples, whose effectiveness in elucidating Dieudonné's story is repeatedly called into question. In addition to the hermeneutical imperative to multiply one's perspectives on Dieudonné's life, however, Condé's text raises questions regarding the power of literature to affect the widespread and persistent desire to identify others in clearly defined terms, even in a global world where identities have allegedly become unmoored. Only the reader is privy to the ambiguity and multiplicity of Dieudonné's story; Dieudonné's dependence on others' visions of him leads to a feeling of emptiness and an inability to project himself into a meaningful future that eventually leads to suicide. Meeting stares wherever he goes, he reflects: "Désormais, il faudrait vivre sa vie, objet d'admiration pour les uns, objet de haine et de terreur pour les autres. Il n'avait pas de vérité, il n'était rien, qu'un bwa-bwa de carnaval, habillé d'oripeaux, travesti des fantasmes de ses compatriotes" (52) [From now on, he would have to live his life as an object of admiration for some, an object of hate and terror for others. He had no truth, he was nothing, only a carnival marionette, dressed in rags, disguised in the fantasies of his compatriots].

While describing the experience of the flattening of time, Condé's text also compels her readers to address the question of historicization. Indeed, regardless of the characters' conscious sentiments regarding history, all are haunted by the past. The excruciatingly hot weather and sandstorms which defy memory are blowing in from the coast of Western Africa, states the narrator in the opening paragraph (13), while the past symbolically resurges in the form of packs of stray dogs that begin to roam the streets and threaten the inhabitants of Port-Mahault once city services cease operations. Dogs, according to the narrator, are heavily charged with negative symbolism in Guadeloupean society:[17]

> C'est une vieille affaire. Au temps de la plantation, les chiens ont poursuivi le nègre en fuite, traqué, fait saigner le marron pour le compte du Maître. En outre, chacun sait que les Esprits adorent se tourner en chiens, prenant, pour jouer leurs mauvais tours, la forme de l'ennemi séculaire. Pis encore, il s'agissait d'un animal tout juste bon à exciter l'hilarité ou la pitié. (68)

> It's an age-old business. In the plantation era, dogs chased the black man in flight, tracked the maroon and made him bleed for the advantage of the Master. Plus, everyone knows the Spirits love to transform themselves into dogs, taking on, in order to play their evil tricks, the form of the secular enemy. Even worse, the dog was an animal only good enough to provoke hilarity or pity.

Dogs intervene in Dieudonné's personal relationship with Loraine as a source of tension and anguish that Dieudonné attempts to erase. When Loraine's excessive affection for her puppy Lili comes between the two lovers, Dieudonné secretly poisons and disposes of the dog, unknowingly reenacting an earlier event, the death of Loraine's childhood pet (also named Lili), who was run over (ostensibly accidentally) by a friend's unapologetic chauffeur. Dieudonné's refusal to relate what actually happened the night Loraine was killed, his mute acceptance of guilt and insistent denial of what ballistic evidence showed (that there had been a struggle [44]), stems from a similar desire to keep his relationship with Loraine pure, to keep her (mis)treatment of him within his own interpretive control, away from the public eye. To confess that Loraine, drunk and angry, "l'aurait abattu comme un chien" [would have shot him down like a dog] had he not defended himself in the course of an argument, would constitute, to Dieudonné's mind, "l'ultime trahison" (227) [the ultimate betrayal]. Keeping silent preserves Loraine's last words to him from scrutiny ("Tu es un vulgaire rien du tout. Tu n'es qu'un petit nègre rempli d'aigreur et de malice comme tous tes pareils. Il te manque la trique dont tu garderas éternellement le souvenir" [224] [You're a vulgar nothing. You're just a nigger filled with bitterness and malice like all the rest. You're missing the cudgel that you'll remember for the rest of eternity]), and allows him to maintain a view of their relationship as one situated outside the history of racial relations, one whose tensions can be explained through psychological or personal reasons. "Est-ce qu'il n'aurait pas dû comprendre qu'elle déparlait?" reflects Dieudonné in the final pages of the novel,

> Parce qu'elle avait trop bu. La bouteille de Glenfiddich à moitié vidée en témoignait. Parce qu'elle était trop seule en cette saison des fêtes. Parce qu'elle éprouvait trop de chagrin du départ de Luc. Peut-être qu'elle ne pensait pas un mot des paroles que sa bouche prononçait et le piquait-elle pour qu'il oublie sa constante réserve. (224)

> Shouldn't he have understood that she was talking nonsense? Because she had had too much to drink. The half-emptied bottle of Glenfiddich testified to that. Because she was too lonely during this holiday season. Because she was too upset by Luc's departure. Maybe she didn't believe one word of what her mouth was saying and was provoking him deliberately to make him forget his constant reserve.

Despite his attempt to efface or reinterpret his own dehumanized or marginalized status as a "dog," dogs continue to haunt Dieudonné throughout his last night, concretely as they follow him through the streets of Port-Mahault, and symbolically, as he is turned away, "comme un chien" [like a dog], by friends and family (109, 213). For the residents of Port-Mahault more generally, dogs, reminiscent of past oppression, reinforce the French administrative hold over the Antilles both on a practical and a psychological level. Representing a threat to life ("une fois même, ils avaient dévoré un bébé endormi dans son berceau" [173] [one time, they had even devoured a baby asleep in his crib]), and to sanitation ("Évidemment, cela n'allait pas sans déjections puantes, dures et sèches comme celles des biques, disséminées un peu partout dans le gazon. Ou au contraire, bilieuses, répandues en purée autour des gerberas et des multipliants" [18]

[Obviously, all this did not come without stinking feces, hard and dry like those of nanny-goats, scattered around all over the lawns. Or, on the contrary, a yellowish purée spread around the gerberas and golden cane palms]), the overpopulation of dogs is the most intolerable consequence of the strikes, seemingly pointing to the breakdown of civil society and state of chaos that would occur should the islands be cut off from metropolitan France. Yet their spectacular slaughter at the end of the novel provokes a change of heart (at the conclusion of the strikes, Animal Control appears with lassos and bags of chloroform, then incinerates the bodies, whose ashes and stench rain down on the city)—"Du coup," the narrator relates, "les esprits les plus endurcis se mirent à regretter la cavalcade de ces bêtes qui leur avaient causé pourtant tellement de répulsion" (248) [At that, the most hardened hearts began to miss the cavalcade of these beasts who had nonetheless sparked in them so much repulsion].

Either reading the dogs as a warning of the potential return of the past,[18] or attempting to efface their memory completely is an unsatisfactory solution for elucidating Guadeloupe's and Dieudonné's present. What *La Belle Créole* calls for is arguably something in between: not just a recognition of the limitations of relying too heavily on the past as a tool for constructing the present and future, but a literary and critical practice that attempts to reconcile historicization with an attention to the often divergent experience of history, to read literature for its ability to elaborate the ambiguous presence of the past in the present, but to read it with its explanatory limits in mind. Such a practice would not jettison postcolonial theory's noted attention to specificity and the past in an age of mutable identities and accelerated (or disappearing) time, but would attempt to engage methods of historicization precisely in order to better analyze the experience of globalization important to any apprehension of the present.

Notes

I would like to thank Zahi Zalloua, Tim Watson, and Thomas Trezise for their helpful comments on earlier drafts of this chapter.

1. Maryse Condé, "O Brave New World," in *Multiculturalism and Hybridity in African Literatures*, ed. Hal Wylie and Bernth Lindfors (Trenton, N.J.: Africa World Press, 2000), 29-36; this quotation, 35.

2. Condé, "O Brave New World," 32. Like the term "modernity," to which it is often related, "globalization," a concept having come into fashion more recently (mainly after Marshall McLuhan's popularization of the idea of the "global village" in the 1960s), has sparked much debate over not only when it began, but whether it exists at all, how precisely it can be defined, and whether it should be celebrated or resisted.

Very generally, globalization theories seek to explain tendencies toward the transnationalization of capital and communications networks, recent increases in population migrations across the globe, and the shifts in conceptions of the nation, culture, and identity that result from such movements. Disputes over the definition of globalization have often centered on the perceived "newness" of such trends, as well the extent to which they indicate increasing cultural homogenization (generally spreading outward from a powerful center) or rather a de-centering of imperialist powers, a breakdown of center-periphery logic, and thus the empowerment of previously "peripheral" and marginalized populations. Michael Hardt and Antonio Negri argue for example in *Empire* that while the currently emerging structure of "Empire" has not been created *ex nihilo*, it is a "new regime" that "has nothing to do with the juridical arts of dictatorship or totalitarianism . . . in other times." *Empire* (Cambridge, Mass.: Harvard University Press, 2000), 26. Arjun Appadurai asserts that "a merest acquaintance of the facts of the modern world" is sufficient "to note that it is now an interactive system in a sense that is strikingly new" (*Modernity at Large: Cultural Dimensions* [Minneapolis: University of Minnesota Press, 1996], 29), while Enrique Dussel ("Beyond Eurocentrism: The World-System and the Limits of Modernity," in *The Cultures of Globalization*, ed. Fredric Jameson and Masao Miyoshi [Durham, N.C.: Duke University Press, 1998], 3-31), views today's world-system on the contrary as governed by a center-periphery logic that has been operative on an "interregional" level since at least 762 C.E., and that is at the root of today's rationalist "practices of domination and exclusion" of the periphery (5, 19). For a philosophical critique of identity and the alternative of nomadism, see Gilles Deleuze and Félix Guattari, *Mille Plateaux* (Paris: Éditions de Minuit, 1980). For a response to the critical evaluation of nomadism in the French postcolonial context see Christopher Miller, *Nationalists and Nomads: Essays on Francophone African Literature and Culture* (Chicago: University of Chicago Press, 1998), in particular chapter 6. See also Simon Gikandi, "Globalization and the Claims of Postcoloniality," *South Atlantic Quarterly* 100, no. 3 (2001): 627-58, for a discussion of disciplinary lines in globalization debates.

3. As Hardt and Negri suggest, "postmodernist and postcolonialist theorists" are "so intent on combating the remnants of a past form of domination [Enlightenment rationality and colonialism] that they fail to recognize the new form that is looming over them" (137-38).

4. Fredric Jameson, "Notes on Globalization as a Philosophical Issue," in *The Cultures of Globalization*, ed. Fredric Jameson and Masao Miyoshi (Durham, N.C.: Duke University Press, 1998), 54-77; this quotation, 55.

5. Arif Dirlik, "Is There History after Eurocentrism? Globalism, Postcolonialism, and the Disavowal of History," in *History after the Three Worlds: Post-Eurocentric Historiographies*, ed. Arif Dirlik, Vinay Bahl and Peter Gran (Lanham, Md.: Rowman and Littlefield, 2000), 25-47; this quotation, 25.

6. Dirlik, "Is There History after Eurocentrism?" 25.

7. Hardt and Negri, *Empire*, 9, 26, xiv.

8. Hardt and Negri, *Empire*, xiv.

9. Maryse Condé, *La Belle Créole* (Paris: Mercure de France, 2001). Henceforth, all references to this work will be stated parenthetically in the text.

10. See Edouard Glissant, *Le Discours antillais* (Paris: Gallimard, 1997).

11. The word *béké* designates white plantation owners and their descendents.

12. All translations from the *La Belle Créole* are my own.

13. *Illuminations*, in Arthur Rimbaud, *Œuvres complètes* (Paris: Gallimard, 1979).

14. Jameson, "Notes on Globalization," 55.

15. Appadurai, *Modernity at Large*, 31 (emphasis in the original).

16. Appadurai, *Modernity at Large*, 30. See Gikandi for a sensitive analysis of the valorization of the imaginary in postcolonial discussions of globalization.

17. An aversion to dogs is of course not a purely Caribbean phenomenon. J. M. Coetzee also makes creative use of the figure of the dog in the South African context in his 1999 novel *Disgrace* (New York: Penguin Books, 2000).

18. A humorous reminder against simply conflating the past and the present through the symbol of the dog comes when we learn that among the artists demanding their due from their white oppressor, Loraine, is the actor Élias Reclus, famed for his performance in *Combat de nègre et de chien* [The Fight of the Black and the Dog] (219). Conversely, however, Loraine's inability to recognize or comprehend the historical reasons for her current relative privilege and the attendant resentment against her is equally problematic. Subscribing to the myth of the "good master," Loraine underestimates the past wrongs of her class, and is only able to describe that class, and her own position in the world, in tragic, metaphysical terms. "[P]our mon malheur, je suis une békée. Les békés sont une race maudite," she complains to Dieudonné. "Nous avons fait le sale travail pour les blancs-France: mettre les nègres d'Afrique au travail, cultiver la canne, essayer de sauver les plantations après l'abolition. Quand même, ceux-ci n'ont jamais éprouvé de reconnaissance. Jamais un mot de merci! . . . Quant aux nègres, ils nous détestent. Jusqu'au jour d'aujourd'hui, ils nous accusent de tous les péchés d'Israël. Ils ne veulent se souvenir que des coups et des humiliations des mauvais maîtres. En même temps d'après eux, les bons maîtres, c'était pis encore que les autres, des hypocrites, des paternalistes. En somme, nous perdons sur tous les tableaux" [It is my misfortune to be a *békée*. The *békés* are a cursed race. We did the dirty work for the metropolitan French: putting the blacks from Africa to work, cultivating the sugar cane, and trying to save the plantations after abolition. And yet they never felt any gratitude. Never a word of thanks! . . . As for the blacks, they hate us. Right up to today they accuse us of all the sins of Israel. They only want to remember the blows and the humiliation from the bad masters. At the same time, according to them the good masters were even worse than the others. Hypocrites, paternalists. In sum, we lose on all fronts.] (138). For a discussion of the notion of the "bon maître," see Caroline Bastide, "Pour en finir avec le bon maître," *Dérades* no. 5 (2000): 41-58.

4

France and the French in the Collective Memory of the Acadians

Jean-Luc Desalvo

THIS STUDY EXAMINES THE WAYS in which France and the French are portrayed in the collective memory of the Acadians in the works of Antonine Maillet and Claude LeBouthillier, two contemporary francophone Acadian authors. Today's Acadians are the descendants of French colonists who settled in the Maritime Provinces of Canada from the seventeenth century onwards before being expelled by the British in the middle of the eighteenth century. As we shall discover, relegated to a minority status having little to no say in their own affairs and left to suffer in silence, the Acadians hold a tremendous grudge against history not only for the humiliations and injustices Acadia and French-speaking Acadians have endured throughout the course of history at the hands of various groups, but also because Acadia has fallen victim to one of the worst forms of historical contempt—neglect—or, as Maillet's narrator, for example, points out ironically in *Le Chemin Saint-Jacques*, "l'histoire d'un peuple sans histoire"[1] [the (hi)story of a people without history]. This remark underscores the importance and urgency in Maillet's and LeBouthillier's works of reinserting Acadia's name within the forgotten lines of history, as well as in the consciousness and collective memory of the Acadians themselves. Or, conversely, as Maillet's narrator notes once again with irony in *L'Acadie pour quasiment rien*: "Je ne vous ferai pas un cours d'histoire, les peuples heureux n'en ont pas"[2] [I will not lecture you on history, fortunate nations do not have any]. In other words, as Maillet herself would say tongue in cheek, the Acadians are not fortunate enough to have any "bisbilles" or squabbles with anyone.

The Acadians seek not only to be included and take part in history, but also to be in a position to write their own historical account, especially when it concerns them. The discussion regarding the historical exclusion of Acadia and of the Acadians in Maillet's and LeBouthillier's works calls into question the criteria employed to judge the merit of what deserves to be included in the pages of history and, likewise, history itself when written by outsiders. For instance, Maillet questions the pertinence and reliability of these criteria by evoking the divergence between history written with a capital H and history, often oral accounts, written with a lowercase h. Maillet's narrator in *L'Acadie pour quasiment rien* highlights the difference in the following manner: "La différence entre la grande et la petite histoire est que l'une traite des grands hommes et des grands événements qui dirigent la vie d'un peuple; et que l'autre raconte la vie de ce peuple qui se fait ballotter par les grands événements et les grands hommes. L'Acadie, pour sûr, c'est de la petite histoire."[3] [The difference between major and minor history is that one is about great, historical figures and events that lead a people's lives; the other recalls the lives of a people who have been tossed about by these great, historical events and figures. Acadia is for sure a case of minor history.] Consequently, Maillet and LeBouthillier both acknowledge their indispensable role with regard to ensuring the authentic transmission of the Acadians' collective memory. However, in view of the historical and political marginalization of Acadia and French-speaking Acadians by diverse groups, including the French, we will also explain the, above all, historical and cultural reasons responsible for the creation in Maillet's and LeBouthillier's works of an often bitter-sweet or ambivalent portrait of France and the French.

A remark in the section entitled "L'Acadie historique" or "Historical Acadia" at the very beginning of Maillet's novel *L'Acadie pour quasiment rien* is in this regard very telling. The novel's ironic title probably draws attention to the fact that, although Acadia was given away for cheap and that it no longer officially exists, the narrator is being generous in offering the reader the scraps or, in any case, what little remains. The narrator's attitude and tone reveal a certain amount of bitterness directed toward the kings of France and, especially, the kings of England and Acadia's other conquistadors who, for the most part, neglected Acadia except when their political interests were at stake: "Elle fut d'abord dunes de sable et forêts vierges pour outardes et goélands; puis colonie des rois de France; puis terrain de chasse des armées anglaises; puis provinces qui entrent à pieds joints dans la Confédération; puis de nouveau forêts et dunes pour outardes et goélands"[4] [It was, first of all, a series of pristine sand dunes and forest lands for Canada geese and seagulls; then a colony of the kings of France; next a hunting ground for the English army; then provinces forced to join the Confederation; after that again forest lands and sand dunes for

Canada geese and seagulls]. This return to a state of wilderness of "forest lands and sand dunes for Canada geese and seagulls," no longer pristine, clearly underscores the neglect which befell Acadia politically and, more recently, economically within the Canadian Confederation.

Likewise, in his collection of poems, entitled *Tisons péninsulaires*, LeBouthillier is desperately in search of answers to Acadia's problems, and the poet expresses perfectly the feeling of frustration and abandonment to which Acadia falls prey:

> Dans l'empremier, les morues sautaient dans les assiettes.
> Aujourd'hui, comme des termites,
> Le désespoir gruge les maisons à vendre
> Abandonnées
> Saisies par les finances, crevassées par les cassures de familles.
> Village fantôme où nous guette le chiendent
> Feuilles glacées dans la pluie froide et le ciel affaissé.
> Chantiers navals désertés, marchés aux puces,
> Soupes de plus en plus populaires.
> [. . .]
> Greffée sur la misère, notre technologie de pointe.
> Hôpitaux
> Cliniques d'hygiène mentale
> Psychologues
> Psychiatres
> Travailleurs sociaux
> Agents de probation
> Conseillers de recherche de non-emploi
> Compagnies de finance
> Déménageurs.
> Si on ne peut briser la résistance de la Péninsule, on la vide.
> Ras le bol de transfuser Toronto, Montréal, Moncton.
>
> Nos ancêtres se sont-ils battus pour mettre ce pays aux
>   enchères?
> Que nous restera-t-il?
> Un doré pourri?
> Un chalutier embourbé?
> Quelques trappes dans un musée virtuel?
> Ras le bol.[5]
>
> In the beginning, cod jumped out from everywhere.
> Today, like termites,
> Hopelessness eats away the houses for sale

Abandoned
Repossessed by financial lenders, cracked by broken families.
Deserted village where trouble awaits
Leaves frozen in the cold rain and the sunken sky.
Deserted shipyards, flea markets,
Soup kitchens springing up everywhere
[. . .]
Grafted on misery, our leading-edge technology.
Hospitals
Mental health clinics
Psychologists
Psychiatrists
Social workers
Probation officers
Unemployment counselors
Financial companies
Movers
If the Peninsula's resistance cannot be broken, liquidation.
Fed up with transfusing Toronto, Montréal, Moncton.
Did our ancestors fight to put this country up for
     auction?
What will we have left?
A rotten wall-eyed pike?
A bogged down trawler?
A few traps in a virtual museum?
Can't take any more of this.

Maillet expresses a similar idea in her novel *On a mangé la dune* when the main protagonist Radi, Maillet's own childhood alter ego, realizes that Acadia is "À vendre!" or up for sale to the highest bidder.[6]

Historically speaking, Maillet's narrator in *Pélagie-la-Charrette* is even more caustic with regard to the notion that Acadia is merely, in the eyes of the kings of France and England, a "jeu de cartes," an amusement in the form of a "card game" or map exercise whose borders they can redraw according to their every whim:

> Car l'Acadie, à force d'être ballottée d'un maître à l'autre, avait fini par se faufiler entre les deux, par les leurrer tous et par mener ses affaires toute seule, juste sous le nez des Louis et des George des vieux pays qui reniflaient encore du côté des épices. Et sans souffler mot, la petite colonie d'Atlantique laissait les rois de France et d'Angleterre se renvoyer des cartes revues et corrigées d'Acadie et de Nova Scotia, pendant qu'elle continuait allégrement à planter ses choux. Ça ne devait pas durer, c'était des choux gras. Et les soldats anglais qui rêvaient d'un coin de terre se mirent à lorgner ces champs-là.[7]

For Acadia, tossed from one royal master to another, had managed to slip between the two and fool them both, going about its own business right under the old-country noses of Louis and George still sniffing the wind for spices. And without breathing a word, the little Atlantic colony had let the kings of France and England send back and forth their revised and corrected maps of Acadia and Nova Scotia, and had gone on happily cultivating its garden. It wasn't to last: The harvests were too good to be true. And the English soldiers, dreaming of a few country acres, began to covet those Acadian fields.[8]

There is an obvious reference here to the Antilles and their spices. Maillet's narrator most likely holds a grudge against France for abandoning its interests in New France in favor of its more lucrative spice interests in Guadeloupe and Martinique. In any case, the Treaty of Paris in 1763 ceded militarily once and for all Canada (New France) to England. This also explains perhaps the remark by one of Maillet's protagonists in *Cent ans dans les bois* who grumbles about "la Martinique qui leur avait fait cadeau d'un fils de pute"[9] [Martinique which had offered them as a present the son of a whore].

A similar phenomenon takes place between the Acadians and the French if one reads Maillet's works carefully. It becomes apparent when reading between the lines that there is an often bittersweet or ambivalent portrait of France and the French. Even though Maillet is proud to be of French heritage, she, as well as a great number of francophone Acadians, hold something of a grudge against the French for abandoning, as we saw above, so readily Acadia and their francophone cousins. For example, in a television interview, Maillet declared in a rather accusatory manner that Acadia and the Acadians were left to fend for themselves: "L'Acadie a été déportée, d'où l'euphémisme 'Grand Dérangement'. Elle a été ballottée, elle a été exilée, elle a été prêtée à tout le monde. On ne savait pas si elle était à l'Angleterre, à la France ou à qui."[10] [Acadia was deported, hence the euphemism the "Great Disruption." It was tossed around, exiled, it was lent to everyone. No one knew whether it belonged to England, France or to whom.] In this same interview, the Acadian critic Pauline Chamberlain also noted that the Acadians faced an uncertain and precarious future when abandoned by a "neglectful motherland": "Pendant un siècle et demi, ils (les Acadiens) le défendent (le sol acadien), souvent seuls, laissés à eux-mêmes par une mère patrie souvent oublieuse."[11] [For a century and a half, they [the Acadians] defend it [the Acadian soil], often by themselves, left to themselves by an often neglectful motherland.]

Likewise, in Maillet's *Les Confessions de Jeanne de Valois*, the narrator also remarks that France has been a "neglectful motherland": "Il ne restait donc à ce petit peuple français abandonné le long des côtes et dans les forêts vierges d'Amérique que l'Église romaine pour tout recours et pour tout soutien.

Mais Rome est loin, plus loin encore que la France ne l'avait été."[12] (The only support that remained for this small French nation abandoned along America's coastline and its pristine forests was thus the Roman Church as a last resort. But Rome is far away, even farther away than had been France.) Nevertheless, in Martine Jacquot's interview, Maillet seems to underscore the idea that the Acadians were able to persevere without France's assistance and, as a result, are all the better for it and stronger: "Je suis très fière de descendre de cette noble race (française), mais très contente d'en être descendue."[13] [I am proud to have descended from this (French) noble race, but nevertheless very happy to have moved on.] Furthermore, the narrator in *Les Confessions de Jeanne de Valois* appears to be somewhat dismayed by Quebec's and France's ignorance and/or lack of interest in Acadia: "Le Québec et la France venaient tout juste d'apprendre que nous étions rentrés du Grand Dérangement"[14] (Quebec and France had only just realized that we had returned home from the Great Disruption).

In Maillet's *Cent ans dans les bois*, it is the written word which is coincidentally held responsible, in large part, for the Acadians' Deportation as a result of the work done by a "scélérat d'arpenteur-géographe" (a rascal surveyor-geographer) who clears the way for the "Anglais":[15]

> Il se disait arpenteur, ou géographe. À d'autres, il aurait même dit cartographe. Mais les Bélonie eux-mêmes ne connaissaient pas bien la différence entre tous ces métiers (graphiques), si métiers c'était. Rien qui ressemblait à un charpentier ou à un marin, en tout cas. Même pas à un coureur de bois. Plutôt un genre de défricheur sur papier. C'est ça, il défrichait les cartes et les titres.[16]

> He claimed to be a surveyor, or geographer. To others, he would have even claimed to be a cartographer. But as for the Bélonies [people of Breton origin] they were not familiar with the difference between all these (graphic) occupations, if these were occupations at all. Nothing like a carpenter or a sailor, in any case. Not even a trapper. More like a sort of land-clearer on paper. That's it, he cleared maps and titles.

This historically true story is all the more tragic and ironic because the surveyor, Des Barres,[17] is himself French: "C'était un Français de France.—Le traître! J'aurions[18] plus aisément pardonné à un étrange d'une autre race. Sûrement. Vaincus et déportés par le roi ennemi de leur roi, passe; mais trahis par un Français, un de leur sang . . . vache!" [He was a Frenchman from France.—The traitor! We would have more easily forgiven a foreigner of a different race. Surely. Had we been defeated and exiled by a king who was the enemy of their (i.e., the French) king, we could have let it pass; but we were betrayed by a Frenchman, one of their own flesh and blood, . . . damn it!]¹⁹

Linguistically speaking, the Acadian identity is clearly critiqued and problematized in an ironic fashion by Maillet's Acadian narrator in *Par derrière chez mon père* who cannot refrain from using an Acadianized form of French as opposed to standard French or Quebecois French:

> Puis on en est venu à nous. Remarquez qu'on n'a pas dit : "Quoi c'est ça, un Acadien ?" Oh! non. Mais : "Un Acadien, qu'est-ce?" Une nuance dans le style et qui change tout. Qui distingue un pays d'un autre.
>
> J'étais prête. Champlain, Poutrincourt, Dollard des Ormeaux, les Iroquois et les trappeurs, c'est matière scolaire, on connaît la réponse juste. Mais un Acadien, quoi c'est ça, un Acadien? C'est pourtant bien facile à dire . . . très facile même . . . très très facile . . . hummmm.
>
> C'est la même chose qu'un Québécois?
>
> Non, c'est pas la même chose.
>
> C'est un Canadien, alors?
>
> Non plus, pas tout à fait.
>
> Un Québécois est-il un Canadien?
>
> De moins en moins.
>
> Un Français?
>
> C'est difficile à dire.
>
> Alors un Acadien n'est ni français, ni canadien, ni québécois; il est quoi, au juste?
>
> Un Acadien.²⁰

Then the attention was turned to us. Notice that no one said: What's that, an Acadian? Oh! No. But: An Acadian, what is it? A stylistic nuance which changes everything. Distinguishing one country from another.

I was prepared. Champlain, Poutrincourt, Dollard des Ormeaux, the Iroquois and trappers, it's an academic subject matter, we know the correct answer. But an Acadian, what's that, an Acadian? It's after all easy to say . . . even very easy . . . very very easy . . . hummmm.

It's the same thing as a Quebecois?

No, it's not the same thing.

He's a Canadian, then?

Not either, not exactly.

A Quebecois, is he a Canadian?

Less and less.

A Frenchman?

It's difficult to say.

So an Acadian is neither French, Canadian, nor Quebecois; what is he exactly?

An Acadian.

The Acadian identity is once again thrown into question and seems to be defined again with reference to the Quebecois identity rather than the French identity in Maillet's best-known play *La Sagouine*:

> Non, je sons pas tout à fait des Français, je pouvons pas dire ça : les Français, c'est les Français de France. Ah! pour ça, je sons encore moins des Français de France que des Amaricains. Je sons putôt des Canadjens français, qu'ils nous avont dit ... Ça se peut pas non plus, ça. Les Canadjens français, c'est du monde qui vit à Québec. Ils les appelont des Canayens, ou ben des Québecois. Ben coument c'est que je pouvons être des Québecois si je vivons point à Québec? ... Pour l'amour de Djeu, où c'est que je vivons, nous autres? ... En Acadie, qu'ils nous avont dit, et je sons des Acadjens. Ça fait que j'avons entrepris de répondre à leu question de nationalité coume ça: des Acadjens, que je leur avons dit. Ça, je sons sûrs d'une chouse, c'est que je sons les seuls à porter ce nom-là.[21]

> Nope, we ain't completely French, can't say that: the French folks is the folks fr'm France, *les Français de France.* 'n fer that matter, we're even less *Français de France* than we're Americans. We're more like French Canadians, they told us. Well, that ain't true either. French Canadians are those that live in Québec. They call 'em *Canayens* or *Québécois.* But how can we be *Québécois* if we ain't livin' in Québec? Fer the love of Christ, where do we live? ... In Acadie, we was told, 'n we're sup- posed to be *Acadjens.* So, that's the way we decided to answer the question 'bout nationality: *Acadjens* we says to them. Now then, we can be sure of one thing, we're the only ones to have that name.[22]

As noted by LeBouthillier's highly defiant narrator in *L'Acadien reprend son pays*, there is the illusion, then the deception, even the trap, of believing that the Acadians are at home or among fellow countrymen wherever French is spoken, such as in France:

> L'Acadien était souvent victime du piège de la langue et de la culture lorsqu'il vi- vait au Québec ou en France; il s'attendait à y trouver un pays identique, alors qu'il y avait beaucoup de différences. En effet, même si la langue et la culture ressemblaient aux siens, les signaux sociaux émis et perçus étaient sujets à des in- terprétations différentes. À l'étranger, l'Acadien avait fréquemment tendance à chercher des repères familiers, en scrutant les foules instinctivement comme s'il allait rencontrer un compatriote.[23]

> The Acadian was often the victim of the language and culture trap when living in Quebec or in France; he expected to find an identical country, whereas there were many differences. In fact, even if the language and culture were similar to his own, the communication signals that were sent and received were subject to various interpretations. When abroad, the Acadian frequently had a tendency to

search for familiar reference points by instinctively scanning the crowds as if to find a compatriot.

In any case, it is apparent that both Quebec and France represent foreign lands where the Acadians are clearly out of place in Maillet's and LeBouthillier's works.

Furthermore, Maillet most likely sympathizes and identifies symbolically with the Bretons' minority status within France rather than with the French in general when casting two Breton characters in two of her plays—the Breton in *Évangéline Deusse* and Olivier in *Margot-la-Folle*. This is similar in spirit to the highly symbolic identification of the Acadians with the fate of the Jews in a great number of her works.[24] Maillet's narrator in *L'Acadie pour quasiment rien* reminds the reader that the Acadians all have Celtic blood running through their veins: "[Nous] avons tous une bonne dose de sang celtique dans nos veines de Bretons expatriés"[25] [[We] all have a good dose of Celtic blood in our expatriated Breton veins]. In a similar way to the Acadians who have rediscovered the wealth and beauty of the Acadian language, Bretons in France have expressed these past few years a growing interest for the Breton language as a means of rediscovering and reaffirming their cultural identity when confronted with France's cultural and linguistic hegemony.[26] That, despite the assertion of Maillet's narrator that the Acadians are all expatriated Bretons, the vast majority of the Acadians do not, in fact, come from Brittany. Whereas the Quebecois come, for the most part, from the Île-de-France and Brittany regions, the Acadians come from the west central part of France, from Poitou, Anjou, and Touraine.

The name and heroics of this downtrodden people conjure up nevertheless the image of a nation proud of its ancestral roots. For example, in *Pélagie-la-Charrette*, the narrator makes no attempt whatsoever to conceal the protagonist's heroic, Gallic lineage: "Il n'avait rien perdu de son vieux fonds gaulois, le Bélonie"[27] [He had lost nothing of his ancient Gaulish roots back in Bélonie][28] Likewise, the identification of the "Puçois"[29] with the Gauls and their struggle against their Roman conquerors, who ravaged Gaul by their sheer numbers and superior weaponry, is symbolically reenacted in several of Maillet's works.[30] Maillet is, therefore, readily disposed to create her own heroic, Acadian figures, some of whom seem to be taken from the popular, animated comic book series *Astérix*, to wage her battles: "On se croirait en présence d'Obélix devant les Romains"[31] [It is as if we were in the presence of Obélix face to face with the Romans].

This symbolic identification is all the more significant insofar as one of LeBouthillier's characters, like David before Goliath, also identifies with this oppressed minority. In *C'est pour quand le paradis . . .*, the narrator notes: "L'après-midi se passa en compagnie d'Astérix le Breton. Je me sentais proche de lui. L'humour breton profond et perspicace semblait s'apparenter de façon indéfinissable à celui des peuples opprimés comme le nôtre."[32] [The afternoon was spent in the company of Astérix the Breton. I felt close to him. Deep and clear-sighted Breton humor seemed indefinably to have certain similarities with that belonging to oppressed people like our own.] Similarly, LeBouthillier's narrator in the foreword to *L'Acadien reprend son pays* speaks of "l'Acadie, ce rêve et ce pays de mes aïeux, îlot de résistance, comme la Bretagne d'Astérix, en lutte pour l'éclosion de son identité"[33] [Acadia, this dream and this nation of my ancestors, a pocket of resistance, like Astérix's Brittany, fighting for the flowering of its identity].

It would appear that Acadia is in need of heroic figures, such as Vercingétorix, the prototypal French national hero, as Maillet's narrator in *Crache à pic* aptly points out: "Il s'appelait Crache à Pic. Un gaillard de sept pieds selon la règle de Clovis tout en muscles, moustaches et poil dans le nez, un Vercingétorix."[34] [His name was Crache à Pic. A seven-foot, strapping fellow according to Clovis's ruler, full of muscles, a mustache and hairs in his nose, a Vercingétorix.] Likewise, Maillet's narrator in *Le Chemin Saint-Jacques* refers to her character's heroic patrimony: "Mais mon père n'appartenait pas à la dynastie des conteurs et me renvoyait chaque fois à son cousin Thaddée qui refusait de s'attarder à ces contes farfelus. Ses géants à lui s'appelaient Charlemagne, Clovis ou Vercingétorix"[35] [But my father was not a member of the storyteller dynasty and referred me back each time to his cousin Thaddeus, who would refuse to dwell on these hare-brained tales. His own giants went by the name of Charlemagne, Clovis, or Vercingétorix.] Contrary to Maillet, LeBouthillier evokes rather pessimistically with regard to Acadia's future his nostalgia for the good old days, an era whose time has clearly passed and where heroic figures, such as Vercingétorix, are nowhere to be found: "Dans cette 'capitale' de l'Acadie Le jour de l'an ne sera plus pareil. La fanfare ne jouera plus la Marseillaise ni *l'Ave Maris Stella*. On ne montera plus *Le marchand de Venise*, *Vercingétorix*, ou *Mon huile de foie de morue*."[36] [In this "capital" of Acadia New Year's Day will no longer be the same. The brass band will no longer play the Marseillaise nor *Ave Maris Stella*. *The Merchant of Venice*, *Vercingétorix*, or *My Cod Liver Oil* will no longer be staged.] In the end, the Acadians' highly symbolic identification with the Bretons' plight in Maillet's and LeBouthillier's works is probably symptomatic of these authors' desire to exclude no one insofar as their writing seeks always to recognize the Other,[37] as Maillet's narrator in *Les Confessions de Jeanne de Valois* so clearly recalls, whether they be "les noirs, les jaunes, les enfants, les déshérités, les femmes, tous ceux en somme qui remplissent les neuf dixièmes de la planète, se coiffent du titre de minoritaires et le font avec défi et ostentation"[38] [the blacks, the yellow races, children, the have-nots, women, all those who all in all make up nine-tenths of the planet, embrace their minority status and conduct themselves defiantly and ostentatiously].

However, this does not paradoxically prevent Maillet's narrator from being filled with admiration for France when recalling nostalgically France's great historical and cultural legacy:

> Puis Sœur Augusta et moi, nous parcourions les rues du Paris d'avant la Révolution, le Paris de la Comédie-Française, de l'Académie, de Notre-Dame, du Louvre, de François Villon. Et nous poursuivions notre rêve jusqu'en France profonde, celle de nos racines et de nos pères, celle de ces hameaux perdus en Charente et en Anjou où sous un toit d'ardoise, pour reprendre du Bellay, nous revenions "pleines d'usage et raison, vivre entre nos parents" retrouvés après trois siècles. La France ancestrale, amicale, fraternelle nous attendait, n'attendait même que nous. J'ai cru que cet été-là ne s'achèverait jamais et que l'automne était au bout du monde.[39]

> Sister Augusta and I, we would travel up and down the streets of pre-Revolutionary Paris, the Paris of the Comédie-Française, of the French Academy, of Notre-Dame, of the Louvre, of François Villon. And we would pursue our dream deep into the France of our roots and of our forefathers, of those out-of-the-way hamlets in Charente and Anjou where under a slate roof, to go back to Du Bellay, we would come back "fully endowed with good manners and reason, to live with our parents" reunited after three centuries. Ancestral, amiable, fraternal France awaited us, awaited even only us. I thought that that summer would never end and that autumn was a world away.

In conclusion, if the portrait of France and the French plays, especially in Maillet's works, an integral role in shaping the Acadian identity through the Acadians' collective memory, these common experiences and recollections, these souvenirs are not, as we have seen, solely positive in Maillet's and LeBouthillier's works insofar as they are sometimes illusory, even perhaps deceptive:

> Je venais en France à la recherche de mon passé, de mon âme essentielle. Et c'est pour cela que je fus d'abord déçue. Car avant de frapper le roc sous les multiples couches sédimentaires déposées par des siècles d'histoire, que de limon gluant et poisseux j'ai dû traverser! J'avais eu tort d'imaginer l'herbe plus verte de l'autre côté de la montagne. Mais ma montagne à moi était si minuscule! Ma connaissance du monde était si limitée que je l'avais paré de splendeurs comme seul un cerveau pouvait en produire. En écoutant, par exemple, le babillage verbeux et arrogant d'une mondaine patronnesse, je n'arrivais pas à me figurer tant de bêtise enveloppée de tant d'élégance.[40]

> I was coming to France in search of my past, my primordial soul. And that is why I was first of all disappointed. Because before striking the rock under multiple

sedimentary layers deposited by centuries of history, such gummy and sticky silt I had to go through! I was wrong to imagine the grass greener on the other side of the hill. And my hill was so tiny! My knowledge was so limited that I had splendidly adorned it as only the mind can. While listening, for example, to the wordy and arrogant babbling of a mundane patroness, I could not imagine such folly shrouded in such elegance.

In a similar fashion, many of Maillet's narrators also reproach the French, such as Malherbe, for their pretentious attitudes, arrogance, and airs and graces.[41] Moreover, in the Acadians' collective memory, Acadia appears to transcend, in the end, France's borders both in space and time:

> L'Acadie n'était pas seulement française, mais acadienne, c'est-à-dire vieille France, France d'avant Louis XIII, France du Poitou et de Touraine, France de Rutebeuf, de Villon, de Rabelais, de Marguerite de Navarre; l'Acadie était mémoire autant que continuité, dépositaire autant que permanence; l'Acadie était comète traînant dans sa queue un répertoire de fables et de fabliaux, de croyances et de traditions, de mots et de proverbes, de légendes et de mythes, et d'une sagesse millénaire restée vivante dans nos tripes et dans nos gorges . . . une comète devenue étoile filante, devenue le chemin de Saint-Jacques qui rattacherait à jamais le nouveau monde à l'ancien continent.[42]

> Acadia was not only French, but Acadian, that is to say France of bygone days, France before Louis XIII, France of Poitou and Touraine, France of Rutebeuf, of Villon, of Rabelais, of Marguerite of Navarre; Acadia was as much memory as continuity, depository as much as permanency; Acadia was a comet tail dragging in its wake a repertory of fables and fabliaux, of beliefs and traditions, of words and proverbs, of legends and myths, and of age-old wisdom kept alive in our gut and in our bosom . . . a comet turned into a shooting star, to become *le chemin de Saint-Jacques* (pilgrimage road to Santiago de Compostela) which would reunite forever the new world and the old continent.

There is an obvious reference in this last sentence to Maillet's following novel, *Le Chemin Saint-Jacques*, corresponding to Maillet's vision or perspective of the universe which catapults itself both toward the past, by returning to her ancestors and her own birth, events actually predating her own birth, and toward the future.[43] In other words, as is often the case in Maillet's works, events have come full circle. In addition, the title attests to the great power which storytelling exerts over Radi, Maillet's childhood alter ego in *On a mangé la dune*, *Le Chemin Saint-Jacques*, *Chronique d'une sorcière de vent* and *Le temps me dure*. Maillet's narrator later refers to this as "mon double, ma mémoire, mon histoire primaire et primitive"[44] [my double, my memory, my primordial and primitive history] in *Chronique d'une sorcière de vent*. The power to immortalize and transcend the present is, furthermore, highlighted by way of two epigraphs at the beginning of each section of her novel *Le Chemin Saint-Jacques*: Jules Renard's statement that "Le bonheur serait de se souvenir du présent" [Happiness would be to remember the present] and that of Marcel Proust, "Éterniser l'instant présent" [Immortalize this present moment]. In other words, as both a political and a cultural entity with French roots, Maillet or, at the very least, her narrator suggests that Acadia is greater than the sum of its parts.

Notes

1. Antonine Maillet, *Le Chemin Saint-Jacques* (Montréal: Leméac, 1996), 332. All translations are my own except where indicated.

2. Antonine Maillet, *L'Acadie pour quasiment rien* (Montréal: Leméac, 1973), 13.

3. Maillet, *L'Acadie*, 15.

4. Maillet, *L'Acadie*, 13.

5. Claude LeBouthillier, *Tisons péninsulaires* (Tracadie-Sheila, New Brunswick: La Grande Marée, 2001), 11-12.

6. Antonine Maillet, *On a mangé la dune* (Montréal: Leméac, 1977), 99.

7. Antonine Maillet, *Pélagie-la-Charrette* (Paris: Grasset, 1979), 17.

8. Antonine Maillet, *Pélagie*, trans. Philip Stratford (Toronto: Doubleday, 1982), 7.

9. Antonine Maillet, *Cent ans dans les bois* (Montréal: Leméac, 1981), 86.

10. Dominique Gallet, *Espace Francophone: Le magazine du monde d'expression française* (Paris: ICAF, 1982), 15. See also Antonine Maillet, *Rabelais et les traditions populaires en Acadie* (Québec: Presses Universitaires Laval, 1971), 5; Jacques Jaubert, "Antonine Maillet s'explique," *Lire* 50 (1979) : 29.

11. Gallet, *Espace*, 16.

12. Antonine Maillet, *Les Confessions de Jeanne de Valois* (Montréal: Leméac, 1992), 95.

13. Martine Jacquot, "'Je suis la charnière' : Entretien avec Antonine Maillet," *Studies in Canadian Literature* 13 (1988): 263. See also Antonine Maillet, *Les Crasseux* (Montréal: Holt, Rinehart and Winston, 1968), 10.

14. Maillet, *Confessions*, 216.

15. It is important to note that the reference to the "Anglais" or English in Maillet's works should not be taken literally because it often refers to any English-speaking character and/or someone in a more favorable socioeconomic situation than the "crasseux" or "filthy ones" evoked in the title of her play of the same name, even if this person is French-speaking. For a discussion of this subject, see Jean-Luc Desalvo, *Le Topos du mundus inversus dans l'œuvre d'Antonine Maillet* (Bethesda, Md.: International Scholars Publications, 1999) 32-34.

16. Maillet, *Cent*, 30. See also 23, 29, 31.

17. The name is taken directly from Acadia's history books. See, for example, Emery LeBlanc, *Les Acadiens* (Ottawa: Éditions de l'homme, 1963), 123.

18. Maillet routinely uses the first person singular subject pronoun with the first person plural conjugation in her works to create and reinforce the notion of collectivity.

19. Maillet, *Cent*, 30.

20. Antonine Maillet, *Par derrière chez mon père* (Montréal: Leméac, 1972), 86.

21. Antonine Maillet, *La Sagouine* (Montréal: Leméac, 1971), 88.

22. Antonine Maillet, *La Sagouine*, trans. Luis de Céspedes (Toronto: Simon & Pierre, 1985), 165.

23. Claude LeBouthillier, *L'Acadien reprend son pays* (Moncton: Éditions d'Acadie, 1977), 28.

24. For example, the heroine in *Pélagie-la-Charrette* is clearly identified with Moses leading and saving his people. See also, for example, *Le Chemin Saint-Jacques*, 280. Likewise, Radi seems particularly moved in *Le Temps me dure* (Montréal: Leméac, 2003) by the narrator's account of Anne Frank's tragic ordeal (see, for example, 192-93 and 202). This identification is also present in LeBouthillier's works. See, for example, *L'Acadien reprend son pays*, 48.

25. Maillet, *Acadie*, 100.

26. See, for example, Henriette Walter, *Le Français dans tous les sens* (Paris: Laffont, 1988), 130, 203, 204.

27. Maillet, *Pélagie*, 79.

28. Maillet, *Pélagie*, trans. Philip Stratford, 55.

29. One of Maillet's many neologisms roughly translated as "the flea-infested people."

30. See, for example, *Don l'Orignal* (Montréal: Leméac, 1972).

31. Maillet, *Rabelais*, 121.

32. Claude LeBouthillier, *C'est pour quand le paradis . . .* , (Moncton: Éditions d'Acadie, 1984), 148.

33. LeBouthillier, *L'Acadien*, 9.

34. Antonine Maillet, *Crache à Pic* (Paris: Grasset, 1984), 74.

35. Maillet, *Chemin*, 289.

36. LeBouthillier, *Tisons*, 13.

37. Even though Maillet's narrators and protagonists frequently refer allegorically to their "premiers occupants" or "first-occupier" status (see, for example, *Cent ans dans les bois* 163, *Don l'Orignal* 163, *Madame Perfecta* (France: Actes Sud) 83, *On a mangé la dune* 156), it should be noted that neither the French nor the English were the first to settle in what would become "Acadia." The Amerindians, such as the Micmacs, are the only ones who can rightfully make such a claim. One of the rare instances whereby one of Maillet's narrators or protagonists comes to the Amerindians' defense is in *Le Temps me dure* (99; see also *L'Acadie* 29). In any case, Maillet's narrator in *Pélagie-la-Charrette* appears keenly aware of a pecking order in Acadia: "L'esclave battu bat son chien; et le loyaliste vaincu rosse le déporté," 237. (The beaten slave beats his dog; and the defeated Loyalist drubs the deportee] trans. Stratford 185. For a further discussion of the polemical portrait of Blacks and Indians in Maillet's works, see, for example, Karolyn Waterson's article "The Mythical Dimension of *Pélagie-la-Charrette*," *Francophone Literatures of the New World* 2 (1982): 43-69.

38. Maillet, *Confessions*, 73.

39. Maillet, *Confessions*, 151.

40. Maillet, *Confessions*, 153.

41. For example, further proof of a certain amount of linguistic animosity on the part of Maillet toward the French is evident in Jaubert's interview of Maillet when he brings to her attention the fact that her novel *Pélagie-la-Charrette* does not provide a glossary of acadianisms to aid the French-reading public. Maillet responds rather indignantly: "Puis il y avait un sentiment d'honneur: pourquoi fallait-il faire une concession aux Français, qu'eux ne feraient pas pour nous?" [Then, it was a point of honor: why did we need to make a concession to the French, which they wouldn't do for us?] (38).

42. Maillet, *Confessions*, 107.

43. Antonine Maillet, *Chronique d'une sorcière de vent* (Montréal: Leméac, 1999), 9.

44. This is especially true in *Le Temps me dure*. See, for example, 30 and 104.

II
AFRICA AND ASIA

5

Film and Colonial Memory
La Croisière noire 1924–2004

Alison Murray Levine

I N OCTOBER 1924, Georges-Marie Haardt and Louis Audoin-Dubreuil set off
in Citroën halftrack automobiles [*autochenilles*] on the Expédition Citroën
Centre-Afrique, an eight-month journey across Africa that is remembered as
La Croisière noire, the title of Léon Poirier's film and Haardt's memoir. André
Citroën turned the expedition into a major public relations enterprise, framing it as a national project and involving French authorities. He conceived of
the mission not only as a demonstration of the superiority of the French automobile industry, but also as a means of publicizing France's African colonies
in the metropole. Covering over 12,500 miles, the expedition would be a
sweeping symbolic gesture linking French possessions in North Africa, West
and Central Africa, and Madagascar.[1]

The Expédition Citroën Centre-Afrique was only one of many automobile
expeditions to cross Africa; since the turn of the century, manufacturers and
explorers had tested many different kinds of vehicles over the continent's diverse terrain. The film was only one of hundreds of documentary films that
were produced during the interwar years to promote the French colonies. And
yet, this particular expedition was extraordinarily popular. The travelers'
progress was reported in newspapers and radio reports, and they returned to
France to considerable acclaim. The film, released in 1926, was one of the few
documentary films of the period to draw huge audiences, and its reverbera-
tions in popular culture were so extensive that it became a cultural icon of the
1920s. What is perhaps more surprising than its popularity in the 1920s is the
continuing popularity of the film's memory in recent years. The film has been
shown at three major festivals in the last ten years, and a series of related

books, internet sites, and museum exhibits have recently appeared. Unlike every other colonial propaganda film from the 1920s, the images and ethos of *La Croisière noire* linger in French culture.

This chapter considers *La Croisière noire* as a case study in the propagation and exploitation of colonial imagery, at the time it was produced as well as in contemporary culture. Whether in the form of colonial exhibitions, posters, postcards, book or magazine illustrations, films, cartoons, or photographs, colonial imagery played an important role in the development of an *idée coloniale* in France, a role that did not disappear with decolonization.[2] A considerable body of recent scholarship has demonstrated that images of overseas France, many of which were designed to rally support for the colonial cause, helped bring ideas about the colonies—many based on cliché and stereotype— into the French collective imagination.[3] It was partly through the mediation of such images that colonial spaces began to be assimilated into the broader notion of the French cultural heritage. As will be demonstrated in the first section of this chapter, *La Croisière noire* was extremely successful in drawing popular attention to France's African colonies.

What has received less attention is the question of how these images continue to circulate and contribute to an *idée post-coloniale*, to extend Girardet's term, as France comes to terms with its history as a colonial power. Henry Rousso uses the term *syndrome de Vichy* to analyze the evolution of France's collective memory of Vichy; in charting different stages in the collective imagination of the former French empire since the independences, it makes sense to use an analogous term, *syndrome d'empire*.[4] The second section of this chapter will examine what the lingering memory of *La Croisière noire* reveals about the larger *syndrome d'empire* in contemporary France.

The resuscitation of texts and sources of representation from the colonial period might be read as participating in a postcolonial project, defined by Leela Gandhi as "a theoretical resistance to the mystifying amnesia of the colonial aftermath . . . a disciplinary project devoted to the academic task of revisiting, remembering and, crucially, interrogating the colonial past."[5] Viewed in this light, scholarly and less scholarly projects preserving the memory of *La Croisière noire* could be seen as acts of anamnesis, which Elisabeth Mudimbe-Boyi proposes as a positive model for coming to terms with memories of colonialism. Anamnesis, she writes, a voluntary evocation of the past, can allow for the construction of a revitalized vision of the future.[6] Jean Halpérin takes a similar view of memory: "La mémoire est, au sens fort du terme, édifiante . . . l'injonction de se souvenir doit susciter un processus dynamique et créatif qui enrichisse le présent et l'avenir."[7] [Memory is, in the strongest sense of the word, edifying. The injunction to remember must incite a dynamic and creative process that enriches the present and the future.]

Memory, however, does not always serve the forward-looking processes described by Mudimbe-Boyi and Halpérin. In contrast to these views, preserving memories of certain moments of the past can also be symptomatic of nostalgia, which Webster defines as "homesickness, a longing to go back to one's home, home town or homeland."[8] In the analysis of the contemporary resuscitation of *La Croisière noire*, I will argue that this case study is suffused with colonial nostalgia, and that despite considerable scholarly attention to the postcolonial project in contemporary France, the current *syndrome d'empire* also contains a considerable element of nostalgia for the empire.

La Croisière noire: 1920s

The original motivation for the Expédition Citroën Centre-Afrique was André Citroën's desire to prove that automobiles could provide a lighter and more efficient alternative to railroads, over any terrain. Taking advantage of the French government's desire to establish an automobile link between French West Africa and Algeria, Citroën began working on the problem of crossing the Sahara as early as 1919. In 1921, Citroën developed the half-track caterpillar system, which consisted of building cars with wheels on the front axle and a moving continuous rubber belt on the rear axles, in order to drive through unstable terrain such as sand. Gasoline could be supplied by sending special convoys of automobiles along the route to drop off reserves at regular intervals. Using this system, a Citroën team completed the first successful Sahara crossing by automobile in 21 days, from December 1922 to January 1923.

Galvanized by this success, André Citroën began to contemplate its implications not only for commercial traffic between the colonies, but also for the development of tourism. He wrote in 1923, "il suffit pour cela d'organiser le ravitaillement et de jalonner les itinéraires"[9] [all that is needed is to organize the supply lines and to mark out the itineraries]. He envisaged a tourist route from Algeria to Timbuktu, with biweekly automobile service and modern hotels along the way. Many of these establishments were actually built in the first year, and Citroën sold hundreds of tickets through an aggressive marketing campaign. Just weeks before the first group was scheduled to leave, however, the project was mysteriously canceled, probably because of security concerns.[10]

The failure of the tourist circuit did not, however, dissuade Citroën from planning an automobile expedition that would cross all of Africa from Colomb Bechar, in Southern Algeria, through West and Equatorial Africa and south to the Indian Ocean. Like the tourist project, Citroën conceived of the Expédition Citroën Centre-Afrique as a national endeavor, and he corresponded extensively with French authorities in many branches of the government to garner their support. In his proposal, he writes, "Le problème de la mise en valeur des Colonies Françaises, où dorment des richesses de toute nature si utiles à refaire le patrimoine national, s'est inscrit depuis plusieurs années parmi les légitimes préoccupations des hommes d'État."[11] [The problem of rational development of the French Colonies, where all manner of riches useful for rebuilding the national heritage currently lie dormant, has for several years been one of the primary preoccupations of political leaders.] He elaborates a host of benefits to the French nation, including demonstrating France's political and military mobility in the colonies, drawing the attention of a broad French and international audience to the richness and diversity of France's African colonies, encouraging investment by demonstrating the ability of automobiles to facilitate the transport of goods and services among the colonies, and furthering the cause of French scientific knowledge of Africa. Citroën even couches his commercial interest in national terms: "Au point de vue national, le succès de cette deuxième mission montrera une fois de plus à l'étranger la place prépondérante prise par l'industrie française automobile dans le monde."[12] [From a national point of view, the success of this second mission will demonstrate internationally the leading role of the French automobile industry in the world.] Finally, Citroën adds, the whole thing will be a grand adventure.

> La formidable randonnée de sept autochenilles munies de leurs remorques à travers l'Afrique, serait l'évènement le plus considérable qui ait jamais été entrepris dans le monde: ... cette lutte des sept autochenilles contre les obstacles successifs ou combinés des éléments et de la nature, sera une merveilleuse leçon d'énergie humaine et de résistance mécanique, dont toutes les nations suivront avec intérêt ou émotion, les péripéties diverses.[13]

> The tremendous excursion of seven automobiles and their trailers all across Africa will be the most considerable event that has ever been undertaken in the world: ... this struggle of seven cars against the successive obstacles of the elements and nature, will be a marvelous lesson of human energy and mechanical strength, whose varied adventures will be followed with interest and emotion by every nation.

Administrative response to Citroën's plans was overwhelmingly positive. Although he did not receive financial support from the state, he met personally with the President of the Republic, and he did receive an official *mission* from the government as well as logistical support along the way.

Baptized *La Croisière noire*, the expedition would use eight of the half-track automobiles and the same system of supply drops that had been successful in the first Sahara crossing. Two of the vehicles were entirely devoted to transporting film cameras, under the direction of Léon Poirier and Georges Specht.

The journey lasted from October 1924 to June 1925 and covered over 12,500 miles of the African continent. Press coverage of the expedition was extensive, as the travelers made regular reports to the metropole via radio and telegraph. At the request of the President of the Republic, Gaston Doumergue, who recognized the symbolic importance of creating a link to Madagascar, the leaders decided to extend the mission all the way to the most distant French possession in Africa.

As predicted, the expedition encountered many obstacles along the way, but all in all, it was considered a huge success. The travelers met up for a triumphal reception in Madagascar in June 1925.[14] They brought back 27,000 meters of film, 8,000 photos, more than 300 drawings, 100 paintings, and 15 sketchbooks chronicling their experiences. Haardt was received by the President of the Republic at the Élysée palace on 22 January 1926.[15] Poirier's film opened at a gala premiere at the Paris Opera on 2 March 1926, in the presence of the President of the Republic.

The documentary film *La Croisière noire* is made up of a series of vignettes taken from the expedition's halts—such as a scene of Iacovleff sketching an African chief, and a long sequence showing a Djerma fantasia—linked together by numerous scenes of the road, including the various ways in which the cars got into—and out of—difficulties.[16] They successively rumble in and out of craters and ravines, float across rivers and lakes balanced on hollowed-out logs, and occasionally get so irretrievably stuck that it takes an army of Africans to pull them out.[17] The film is action-packed from beginning to end: from festival to lion hunt to the final arrival in Madagascar, the travelers, and the viewer, are constantly on the move.

While not a government project, the film is nonetheless embedded in the colonialist propaganda of its time, following many of the conventions of government propaganda films. Some references to the colonial enterprise in Africa are explicit; in the opening credits, we learn that the film is dedicated to French youth, and Citroën explains in a letter to the Minister of Education that one of its goals is to create "une propagande coloniale [pour . . .] éveiller chez nos jeunes gens le goût des voyages et de provoquer même des vocations coloniales"[18] [colonial propaganda [to . . .] awaken a taste for travel in our youth and to inspire colonial vocations]. Other elements of colonial propaganda are rhetorical rather than explicit. By bringing diverse locations into the standard format of the film frame, under the French flag, the film rationalizes the empire, making it into a "consumable" commodity for metropolitan audiences. Peter Bloom has argued that cinema was an ideal medium for propagating the colonial idea because of its ability to produce the empire as a coherent represented object and no longer an object of conquest.[19] As with many colonial travel texts and films from the interwar period, the travelers are engaged not in conquest but in "anti-conquest," as Mary Louise Pratt writes, seeking "to secure their own innocence in the same moment as they assert European hegemony."[20] Unfettered by the exigencies of a particular civilizing mission, the travelers simply pass through, sketching, filming, writing, and chatting with their hosts. They assert their hegemony by demonstrating the kind of technological mastery over nature that Alice Conklin argues is central to the French version of the civilizing mission.[21] They use guns to kill wild animals, all-terrain automobiles to cross roadless areas, floodlights to divert malaria-carrying mosquitoes, as well as cameras, collecting equipment, and scientific classification systems to amass images and knowledge. The film medium allows them a further triumph over space and time, since images can be cut and rearranged, creating a completely new time line for the expedition.

The success of the technology is exaggerated for the public relations enterprise: for example, when the vehicles reach the tropical rainforest, in the film, the cars slip gently and easily into "l'inconnu de la forêt équatoriale"[22] [the unknown reaches of the equatorial forest]. In reality, they are only able to complete this leg of the journey because 40,000 Africans have spent months cutting a path for them through the jungle.[23] However, the image of mastery is untarnished, and the film ends where it began, under the tri-colored flag of France, encompassing the entire African continent in one sweeping rhetorical flourish.

The film drew unprecedented crowds, and unlike most documentaries of the time, *La Croisière noire* was separately billed as a full-length feature. Full-page photo spreads were splashed all over the film magazines of 1926; this film was the only documentary on Africa that made it onto the cover of *Ciné-Miroir* during the interwar years.[24] The film was screened in over forty French cities in 1926 alone; articles and film reviews appeared in at least fifty-five publications.[25] Gaumont-Palace organized a series of free film screenings for schoolchildren throughout the country.

The reviews are overwhelmingly positive. The reviewer in the *Journal de Rouen* writes, "Mieux que le plus captivant et que le plus imagé des livres d'aventures . . . , il fera vivre aux spectateurs deux heures d'existence hasardeuse à travers les brousses sauvages et les grands déserts silencieux."[26] [Better than the most captivating illustrated adventure books, . . . this film will allow spectators to experience two hours of dangerous existence in the wild bush and the great silent deserts.] One reviewer even explicitly mentions the film's effect on the memory:

Notre imagination éprouve les sensations heureuses d'un enrichissement féerique en s'annexant le souvenir de tous ces paysages, de toutes ces races mystérieuses, de ces danses indigènes, et surtout de ce miracle moderne que

réalise la roue mécanique en gravant son empreinte souveraine dans le sable d'un
continent vierge à la façon d'un tyran imprimant son sceau sur l'épaule d'une
esclave.[27]

Our imagination experiences the sensations of enchanting enrichment, appropriating the memory of all these landscapes, of these mysterious races, of these
native dances, and especially of this modern miracle achieved by the mechanical
wheel, engraving its sovereign imprint in the sand of a virgin continent like a
tyrant imprinting his seal on the shoulder of a slave.

As these reviewers suggest, the film allows audiences a moment of escapism
and adventure in exotic locales, indeed, to "appropriate memories" of Africa,
while remaining under the comforting tricolor flag of France. Its popularity
was primarily due to the fact that as Citroën predicted, the expedition was a
great adventure. The film presented a rich variety of cultures and landscapes
at a brisk pace that sacrificed depth for breadth and privileged the human an-
ecdote over the didactic explanation. Suspense is maintained through the repetition of difficulties and hazards; the viewer is kept wondering whether the
cars will actually make it. In the end, the success of the expedition becomes
symbolically associated with the success of the larger colonial project that
serves as backdrop for the film.

The comic book *Tintin au Congo* was inspired by *La Croisière noire*: Tintin,
boy reporter, drives around Africa in an automobile, carrying a film camera
that looks exactly like Poirier's, filming scenes of animals and daily life for his
"documentary film."[30] The persistence of *La Croisière noire* as a cultural icon
is further confirmed by a student's notebook held by the Musée National de
l'Éducation, which contains a whole illustrated study unit on the film and expedition (Figures 5.3 and 5.4). This notebook is dated 1945, fully twenty years
after the expedition, showing that the story was still being taught—and the
silent film was still being shown—in at least one school, on that date. The student's concluding essay finishes thus: "Que c'est beau, l'Afrique! Et que les
Français y ont fait de grandes choses!"[31] [How beautiful Africa is! And what
great things the French have done there!]

Figure 5.1.　The January 1927 issue of the fashion magazine *L'Officiel de la Couture* featured designs inspired by *La Croisière noire*, titled "La Croisière noire peuplade indigène d'Agnésville." PHOTO D'ORA. *L'Officiel de la Couture, de la mode de Paris*, no. 65 (January 1927).

Figure 5.2.   Velvet hats inspired by the African hairstyles seen in *La Croisière noire*.
Modes de la femme de France, 30 January 1927.

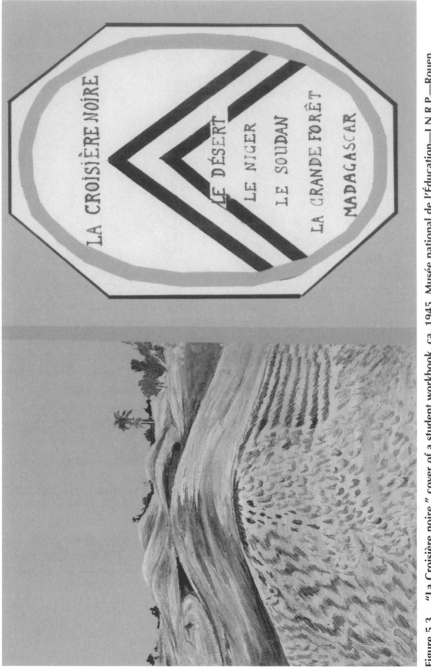

Figure 5.3.   "La Croisière noire," cover of a student workbook, ca. 1945. Musée national de l'Éducation—I.N.R.P.—Rouen.

Figure 5.4. "Elephants," illustration from a student workbook on *La Croisière noire*, ca. 1945. Musée national de l'Éducation—I.N.R.P.—Rouen.

From the above evidence, it is clear that *La Croisière noire* had some impact on the colonial idea in France during the interwar period. At the very least, it gained widespread attention and attracted viewers of all ages. Given the discredit into which colonial discourse has fallen since decolonization, however, it seems curious that such a document should still be in circulation in the 1990s and today.

La Croisière noire: Present

An internet search in 2004 reveals at least thirty websites that mention either the expedition or the film. These sites include four new books: a coffee table book of Iacovleff's drawings, a semi-scholarly history, and two other glossy photo books about the Citroën expeditions of the interwar period.[32] Among the other sites are the official Citroën webpage, which gives a description of the journey; a chronicle of the expedition on the "l'Histoire par l'Image" website created by the Ministère de la Culture; and three amateur sites, one by students of the Lycée Audouin-Dubreuil and two by Citroën car enthusiasts. In addition to these image-laden books and websites, there is an excerpt from Haardt's memoir on a Central African press site, an article on the Paris-Dakar and its relationship to *La Croisière noire*, and a site selling a diorama of the expedition with thirty-six, thirty-seven, or one hundred lead figures. Two different versions of the film poster are available on e-Bay. Another site tells the story of a 1991 expedition that followed the same route as Haardt and Audouin-Dubreuil in Citroën 2CVs. Two additional expeditions plan to celebrate the 80th anniversary of the journey in 2004 by crossing the African continent in automobiles. One of these plans to travel in vintage Citroën Traction Avants, the wildly popular "gangster car" that came out in 1934.[33]

Websites and publications are not the only indicators of a revival of interest in the Citroën expedition. The film was shown at three French film festivals in 1995 and 1996, and also at Africa's premier film festival, the Fespaco (Festival panafricain du cinéma et de la télévision d'Ouagadougou), in 1995.[34] The Musée des années 30, opened in 1998, contains an exhibit of Iacovleff's paintings from the journey. *Tintin au Congo* has been reprinted many times, including a 2002 edition in English published in San Francisco. France-Inter aired a radio program on the expedition on 8 August 2000. The Musée des Blindés de Saumur held an exhibit on the Citroën expeditions from 3 June to 30 September 2003. Ariane Audoin-Dubreuil showed the film and gave a lecture on *La Croisière noire* at the Société de Géographie in Paris on 12 October 2004. Clearly, the Citroën mission and the images of Africa it purveyed continue to fascinate the popular imagination.

There are several explanations for the continuing popularity of *La Croisière noire*. The first and most prosaic is that the expedition involved Citroëns. Car enthusiasts are widespread in many countries, and the particular love for Citroëns in France exceeds any level of nostalgia that exists for other makes of automobile. Eric Massiet du Biest, founder of the company that plans to cross Africa in Citroën Traction Avants, writes of "cet incroyable capital de sympathie qu'inspire cette voiture"[35] [the incredible level of instinctive attraction that this car inspires]. Renault lovers have not fanned the flames, for example, of the Mission Gradis-Estienne, which also crossed the Sahara in 1924 to 1925, in six-wheeled, ten-horsepower Renault vehicles. The memory of *La Croisière noire*, like that of *La Croisière jaune* and *La Croisière blanche*, the Citroën missions to Asia and North America, has in part been kept alive by Citroën lovers.

The second explanation for the continuing popularity of the Black Journey is that through the creation of a visual archive, it was actively involved in the construction of its own memory. André Citroën, already a past master at public relations, created an audience for his project before the journey even began. As discussed above, Citroën was attentive to relationships with the press and with the French authorities, in order to give the impression that the expedition was a grand national project. In addition, the travelers produced a tremendous amount of documentation in the form of text, photos, film, and paintings, mostly of excellent quality. These archives, some of which Citroën has allowed to pass into the public domain, have continued to make the expedition easy to illustrate and commemorate.

The third reason for the persistence of references to *La Croisière noire* is that the expedition was a fantastic adventure story, allowing young men and their young technologies to test themselves in "uncharted" territory. Because of the driving force of the expedition narrative, it is easy for the audience to ignore the potentially disturbing power relations inherent in such a tale of mastery and domination from the imperial period. Indeed, automobile rallies such as the Paris-Dakar continue to exploit the image of Africa as a virgin continent where the ultimate limits of man and machine can be tested. The historian Maurice Guimendego finds this deeply problematic, arguing that clichés and stereotypes continue to be perpetrated because visitors, and the media, take an intense but fleeting interest in the continent while remaining studiously indifferent to the fact that its internal troubles are tearing it apart.[36]

In short, the reasons for the popularity of *La Croisière noire* today are very similar to the explanations for its popularity in the 1920s: the rich imagery that accompanied it, an energetic public relations campaign on the part of its leaders, and the chance it offered its audience to experience a moment of escapism and high adventure that associated French technology with exciting, exotic backdrops. The fact that the entire project was conceived as a way of furthering

French colonial domination of Africa has been virtually written out of its memory. A specific example of this erasure is the action taken by the Citroën company to hide the imperial rhetoric associated with the expedition. When asked for a copy of the film, the company's standard response is to send out a videotape that contains a shortened and "sanitized" version of the film, with all colonial references erased from the commentary, and many scenes simply excised altogether. The dedication to France's youth is gone, as is the stated goal of colonial propaganda. Also sliced out are politically incorrect references to "barbarous" traditions such as human sacrifice, to "civilization's conquests," to white "sorcerors" amazing Africans by their technical prowess, to astonished Africans who have never seen themselves in a mirror, to "strange little gnomes" in the forest, and to rainforest trees being cut down by the French. The entire last scene, which consists of a montage of images from the journey superimposed on the French flag, is gone.[37] It was not until pressed on the subject that a Citroën public relations official admitted that this was not the 1926 cut, writing, "Le film a été remonté en 1984 pour éliminer les propos colonialistes mal vus à l'époque."[38] [The film was reedited in 1984 to eliminate the colonialist discourse that was considered unacceptable at the time.]

The sanitization of *La Croisière noire* suggests a more sobering interpretation of this case study and its implications for the larger question of the "colonial syndrome" in contemporary France. Clearly, it has become necessary for Citroën to improve its public image by erasing from its archives all references to the colonial project. And yet, this has not meant complete erasure of the film. Indeed, as with many other forms of colonial imagery, the film is still in demand because of a broader phenomenon of nostalgia for the empire that inhabits contemporary French culture. Much of the postcolonial scholarship that has sought to denounce the injustices of colonialism and study the culture of colonialism, colonial discourse, colonial urbanism, and even colonial tourism has not had much influence outside the academy. Works focusing on colonial imagery, such as *Images et Colonies, Images d'empire,* and *L'Autre et nous* seem more concerned with providing excellent reproductions of the images than with extensive analytical interpretations of them.[39] Fascination with colonial images is rampant in popular culture; in addition to the books and websites mentioned above, colonial nostalgia films such as *Chocolat* (1988), *Outremer* (1990), and *Indochine* (1991) have flourished, as have novels and memoirs by Europeans growing up in overseas territories.

Perhaps this fascination with colonial imagery is simply an interest in the past as history, with no desire to glorify a particular moment, but simply to remember it. One might buy a poster of *La Croisière noire* as one might of *Birth of a Nation,* out of a simple interest in vintage images (or, in this case, vintage cars). However, whether an image can ever be emptied of its historical content is in itself a problematic question; the Stars and Bars, which some Southerners see as a glorious symbol of Southern identity, remains for many a symbol of the slave system, and the swastika, seen by Hindus as a sign of a prosperous future, is for many people indissociable from Nazism and the Holocaust. These examples, while extreme, demonstrate the cultural problems that nostalgia for certain images, and the desire to dissociate them from their historical context, can create.

The example of *La Croisière noire*, and much of the spillover into popular culture, borders on a nostalgic view of Africa in particular, and the colonial past in general, as a kind of lost homeland. Perpetuation of a sanitized, commercialized, and commodified version of the Citroën memory depends on representational strategies that exemplify, as Marina Heung has written, "the revisionist tactics of postcolonial representation."[40] Through the process of rewriting and erasure, and also commercialization, images of the empire become "fixed" in memorial timelessness rather than in historical time, a practice that Homi Bhabha identifies as one of the fundamental characteristics of colonial, and not postcolonial, discourse.[41] Rather than opening up a new space within which to examine colonial history, these sanitized and commodified images fuel nostalgia as Fredric Jameson defines it, a "desperate attempt to reappropriate a missing past" through "stylistic connotation" and memory process rather than actual historical content. Jameson claims that the postmodern love for the past—which he calls historicism—is fundamentally ahistorical, and furthermore is "omnipresent, omnivorous and well-nigh libidinal."[42] I would argue that an element of this kind of nostalgic historicism is part of the colonial syndrome in present-day French culture. I would add that the recourse to nostalgia is an attempt to rescue individual memories of empire from a collective memory that has become socially unacceptable. The persistence of memories such as those discussed in this chapter are clear indicators of this trend.

Notes

1. Archival sources will be cited as follows: MAAO (Fonds Haardt, Musée des Arts Africains et Océaniens, Paris); MNED (Musée National de l'Éducation, Rouen). I viewed the film at the Archives du film, Centre national de la Cinématographie, Bois d'Arcy. My thanks to the staff at all three of these institutions.

2. For the colonial period, see Raoul Girardet, *L'idée coloniale en France de 1871 à 1962* (Paris: La Table Ronde, 1972).

3. See, for example, Tony Chafer and Amanda Sackur, eds., *Promoting the Colonial Idea: Propaganda and Visions of Empire in France* (New York: Palgrave, 2002); P. A. Morton, *Hybrid Modernities: Architecture and Representation at the 1931 Colonial Exposition,*

Paris (Cambridge, Mass.: MIT Press, 2000); Nicolas Bancel, Pascal Blanchard, and Francis Delabre, eds., *Images d'empire 1930-1960: Trente ans de photographies officielles sur l'Afrique française* (Paris: Éditions de la Martinière-La documentation française, 1997); Frederick Cooper and Ann Laura Stoler, eds., *Tensions of Empire: Colonial Cultures in a Bourgeois World* (Berkeley: University of California Press, 1997); Nicolas Bancel, Pascal Blanchard, and Laurent Gervereau, eds., *Images et colonies: Iconographie et propagande coloniale sur l'Afrique française de 1880 à 1962* (Paris: BDIC-ACHAC, 1993).

4. Henry Rousso, *Le Syndrome de Vichy: De 1944 à nos jours* (Paris: Seuil, 1990).

5. Leela Gandhi, *Postcolonial Theory: A Critical Introduction* (New York: Columbia University Press, 1998), 4.

6. Elisabeth Mudimbe-Boyi, "Introduction," in *Remembering Africa*, ed. Elisabeth Mudimbe-Boyi (Portsmouth, N.H.: Heinemann, 2002), xv-xvii.

7. Jean Halpérin, "Introduction," in *Mémoire et histoire: données et débats*, ed. Jean Halpérin and Georges Levitte (Paris: Denoël, 1986), 8, 10.

8. *Webster's New World Dictionary, College Edition*, s.v. "nostalgia."

9. Fabien Sabatés, *1924-1925: La Croisière noire Citroën* (Paris: Eric Baschet, 1980), 9.

10. For more details on the tourist circuit, see my article, "Le Tourisme Citroën au Sahara (1924-1925)," *Vingtième Siècle* 68 (2000): 95-107.

11. André Citroën, *Projet d'organisation des grandes lignes de communications africaines*, 1924. MAAO, 4°GMH 24.

12. André Citroën to the Président du Conseil, 2 May 1924. MAAO, 4°GMH 24.

13. *Expédition Centre-Afrique; 2ème mission Haardt-Audouin-Dubreuil—de la Méditerranée à l'océan Indien par le Niger, le Congo, et le Nil*, 1924. MAAO, 4°GMH 24.

14. Georges-Marie Haardt and Louis Audoin-Dubreuil, *The Black Journey: Across Africa with the Citroën Expedition* (New York: Cosmopolitan Book Corporation, 1927), 316.

15. MAAO, 4°GMH 26.

16. Sequences from the film are cited by reel number and time code. 2/3:30, 5/2:30.

17. Poirier, *La Croisière noire*, 3/8:00.

18. Poirier, *La Croisière noire*, 1/0:00, and André Citroën to M. Daladier, Ministère de l'Instruction Publique et des Beaux-Arts, 26 Feb. 1926. MAAO, 4°GMH 26.

19. Peter Bloom, "Networks of Empire: The French Colonial Archive, 1889-1933" (Ph.D. dissertation, UCLA, 1997), 203.

20. Mary Louise Pratt, *Imperial Eyes: Travel Writing and Transculturation* (New York: Routledge, 1992), 7.

21. Alice Conklin, *A Mission to Civilize: The Republican Idea of Empire in France and West Africa, 1895-1930* (Stanford, Calif.: Stanford University Press, 1997), 5.

22. Poirier, *La Croisière noire*, 5/0:00.

23. Haardt, *The Black Journey*, 153.

24. *Ciné-Miroir*, founded in 1922, was the most successful magazine of its type, with a circulation of 110,000 in 1930. Claude Bellanger et al., eds., *Histoire générale de la presse française*, Vol. 3 (Paris: Presses Universitaires de France, 1972), 599.

25. MAAO, 4°GMH 87-95.

26. *Journal de Rouen*, 9 October 1926.

27. *Le Réveil du Nord*, 9 October 1926.

28. *Le Petit Journal,* 12 December 1927.

29. Figure 5.1: *L'Officiel de la Couture de la Mode de Paris,* January 1927. Figure 5.2: *Modes de la femme de France,* 30 January 1927. MAAO, 4°GMH 92-3.

30. *Les Aventures de Tintin, reporter du Petit Vingtième au Congo* was first published as a black-and-white serial comic in *Le Petit Vingtième* in 1930. It appeared in book form in 1931 (Brussels: Éditions du Petit Vingtième and Éditions Casterman). The more widely circulated *Tintin au Congo* is a color edition that Hergé redrew in 1946, removing some of the colonialist references (for example, when Tintin teaches in the missionary's classroom, his subject in 1930 is "votre patrie, la Belgique" [your country, Belgium]. In the 1946 version, he gives a math lesson.)

31. Album d'élève, Dontucat, 1945. MNED, 1945 (V) 3.2.03 99.00669.

32. Jacques Wolgensinger, *L'Aventure de la croisière noire* (Paris: Éditions Robert Laffont, 2002); Eric Deschamps, *La Cuisine des croisières Citroën,* (Paris: Éditions de l'envol, 2001); Caroline Haardt de la Baume, *Alexandre Iacovleff: L'Artiste voyageur* (Paris: Flammarion, 2000); Eric Deschamps, *Croisières Citroën: Carnets de route africains* (Paris: Éditions ETAI, 1999).

33. Eric Massiet du Biest, "La Croisière noire 2004," www.globe-driver.com/tracbar/2004-cr-noire (26 Jan. 2004).

34. It was shown in 1995 at the festival of silent film and music at the Musée d'Orsay and also, in the same year, at the Fespaco in Ouagadougou; it was shown again at the 1996 Cinéma du réel festival at the Centre Pompidou and at the Semaine du cinéma ethnographique in Normandy.

35. Du Biest, "La Croisière noire 2004."

36. Maurice Guimendego, "De la Croisière Noire au Paris-Dakar: historique d'un raid sportif," www.africultures.com (3 Oct. 2003).

37. According to film reviews, the original documentary that swept France was two hours in length; the version that is now available in film archives and was shown at recent festivals is fifty-two minutes. Citroën's politically correct version is thirty minutes long.

38. Christian Perdrizet, manager of the Citroën media library, e-mail communication with author, 16 October 2003.

39. See note 3.

40. Marina Heung, "The Family Romance of Orientalism: From *Madame Butterfly* to *Indochine,*" *Genders* 21 (1995): 241.

41. Homi Bhaba, "The Other Question: The Stereotype and Colonial Discourse," *Screen* 24, no. 6 (1983): 18.

42. Fredric J. Jameson, *Postmodernism, or, The Cultural Logic of Late Capitalism* (Durham, N.C.: Duke University Press, 1991), 18-19.

6

Trespass of Memory
The French-Indochina War
as World War II

Hee Ko

IN JEAN LARTÉGUY'S NOVEL *The Centurions*, the Viet Minh capture protagonist Lieutenant Pinières after the fall of Dien Bien Phu in 1954. Shaken, he compares this war to another in his past:

> Ever since My-Oi [his Vietnamese mistress] had betrayed the Vietminh terrorist organization, Pinières had often remembered this incident: at the liberation of France he had ordered his men to shave the scalp of a beautiful, rather silly girl who had openly flaunted her liaison with a German officer. While the operation was being performed, she had looked him straight in the eye:
> "I loved my German, I'd got him under my skin. I'm only a woman. I don't give a damn about politics . . . and to protect him I would have sold the lot of you."
> Pinières had slapped her across the face until she sank to her knees and his men had then made free of her.
> For four days and nights he had been tracking down a band of guerrillas and had set fire to the village that they had used as a hideout. The stench of the burning flesh was still in his nostrils. When he came back . . . he made up his mind to marry My-Oi, the "collaborator."[1]

In choosing to rhetorically situate the French-Indochina War (1945-1954) as analogous to the Nazi occupation of France, Lartéguy may be faulted for overextending the limits of fictional representation. That is, how could he understand the Viet Minh's colonial war of independence from France as comparable to the events in World War II except in the broadest terms? Lartéguy, however, was not the only one to draw such a parallel.

In the December 1946 issue of *Les Temps modernes*, Jean-Paul Sartre described the French-Indochina War in the following manner:

> It is unimaginable that after four years of occupation, the French don't recognize the face of Germans in France that is today theirs in Indochina. Certainly, there, we are the Germans—granted without a Gestapo or concentration camps—at least we hope.[2]

Here, as in the extract quoted above from Lartéguy's novel, events in Indochina are seen to replicate those in Nazi-occupied France, with a foreign force occupying a nation without its consent. In this case, the French, once victims, now terrorized their colonial subjects in a manner all too similar to their former Nazi occupants. Sartre asked how Frenchmen who now knew intimately the tyranny of foreign rule as well as the desire for liberation could condone such actions and support the war in Indochina. By doing so, he argued, the French people risked forsaking the memory of the resistance and tarnishing Republican values. Indochina, thus, became a mnemonic site where France's political heritage would again be called into question.

This chapter seeks to address the narratives that the French used in describing the French-Indochina War to bolster claims to political legitimacy. It explicates how those who supported and opposed the war sought to clarify and understand the Vietnamese war for national liberation in relationship to their memory of the French resistance during the Vichy period. For political expedience and commercial appeal the Left and the Right made analogies between the German occupation of France and the French occupation of Indochina. In so doing, they were able to render intelligible a war in an exotic part of the world to the vast majority of the French public who cared little about affairs in Asia. This chapter describes the trespass of the memory of one event into the territory of another.

After the liberation of Paris, the future of France still remained uncertain for vast numbers of French people. Food and housing were in short supply. The Fourth Republic, which replaced de Gaulle's provisional war government, continued to be in a protracted state of instability. In addition, France had yet to be reconciled with its past experience of Hitler's Germany and Vichy. Purges enveloped the nation against those who had collaborated with the Vichy State. The French people were frantically trying to regenerate their nation during this economic and political chaos. The resistance myth, that all but a few Frenchmen had remained loyal to the Republic, was central to this postwar political endeavor. In the midst of this upheaval, the nationalist revolution in Indochina erupted.

The French-Indochina War stirred passions released during World War II. The French Communist Party (Parti communiste français, PCF), enjoying popular support as newly anointed saviors of the French Republic after World War II, opposed the French escalation of violence in Indochina. But bounded by their tripartite partnership with the Socialists (Section française de l'Internationale ouvrière, SFIO) and the Christian Democrats (Mouvement républicain populaire, MRP), and their concern for protecting Russo-European relations, the PCF was not able to halt the war while working within the government. It marshaled, however, a propaganda campaign against the Indochina War by making analogies with the French experience in World War II. The PCF appealed to the public by employing the antifascist rhetoric that was so successful in World War II, but removed from its historical context. In doing so, the PCF did not condemn outright the government policy in Indochina, since they were now part of the government.[3] But, by using the language of resistance to oppose the war, they were able to recast the war as unpatriotic, thus avoiding a break with the coalition government and maintaining a fictional representation of governmental solidarity. Moreover, for the PCF, the Indochina War was a chance to rewrite its own ambiguous relationship to the history of the resistance. The signing of the Nazi-Soviet Pact in 1939 had delayed the PCF's joining of the resistance, and in turn raised lingering questions about its patriotism and commitment to France. By using the language of the resistance in the context of Indochina, the PCF could both advance a critique of foreign policy and shore up its political position at home.

In fact, the use of resistance rhetoric was common to the broader Left. *Le Franc-Tireur* argued that Ho Chi Minh "was a friend of France, the France of '89, the France of the Resistance . . ."[4] Ho Chi Minh had refused to "collaborate" with the Vichy government in Indochina, according to *Ce Soir*.[5] Throughout the left-wing press, Ho Chi Minh was portrayed as one who had remained loyal to the ideas of the Republic. Rarely, if ever, did the PCF newspapers directly address Ho Chi Minh's communist sympathies. Instead, the Communist press chose specifically to use the language of resistance to describe the goals and actions Vietnamese nationalists took. Every parallel was drawn to compare the German occupation of France to that of the French occupation of Indochina. The PCF presented colonial elites as Pétainist collaborators and the Viet Minh as members of the resistance who fought against Japanese fascism and the Vichy state. By narrating the war as a fight against occupation and the forces of fascism, the PCF argued that it was incumbent on the citizens of France to support the Republic of Vietnam.

The Left's use of this analogy was simplified by the installation of Vichy sympathizers in Indochina during World War II. In June of 1940, Japanese forces had invaded an ill-prepared French Indochina. Faced with political isolation and lack of military assistance from either the French or the Allied fleet, the Governor of Indochina acquiesced to Japanese demands for a negotiated peace. The treaty guaranteed French sovereignty in Indochina in exchange for the stationing and safe passage of Japanese troops into China.[6] Despite the unwelcome and uneasy alliance with Japan, the French colonial administration was able to eke out a large degree of autonomy. As a consequence, Indochina, like a number of other French colonies, was able to implement Marshal Philippe Pétain's National Revolution.

Both historians and contemporaries of Vichy have commented on the colonists' fervent loyalty to the National Revolution.[7] By July 1940, the Governor of Indochina, Jean Decoux, an ardent Pétainist, proceeded to disband elected assemblies, censored the press, and implemented exclusionary measures against Jews.[8] Indeed, many of the French colonists, comparable to Parisian ultra-collaborators, advocated more repressive and uncompromising strategies for national renewal than the *métropole*.[9] Thus, during World War II, Indochina stood out as the quintessence of Vichy *Outre-mer*.

During the Second World War, calls to liberate the Indochinese from the Japanese imperialists came from both French Communists and de Gaulle.[10] The Party encouraged its members to fight the Japanese fascists on French territory. De Gaulle, likewise, pushed to save Indochina from Japan, believing that Empire was absolutely necessary for France's grandeur.[11] "Not for a single hour," said de Gaulle, "did France lose the hope and the will to recover free Indochina."[12] Hence, in the summer and fall of 1945, French partisans enlisted to continue the struggle against fascism in the Orient.

But Japan's occupation of Indochina had de facto ended before the arrival of French troops. After seizing power from the French colonial authorities in March 1945, the Japanese military had by August capitulated to Vietnamese nationalist groups led by the Indochinese Communist Party (ICP). By 2 September, Ho Chi Minh had proclaimed the Democratic Republic of Vietnam (DRV). When Free French troops were dispatched to Indochina in September 1945, they faced the newly established Viet Minh government, not a fight against Japanese fascists.

According to the PCF, French soldiers who had innocently gone to Indochina believing they were going to fight Japanese fascists were forced to commit Nazi-like atrocities against an occupied people. *Le Franc-Tireur* maintained that French soldiers learned only later that they were to wage a colonial war against the Vietnamese.[13] Jean-Henri Roy, a veteran of the Franc-Tireurs et Partisans (FTP) resistance group, explained:

No one among us expected that the Alsatian and German campaigns would take place in the battlefields of Vietnam. Like me, nobody who set sail in October 1945 for Saigon had signed up for a colonial engagement. We had simply signed up for the duration of hostilities, an engagement against Germany and against

Japan [. . .]. Arriving in Saigon, another surprise awaited us. An armed Japanese soldier welcomed us on solid ground, saluting us respectfully. The whites that had deigned to speak to us stated that they owed their lives to the Japanese troops . . . [They claimed] the enemy was the Vietnamese people . . .[14]

According to the left-wing press, only a small handful of men instigated the war for their own profit, betraying the Republic and the French people.[15] Vichy loyalists who remained unpurged from the French colonial administrative apparatus had masterminded the effort. *Ce Soir* reported that the President of the Bank of Indochina had served as Minister of Foreign Affairs for Pétain.[16] The Commissioner of the Republic of Cochinchina was a former Vichyite who in 1944 passed into the resistance once the Allies were sure to win, according to *Le Franc-Tireur*. He remained detested by the Vietnamese, who held him responsible for a horrific repression in 1940.[17] Moreover, the paper argued that the colonial elite in Indochina remained traitors to the new republic; over 90 percent had voted against its constitution.[18]

This rhetoric is unmistakably the *résistancialisme* that historian Henry Rousso describes in his work *The Vichy Syndrome*.[19] Again, Indochina, like France during World War II, was a victim of a small handful of unscrupulous Nazi collaborators. In allowing the war to continue, the PCF and others suggested, these outlaws threatened the ideals and the people of the Republic. Thus they were making the explicit argument that by condoning the colonial elite's war in Indochina, the French public was directly supporting Vichy policy.

Anyone who supported the war, according to this logic, collaborated with Vichy and betrayed true France. This included the press. Newspapers who defended the war in Indochina were "shooting the back of France, of the Republic and of peace and harboring unwashed collaborators [collaborateurs mal blanchis]."[20] Calling for an immediate cease-fire, Albert Bayet wrote in *Le Franc-Tireur* that those in favor of the war spoke grandiloquently of the "integrity of the Empire," "honor," and the "flag" but among those men, he saw those who had "during the period of aggression against Spain sent swords of honor to Franco's men, who at the time of Munich groveled before Hitler, who at Montoire bowed before Pétain."[21] *L'Aurore*, *Le Pays*, and even *Le Monde* were said to participate in the strangulation of the French Republic. Accusations that those in favor of the war in France were aligned with Vichy and Japanese fascists continually filled the pages of *Le Franc-Tireur* and *Ce Soir*.

At the same time, these press accounts deemed anyone who opposed the Indochina War as having the character and values of the resistance. For example, *Le Franc-Tireur* reported the arrest of journalist Jacques Dauphin of *France-Presse* for treason. Dauphin was to face a military tribunal in Saigon. *Le Franc-Tireur* declared that Dauphin was innocent of wrongdoing not by giving facts to the contrary, but by alluding to his resistance record. They reported that back in 1940, the Governor of Indochina, "a representative of Pétain," had arrested Dauphin for seditious activity.[22] In describing the Dauphin affair in such a manner, *Le Franc-Tireur* clearly wanted to demonstrate that a person who had fought against Vichy rule and Japanese tyranny held only the most loyal of Republican convictions. Thus, in opposing the state now, men like Dauphin were actually protecting Republican values against those men in government who betrayed them (as had Pétain).

On the other hand, right-wing newspapers hawked the memory of the French resistance just as vehemently as the Left. *L'Aurore*, known for its fervent anticommunist stance, initially described the war in Indochina as a fight against communism, condemning the PCF support of Ho Chi Minh's forces as anti-French and anti-West.[23] It was unmistakably irked by the communist newspapers' use of anti-Vichy rhetoric. *L'Aurore* called for the French government to implement its own propaganda machine to "combat the ubiquitous communist propaganda."[24]

Almost immediately, the conservative press selectively used resistance language to describe the Indochina War, from simple name-calling—Ho Chi Minh was the "Führer" and his "terrorist organizations" the "Gestapo"—to drawing explicit historical parallels with World War II.[25] For example, *L'Aurore* splashed as a headline Admiral Argenlieu's remark that "France will assure the protection of ethnic minorities that are entrusted to her," referring to the annexation of Cochinchina by the Hanoi government against its wishes and reminding readers how German annexation of nations during World War II led to the Holocaust.[26] Furthermore, it reminded the general public of embarrassing errors made by the Communist Party before and during World War II. *Le Franc-Tireur*'s appeals to negotiate with the Viet Minh, according to the Right, were suspiciously similar to communists who advocated a détente with Germany in 1940 during the Nazi-Soviet Pact.[27] In short, the conservative press naturalized the relationship between Vichy and the Viet Minh, albeit in antithetical ways from the communists.

What complicated the colonial war further and justified the analogy to some were the presence of Japanese deserters in the Viet Minh and the enlistment of German soldiers in the French Foreign Legion. *L'Aurore* pointed out instances where Japanese soldiers working with the Viet Minh committed atrocities. Moreover, details of the mutilation of French soldiers often accompanied explanations that Japanese soldiers and technicians as well as Japanese artillery had assisted the Viet Minh.[28] Throughout the war, *L'Aurore* and *Le Pays* noted that Viet Minh forces were often found next to Japanese deserters "who spread their hatred of whites."[29] In December 1946, *L'Aurore* noted that after a French assault on the residence of Ho Chi Minh, Japanese bodies were found around those of Viet Minh troops: "One more proof in the duplicity of the so-called 'resistant' Ho Chi Minh."[30] Newspapers reported how former Japanese officers "devise the attacks."[31] Journalists' reports, however, overrated Japanese power and underestimated the autonomy of the native Vietnamese opposition. For example, *Le Pays* stated that the Vietnamese "bands were surrounded by veteran instructors of the old army of Mikado . . ."[32] But according to Christopher Goscha's insightful study on Japanese soldiers in Vietnam, relatively few Japanese deserters served with the Viet Minh.[33]

While the French conservative press used descriptions of Japanese and (less often) German soldiers leading the Viet Minh insurrection, the communists counterattacked by publicizing the enlistment of Nazi officers in the French Foreign Legion. The colonial elites in Indochina, according to the communist press, welcomed former Nazis and Vichyites. In 1945, a Communist deputy accused the French Army of recruiting Germans from prisoner of war camps.[34] In the French Assembly, members of the PCF claimed that two German soldiers who had participated in the Oradour massacre had escaped prosecution by serving in the French Foreign Legion.[35] The left-wing paper *Le Franc-Tireur* speculated that 231 German prisoners who arrived in Marseille to join the French Foreign Legion were going to be used as reinforcements in Indochina.[36] These rumors were meant to cast doubt upon the Fourth Republic's commitment to purging Vichy sympathizers.

As early as 31 October 1945, the French government, in the face of these rumors, admitted they had been recruiting German prisoners of war for the French Foreign Legion. But they carefully stated that extreme precautions were taken to investigate the background of all recruits, banning automatically recruits with SS, Hitlerjugend, Nazi, or pro-Nazi associations from enlisting.[37] Moreover, the government stated that the number of German prisoners of war admitted into the Legion did not exceed twenty for every 1000 recruits, certainly far less than in previous years.[38]

The French Foreign Legion had had a long tradition of using German mercenaries.[39] French authorities believed Germans were highly trained and instilled discipline.[40] In 1939, Germans comprised about one-fifth of the Foreign Legion.[41] During Vichy, the German government had demanded the repatriation of its soldiers. It is unclear, however, after the liberation of Paris, how many Germans the Legion admitted, let alone whether any were SS officers.[42] In a comprehensive study of soldiers who fought in the French-Indochina War, Michel Bodin demonstrates the difficulty of obtaining accurate figures, primarily because the personnel files of recruits are still closed, but he estimates that about 40 percent of the Legion during the Indochina War were of Germanic origin.[43]

Concern with the presence of Nazis in the French military spread outside the PCF propaganda mill. Historian R. C. Hudson has most thoroughly studied the prevalence of Nazi-like atrocities committed by French troops in Indochina in his examination of the periodical *Les Temps modernes*.[44] Although the Indochina War was never a primary topic in this journal, protests against it appeared regularly.[45] Editors Jean-Paul Sartre and Maurice Merleau-Ponty used contributions from former soldiers, anthropologists, journalists, and Vietnamese writers, challenging the war's legitimacy through a series of first-hand accounts asserting the presence of former SS men in French troops. Jeanne Cuisinier, anthropologist and member of the SFIO, described the French colonists' acceptance of and complacency toward Germans on French territory in the following manner:

> These SS men were singing the Horst Wessel Lied right in the middle of a Saigon Street. . . . It wasn't the least surprising to the French (colonist) to hear German spoken each time they met up with the legionnaires in the streets of Saigon.[46]

Moreover, journalists and returning soldiers commented on how the war brought out the worst instincts among Frenchmen, comparable to those of Nazi soldiers. In particular, the contributors and editors of *Les Temps modernes* were gravely concerned about how the presence of German Nazis in the French military could influence French soldiers' behavior. The resistance experience of the French soldiers should have naturally made them empathetic to the Viet Minh cause, argued Sartre: "And who is in a better place to understand the Vietnamese resistance than the [French] resistant? Who better than a Frenchman to feel the horror of Occupation?" But instead, Sartre worried about French soldiers abandoning Republican notions of liberty and equality to mutate into German Nazis. Sartre continued: "In each of his enemies he has found in them what he once was; in each of his comrades he fears finding a German. And himself."[47]

It was in this context that the Henri Martin Affair exploded. The French government had charged Martin with treason for masterminding a plot to sabotage a French aircraft carrier ready to embark on mission to Indochina in 1950. Martin, a former combatant in Indochina, admitted to distributing tracts against the war but denied the charge of sabotage. Martin's supporters used a familiar set of references to persuade the public of his innocence. They argued that a man such as Martin could never be a traitor to his country because of his resistance past.

The "Coordinating Committee for the Defense of Henri Martin" was made up of communist organizations that specifically used Martin's affiliation with the resistance during the Second World War as a defense strategy.[48] Posters and newsletters recounted his resistance past and described him as an "exemplary patriot." By calling him a patriot, the committee tried to establish two things: first, his resistance past as a member of the FTP, second, his conduct in disobeying the law for the greater good of the Republic. PCF leader André Menstrier appealed for the release of Martin based solely on his resistance record, describing how "at the age of seventeen, already a sailor, he disobeyed the traitors Pétain and Darlan who delivered the French fleet to Hitler's Germany [. . . and . . .] took arms as a Franc-Tireur and French partisan."[49] Menstrier argued that just as during Vichy, Martin's refusal to follow the orders of a misguided government and the will of the majority demonstrated his patriotism.

The PCF's calls to support Henri Martin's fight against charges of sabotage were heard throughout France. The articulation of his innocence and support for him followed the same pattern. For example, on 24 August 1952, the Mayor of Silvareccio, Corsica, sent a letter and petition to the President of the Republic requesting the immediate release of Martin.[50] He noted that in the month of August, "patriots" from all over the island of Corsica assembled around the tombs of resistance martyrs and heroes, commemorating their sacrifice for the liberation of their nation. In addition to the numerous ceremonies held on the island to commemorate the Liberation, the mayor described a smaller assembly held for Dominique Vincetti, who died at the age of twenty-seven at the hands of the Germans.

> While rendering a solemn homage to our dead, we do not forget the living. Our thoughts, Mr. President, go . . . towards Henri Martin. At the age of sixteen, Henri Martin fought for the same cause of Dominique Vincetti: The liberation of the *Patrie*.

Thirty-two local government officials, civil servants, and businessmen, all of them denoting their occupation and more importantly their involvement in the resistance, as well as the various medals of honor they received as members of the resistance, signed the letter.

Protests against Martin's treatment did not flow only from the French Communist Party. Intellectuals such as Sartre and Simone de Beauvoir, university professors, and politicians such as Paul Reynaud organized a campaign for Martin's defense while publicly denying any ties to the PCF.[51] All of these public entreaties began with or included Martin's connection with the resistance during World War II as proof of his innocence. Sartre published Henri Martin's letters to his family from Indochina as evidence of Martin's loyalty to France. In the introduction, Sartre dramatically recounts Martin's decision to join the resistance, and to risk his life to save France from the Nazis. Moreover, Sartre suggests that after the Liberation in 1944, Martin remained more patriotic than most by continuing his fight against fascism in the Far East, by joining the navy in its campaign against the Japanese occupation of Indochina. Another contributor to the collection, Marcel Ner, wrote:

Nothing in these letters has an embittered or undisciplined character or a sectarian spirit. He [Martin] is an average Frenchmen inspired by our traditions of patriotism and liberty, honored by the Resistance and full of admiration for his commander in chief.[52]

Hence, it was not his suspected communist ties that prompted Martin's actions. Rather, Martin's commitment to the ideals of France and the resistance led him to protest the war.

Martin, according to Sartre, was unaware of what was happening in Indochina, or more exactly, he believed what they had told him—he was going to Indochina to fight fascism. Consequently, Martin could not understand the overwhelming presence of Vichyites in his crew.[53] Martin wrote to his family that there was

a total lack of purges . . . there are some second mates who were sergeants in Pétain's G.M.R.[54] And there are some who are still more notorious than them. Here, guys from the maquis would have to hide themselves (from their own crew) as at the time of the *Boches*.[55]

The combination of Pétainists and Germans formed a dangerous mix, according to Martin: "In Indochina, the French army behaves like the *Boches* did in France. I am completely disgusted in seeing this. Why do our planes shoot (all the time) defenseless fishermen? Why do our soldiers loot, burn, and kill? In order to civilize?"[56]

Martin's legal defense strategy did not differ from the propaganda. When Martin was finally brought to trial, he invoked the resistance tradition as fundamental in guiding his decision to oppose the French-Indochina War. When the judge asked why he chose to disobey the laws of his country, he replied, "It is not considered disobedience when it concerns the struggle against a government which betrays the interests of France. Those who fought against Vichy were not [considered] traitors." The judge asked: "But does that mean that anyone can do whatever he pleases?" Martin answered: "There is a fundamental difference between doing whatever one wants and defying the orders of criminals. As for me, what I saw in Indochina was sufficient [to prove the latter]."[57] By stating that his cause was the same as that of the resistance against Nazi-occupied France, Martin and the PCF also implied that the Fourth Republic held much in common with the Vichy Regime. Martin and other antiwar activists attempted not only to stop the war in Indochina but also to challenge the leaders of the Fourth Republic by convincing the public that its government had once again abandoned the principles of true France.

After 1947, though, much had changed. The communists had been ousted from government, thus transforming their political strategies and need for compromises. In addition, the international situation had shifted, with the founding of the Cominform, the release of the Jdanov paper, the Truman Doctrine, the outbreak of the revolution in Greece, and the Korean War. An exceptional divide separated East from West. But the Henri Martin Affair in the early 1950s demonstrates how little French rhetoric had changed in describing the Indochina War to the French public.

Similarly, French intellectuals, the PCF, and the conservative press all misunderstood the complexities of the situation in Indochina. By grafting the *résistancialisme* rhetoric onto a colonial war for independence in the midst of the Cold War, they abandoned the integrity of the historical moment. The analogy between Vichy and Vietnam left little space for a serious reconsideration of French colonialism. Rather, it suggested that the evil that emanated from colonialism came from Nazi Germany. Ho Chi Minh thus became a resistance fighter or a Hitler, depending on one's political allegiance. As Pierre Nora has observed, "Memory, being a phenomenon of emotion and magic, accommodates only those facts that suit it. It thrives on vague telescoping reminiscences, on hazy general impressions or on specific symbolic details."[58] The reworking of World War II memories in the context of the French-Indochina war provides a striking illustration of this process.

Notes

1. Jean Lartéguy, *The Centurions*, trans. Xan Fielding (New York: Dutton, 1962), 87.

2. Jean-Paul Sartre, "Et bourreaux et victimes," in *Les Temps modernes* 15 (December 1946): unpaginated editorial preceding page 385. Unless otherwise noted, all translations are my own.

3. François Goguel, *France under the Fourth Republic* (Ithaca, N.Y.: Cornell University Press, 1952), 25.

4. Albert Bayet, "L'Union française ?" *Le Franc-Tireur*, 25 December 1946, 1. Hereafter cited as *FT*.

5. René Andrieu, "Fontainebleau cadre historique de tant d'événements où s'ouvre aujourd'hui la négociation France-Viet-Nam," *Ce Soir*, 7-8 July 1946, 2.

6. Alain Ruscio, *La Guerre française d'Indochine* (Brussels: Éditions Complexe, 1992).

7. Eric T. Jennings, *Vichy in the Tropics: Pétain's National Revolution in Madagascar, Guadeloupe, and Indochina, 1940-1944* (Palo Alto, Calif.: Stanford University Press, 2001); Robert Paxton, *Vichy France: Old Guard and the New Order 1940-1944* (New York: Columbia University Press, 1972).

8. Jacques Dalloz, *The War in Indochina: 1945-54*, trans. Josephine Bacon (Savage, Md.: Barnes & Noble, 1990), 36-37.

9. Jennings, *Vichy*, 131-133.

10. Marius Magnien, "Québec et la libération de l'Indochine," *L'Humanité*, 17-18 September 1944 and "Politique extérieure réaliste," *L'Humanité*, 25 October 1944; see

also Edward Rice-Maximin, *Accommodation and Resistance: The French Left, Indochina and the Cold War 1944-1954* (Westport, Conn.: Greenwood, 1986).

11. Alain Ruscio, *Les Communistes français et la guerre d'Indochine, 1944-1954* (Paris: L'Harmattan, 1985), 73.

12. As quoted in Bruce C. Marshall, *The French Colonial Myth and Constitution-Making in the Fourth Republic* (New Haven: Yale University Press, 1993), 135.

13. Bayet, "Union française," 1.

14. Jean-Henri Roy, "Un abus de confiance," in Jean-Paul Sartre et al., *L'Affaire Henri Martin* (Paris: Gallimard, 1953), 123-125.

15. Georges Altman, "Jusqu'à quand le sang va-t-il couler en Indochine," *FT*, 28 November 1946, 1.

16. J. Dresch, "Le Viet-nam république amie," *Ce Soir*, 23-24 June 1946, 1-2.

17. Altman, "Jusqu'à quand," 1.

18. Léon Boutbien, "Je reviens d'Indochine," *FT*, 16 January 1947, 4.

19. Henry Rousso, *The Vichy Syndrome: History and Memory in France since 1944*, trans. Arthur Goldhammer (Cambridge: Harvard University Press, 1995). In Rousso's analysis, it was only with the Algerian War that memories of Vichy affected events outside the Hexagon. While Rousso contributes invaluably to the history of postwar France, his focus on domestic events neglects a critical juncture where the memory of Vichy collided with events in Indochina.

20. "Nous Accusons," *FT*, 22-23 December 1946, 1. The term is used to describe collaborators who were not "washed" from their associations after the war. Cf the phrase "argent blanchi" to signify money the provenance of which is hidden through money laundering.

21. Albert Bayet, "Rappelez d'Argenlieu," *FT*, 7 December, 1946, 1.

22. "Un journaliste français arrêté par d'Argenlieu!" *FT*, 28 January 1947, 1.

23. "Les Communistes complices de l'assassin Ho Chi Minh," *L'Aurore*, 19 March 1947, 1 and 4; *L'Aurore*, 19 January 1948, 1; "Nouvelle reculade du gouvernement dans l'affaire Duong Bac Mai," *L'Aurore*, 27 March 1947, 1.

24. Dominique Pada, "Halte! À la trahison. On autorise le Viet-nam à publier à Paris la liste des soldats français qu'il assassine en Indochine," *L'Aurore*, 18-19 January 1948, 1.

25. "Partout en Indochine les chefs du Viet-minh font leur soumission," *Le Pays*, 17 March 1947, 1.

26. "La France assurera la protection des minorités ethniques," *L'Aurore*, 26 December 1946, 4.

27. Discussed in Georges Altman, "D'Argenlieu donne-t-il ses instructions à Moutet," *FT*, 28 December 1946, 1.

28. Altman, "D'Argenlieu," 1.

29. "Le Drame d'Indochine," *L'Aurore*, 29 November 1946, 1 and 4; "L'Insurrection vietnamienne éclate dans le nord de l'Indochine," 21 December 1946, 1 and 4; "Désaccord entre les troupes d'Ho Chi Minh," 19-20 January 1947, 4; "Plus un Français en Indochine dans deux ans," *Le Pays*, 4 March 1948.

30. *L'Aurore*, 24 December 1946, 4.

31. "Le Sous-Lieutenant Le Clerc dénonce la propagande criminelle des partisans français d'Ho Chi Minh," *L'Aurore*, 30 January 1947, 4.

32. *Le Pays*, 20 December 1947, 1.

33. Christopher E. Goscha, "Belated Allies: The Technical Contributions of Japanese Deserters to the Viet Minh, (1945-1950)," in *A Companion to the Vietnam War*, eds. Marilyn Young and Robert Buzzanco (Malden, Mass.: Blackwell Publishers, 2002) 37-64. See also David Marr, *Vietnam 1945: The Quest for Power* (Berkeley: University of California Press, 1995), 543.

34. Michel Bodin, *Les Soldats d'Indochine*, 1945-54 (Paris: L'Harmattan, 1997), 19.

35. *Journal Officiel*, 9-10 June 1949, 3239-3243, 3303-3307.

36. "231 Allemands arrivent à Marseille encadrés par des policiers," *FT*, 31 December 1946, 1. Tass and other Soviet orbit press agencies also publicized the French use of ex-SS men in the French Legion. Bodin, *Soldats*, 84. In addition, German periodicals such as *Der Spiegel* and *Christ und Welt* began to publish reports that German SS officers were serving in the French Foreign Legion in large numbers. See for example *Der Spiegel*, 8 August 1951, 12-16; "Die Armee der Enttäuschten," *Christ und Welt*, 5 January 1950; Adrien Liddell Hart, "Die Deutschen in der Fremdenlegion," *Christ und Welt*, 28 August 1952, 8. See also the Bundestag debate 21 February 1952.

37. "Armée," *Le Monde*, 31 October 1945, 2. See also French Minister Counselor to the United States Robert Seydoux's letter to the editor regarding the numbers of Germans in the Legion, *New York Times*, 15 May 1952. According to Janos Kemencei's memoir of the French Foreign Legion, Legion officials disallowed any SS soldiers from enlisting by checking the left armpit for Waffen SS tattoos: Janos Kemencei, *Légionnaire en avant!* (Paris: Jacques Grancher, 1985), 137.

38. "Armée," 2.

39. The Society for the Protection Against the French Foreign Legion (Schutzenband gegen die französische Fremdenlegion) was formed in 1932. German newspapers accused the Foreign Legion of having Germans as four-fifths of its ranks, exhausting and infecting them with disease during their contract, and finally leaving the Germans to care for them, costing the government six million marks annually. David Del Testa, "'The Enemy Within': German Legionnaires and the World War II Foreign Legion," (Department of History, University of California, photocopy), 6.

40. Bodin, *Soldats*, 141.

41. Del Testa, "The Enemy Within," 14.

42. Vichy sympathizer and LVF member Christian de la Mazière, having joined the French division of the Waffen SS, described how Legion agents came to the political prison where he was interned in an effort to recruit his fellow prisoners. Christian de la Mazière, *The Captive Dreamer* (New York: Saturday Review Press/E.P. Dutton, 1974). Mazière, a former journalist for the fascist paper *Le Pays Libre*, joined the Charlemagne division of the Waffen SS after the liberation of Paris. He became a public personality when he appeared in Marcel Orphul's documentary *The Sorrow and the Pity* as one of the few willing to acknowledge publicly his role during Vichy.

43. The Legion gathered only information on the primary language of its recruits for training purposes. Bodin, *Soldat*, 141.

44. R. C. Hudson, "*Et Bourreaux et victimes!* Eyewitness reactions to the first phase of the French war of decolonization in Indochina, 'Les Temps modernes' 1946-1950," *Journal of European Studies* 19 (1989): 191-204.

45. Hudson, "*Et Bourreaux et victimes*," 193.

46. Claudine Chonez, "Petit réquisitoire indochinois," *Les Temps modernes* (February 1950), 1488. Also quoted in Hudson, "*Et Bourreaux et victimes*," 197.

47. Sartre, *L'Affaire*, 121.

48. Letter from Maurice Renaudat, Bourges, to Cell Secretaries, 19 September 1950, *Archives of André Marty* (microfilm, Hoover Institution on War, Revolution and Peace, Stanford University). Hereafter cited as *AAM*.

49. *AAM*, "Pour la Libération d' Henri Martin," signed by André Menstrier.

50. *AAM*, Letter from Silvareccio, Corsica, to the President of the Republic, 24 August 1952.

51. "Note sur les interventions d'écrivains d'universitaires ou démarches diverses auprès de M. Le Président de la République," Sartre, *L'Affaire*, 214-216.

52. Marcel Ner, "Henri Martin et ses 'Lettres d'Indochine,'" in Sartre, *L'Affaire*, 67.

53. Letter from Henri Martin to his family 16 April 1946, in Sartre, *L'Affaire*, 38.

54. Formed in 1941, the Groupes Mobiles de Réserve or G.M.R. served under the discretion of regional prefects and police to round up Jews and members of the Résistance.

55. Letter from Henri Martin to his family 16 April 1946, in Sartre, *L'Affaire*, 38-39.

56. Sartre, *L'Affaire*, 41.

57. Minutes of 17 October 1950 meeting, in Sartre, *L'Affaire*, 28.

58. Pierre Nora, "General Introduction: Between Memory and History," in Pierre Nora, general editor, *Realms of Memory: Rethinking the French Past*, ed. Lawrence D. Kritzman and trans. Arthur Goldhammer (New York: Columbia University Press, 1996), 1:3.

7

Memory and Continuity

The Resistance, the Algerian War, and the Jeanson Network

Marie-Pierre Ulloa

MARCH 18, 2002 MARKED THE FORTIETH ANNIVERSARY of the end of the Algerian War. A few weeks before, Paul Aussaresses, former French general who acknowledged his use of torture during the war in his memoirs *Services Spéciaux. Algérie 1955-1957*,[1] was convicted of "trying to justify war crimes" and fined $6,500.[2] The former general was not pursued for the act of torture itself, which has long been covered by the 1962 Gaullist amnesty, but for having spoken in favor of it. On 22 March 1962, a decree granted amnesty to "les faits commis dans le cadre des opérations de maintien de l'ordre dirigées contre l'insurrection algérienne" [all acts perpetrated in the context of operations to maintain order against the Algerian insurrection][3] and in June 1966 another law gave amnesty to the French opponents of the Algerian War, the "porteurs de valises" (suitcase carriers). The "suitcase carriers" were a network of French intellectuals, mostly leftists, communists, artists, worker-priests, and Catholics "en rupture de ban" (dissidents), led by the philosopher Francis Jeanson. Their actions consisted mainly of hiding Algerian activists in France, helping them cross the border between France and its neighbors, publishing a bulletin named *Vérités Pour*, and last but not least, handling funds contributed to the cause by Algerians in France and transmitting them in suitcases—hence the name *porteurs de valises*—to the FLN (Front de Libération Nationale [National Liberation Front]) abroad where it was used mainly to purchase arms.[4]

In February 1960, French police arrested eighteen French members of the network and six Algerians from the FLN working with them. In September 1960, the Jeanson trial, also known as the trial of the Jeanson Network, took place at the "Tribunal permanent des forces armées de Paris" [the Permanent

Military Court in Paris]. The members were tried in Paris, but Jeanson managed to escape and fled to Switzerland. He was tried in absentia as the brain of the organization. Fourteen activists were convicted, among them Francis Jeanson and the number two in his network, Hélène Cuénat, to:

- ten years in prison (in absentia for Jeanson)
- loss of their civil rights
- a fine of 70,000 nouveaux francs
- five years during which Jeanson was forbidden to enter French territory.

However, the convicted, including Jeanson's spokesperson, Hélène Cuénat, succeeded in turning the tables with the help of their lawyers. Their legal team was headed by Roland Dumas and collaborated with their Algerian counterparts' lawyers, led by the Collectif FLN, of which Jacques Vergès was the most provocative figure. Soon the members of the Jeanson Network began to use the court to put the Algerian War on trial. The trial of the Jeanson Network became the trial of the war. The detainees were accused of threatening the safety of the state and were widely considered to be traitors, but they were not accused of treason because officially there was no war since Algeria was still part of France.

With the upcoming trial in mind, Jeanson had already defended himself against treason in his pamphlet *Notre Guerre*, written in June 1960, which was censored and seized a week after its release for its strong words:

> Il nous fallait à la fois "trahir" les Français en faisant cause commune avec les Algériens et "trahir" les Algériens en demeurant résolument français. Cette double "trahison," c'est notre fidélité: à la cause française et à la cause humaine, qui justement ne devraient être qu'une seule et même cause.[5]

> We simultaneously had to "betray" the French by supporting the Algerians and "betray" the Algerians by staying resolutely French. This double "betrayal" is our allegiance to the French cause and to the human cause, which should rightly be one and the same.

The trial gave the network publicity that Jeanson could not have imagined in his wildest dreams. With the arrests, the French learned at once of individuals who were opposed to the war and were helping the Algerians in the name of France.

One of the reasons invoked by the Jeanson network in order to legitimize its involvement with the FLN was a historic precedent: the French Resistance during World War II. Many of the militants of the Jeanson Network believed themselves called upon to rekindle the flame of the Resistance. Nevertheless, this Resistance paradigm was not a unifying theme within the Jeanson Network. In fact, its leader, Francis Jeanson, disavowed this parallel. He did not justify his commitment to the Algerian cause by the appeal to the Resistance model of World War II. This caused a tension inside the Jeanson Network between, on one hand, the suitcase carriers who invoked the call of the Resistance and, on the other hand, their leader who did not brandish the memory of the Resistance against the Nazis and Vichy France in order to justify his actions during the Algerian War.

This chapter investigates the impact of the memory of the Resistance in the creation of the Jeanson Network and assesses the extent to which the suitcase carriers considered themselves the heirs to the Resistance. Did the Jeanson Network stand for a new Resistance?

Also considered here are activists among the Jeanson Network who claimed a different moral standard in order to legitimize their involvement in the Algerian War.

I conclude by examining the case of Francis Jeanson himself. Jeanson's relationship with the memory of Resistance and its legacy was complex and tortuous, because Jeanson was one of the only members of the network to have been actively involved in the Resistance during World War II, yet his dissidence during the Algerian War was not motivated by his own past Resistance activities. Why?

The Resistance Resurrected?

Among the militants of the Jeanson Network the most inclined to claim affiliation with the Resistance was the number two in the network, Hélène Cuénat. Born in 1930, Hélène Cuénat was a Communist teacher when she became involved with the Jeanson Network. She was first solicited to be part of the network by a friend of Francis Jeanson, Étienne Bolo, but she turned him down because she was a Communist and did not want to commit herself to a political adventure not approved of by the PCF (Parti Communiste Français [French Communist Party]). Nevertheless her political thinking evolved when she was disappointed and even depressed by the chilly attitude of the PCF toward the revelation of the use of torture by the French army in Algeria and by the party's support for the March 1956 Special Powers Act. It was in 1956 that Cuénat decided to act and become part of the network. There were two main reasons why she decided to become an outlaw: first there was the scandal of torture and second the inspiration provided by anti-Nazi resistance. Cuénat had grown up with heroic tales of the Resistance. She admired the resisters so much that she could not help asking herself this haunting question: "J'étais étudiante à la Sorbonne et confrontée à la question : est-ce que moi j'aurais résisté à la torture ?"[6] (I was a student at La Sorbonne and confronted by the question: would I have resisted torture?)

Cuénat was not the only one to ask herself such a question. She was joined in her existential quest by another prominent member of the Jeanson Network, Jean-Louis Hurst. Like Cuénat, Hurst was a Communist and a schoolteacher. He was sent to Algeria as a second lieutenant and he deserted in 1958. He then wrote *Le Déserteur* under the pseudonym Maurienne. Hurst chose this pen name as a tribute to the Resistance; Maurienne was the name of a *Maquis* (Resistance) group during World War II.

Thanks to the Catholic intellectual André Mandouze, a great resister and friend of Jeanson, Hurst joined the network and was immediately appointed by Jeanson to run the branch of the young deserters. Hurst was in charge of organizing the escape of soldiers who wanted to flee the war and of finding them a secure place to hide in Switzerland or Germany. The Jeanson Network delegated this task to a new division inside the network, named Jeune Résistance (Young Resistance). The new name was emblematic because it created a direct affiliation with the Resistance. As World War II had its Resistance, so did the Algerian War, this time baptized Young Resistance. The old Resistance was rejuvenated by new blood in the new historical context of the colonialist war. Hurst completely identified himself with the Resistance and even declared, "Jeune Résistance, c'est l'idéologie de la Résistance renouvelée."[7] (Young Resistance is the ideology of the Resistance renewed.)

It was through its underground publication *Vérités Pour* that the Jeanson Network announced the launch of Jeune Résistance and orchestrated its propaganda. Starting in 1960 *Vérités Pour* put on its front page an extract from the famous Resistance song *Le Chant des Partisans:* "Ami si tu tombes un autre sort de l'ombre à ta place . . ."[8] (My friend, if you fall, someone else will emerge from the shadow to replace you . . .).

Vercors, author of the 1942 masterpiece of Resistance literature, *Le Silence de la mer*[9] (*The Silence of the Sea*), had given an interview to Jeanson, published in *Vérités Pour* in 1959. In this interview, Vercors—whose real name was Jean Bruller and whose pen name was a homage to the Vercors *Maquis* group of the Resistance—put his perspective on the dilemma faced by the French during the Algerian War: in doing so, Vercors immediately established a legitimate parallel between his resistance, anti-Nazi Resistance, and the Jeanson Network's new Resistance. Vercors stated that the existence of the Jeanson Network reminded him of "les liaisons souterraines comme au temps où s'organisait la Résistance"[10] (the underground contacts during the making of the Resistance). The foundation of *Vérités Pour* squared with the practice of the "bulletin de liaison" used during World War II. The bulletin was a mouthpiece for Young Resistance. Inside the columns of *Vérités Pour*, Young Resistance could proclaim that it brought together 3,000 deserters and draft evaders. The minister of the army advanced the number of 200 deserters whereas the investigators Hervé Hamon and Patrick Rotman in their survey estimated the number of rebellious soldiers at 300 to 400.[11]

Under these circumstances, in declaring his support both to the underground form—*Vérités Pour*—and to the content of the network, Vercors brought his moral authority to the defense of the Jeanson Network. The Algerian War gave him a powerful sense of déjà vu. In September 1960, Vercors testified at the Jeanson trial and reaffirmed his appraisal of the actions of the network. Questioned during his testimony by the Algerians' lawyer, Jacques Vergès, Vercors proclaimed:

> Lorsqu'on se bat, en effet, pour l'indépendance de son pays, comme nous nous sommes battus, tout le respect est dû à ces Résistants et non seulement tout le respect, mais toute l'aide qu'on peut leur apporter.[12]

> When one is fighting, indeed, for the independence of one's country, as we ourselves fought, all respect is due to these resisters and not only all respect, but all the help that we can provide them.

Another famous resister, André Mandouze, justified the Jeanson Network's approach during the hectic hours of the trial. He declared:

> Il y a maintenant un autre problème qui n'est pas seulement celui du lieu de la patrie, mais du temps de la patrie. Certaines gens sont toujours en retard. D'autres sont exceptionnellement en avance. Quand on est trop en avance, cela vous vaut généralement un certain nombre d'ennuis. Nous étions en avance en 1940 quand nous avons cru en la parole d'un homme qui est maintenant à la tête de l'État, alors qu'on aurait pu penser qu'il était fou en abandonnant la France— "desherere"!—Premier Résistant, premier déserteur, on aurait pu croire qu'effectivement il désertait la France, qu'il la transportait ailleurs. Or, c'était lui qui avait vu juste, et c'était lui qui incarnait la France.[13]

> Now there is another problem, which is not only that of location of country but also of time of country. Certain people are always late. Others are exceptionally early. When one is too far ahead of one's time, it can be something of a nuisance. We were ahead of our time in 1940 when we believed in the speech of a man who is now the head of state, although one could have said that he was crazy in abandoning France—"desherere"!—The first resistant, the first deserter, one could have believed that he effectively deserted France, that he took it elsewhere. But he saw clearly, and he embodied France.

Vergès asked Mandouze to give his opinion of the words of Jean-Paul Sartre, who had declared:

> Si Jeanson m'avait demandé de porter des valises ou d'héberger des militants algériens, . . . je l'aurais fait sans hésitation.[14]

> If Jeanson had asked me to carry suitcases or to shelter Algerian militants, . . . I would have done so without any hesitation.

Mandouze answered:

> J'apprends la phrase de Jean-Paul Sartre, mais je crois avoir répondu d'avance. Je crois avoir revendiqué mes responsabilités. . . . J'approuve, et j'appuie ceci par une expérience qui est celle de la Résistance.[15]

> I had not previously heard Jean-Paul Sartre's comment, but I believe I have already answered it. I think I have asserted my responsibilities. . . . I agree, and I support it on the basis of the experience of the Resistance.

There was a subtext to André Mandouze's declaration: he agreed with Sartre and subtly added that he, unlike Sartre, could evoke his resistance past in order to support the *raison d'être* of the Jeanson Network, whereas Sartre lacked these credentials.

In Search of Another Legacy

However, not all the comrades of Jeanson in his network claimed their affinity with the rhetoric and the memory of the French Resistance in order to legitimize their Algerian commitment. Indeed, some of them claimed another legacy. This was the case, for example, of Christiane Philip and Robert Bonnaud. Christiane Philip could have easily and demonstrably invoked a direct link—a filial connection—between her involvement within the Jeanson network and the Resistance, since she was the daughter of André Philip.

André Philip was a law professor, a leader of the Christian socialists inside the SFIO (Section Française de L'Internationale Ouvrière [the French Socialist Party]) and one of the eighty deputies who refused to vote for Marshal Pétain on 10 July 1940. He became the leader of the underground Resistance movement Libération-Sud. He then joined de Gaulle in London and was appointed by him to a senior Resistance position inside France in July 1942.[16]

However, before going underground, fighting beside de Gaulle and subsequently leaving France, Philip sent his children to a safe place. He sent them to the United States of America, where Philip had developed some close friendships within the academic and journalistic worlds. Consequently, Christiane Philip, born in 1928, spent the war years in Chicago—from 1941 to 1943—with an American family, Clifton and Frayn Utley.[17] For the young Christiane, the Resistance meant something very concrete and harsh, the absence of her parents, the distance from the events taking place in France, and the deep fear of not seeing her parents again. She did not experience the tragic and heroic story of her parents as resisters. According to her, if her father's figure as a great resister did not motivate her own resistance during the Algerian War, the influence of her father was still present but manifested itself differently. It was not André Philip the resister who made his mark on her political thinking, but André Philip, Minister for the Economy in several Fourth Republic governments, expelled from his own party, the SFIO, in 1957 because of his incendiary writing *Le Socialisme trahi*[18] [*Socialism Betrayed*].

André Philip denounced in his pamphlet the murderous politics of the French government in Algeria. He very strongly criticized Guy Mollet and his failure to condemn the use of torture by French paratroopers in Algeria. Indeed, Christiane Philip decided to go underground and to become a member of the Jeanson network after a dinner at her parents' house where Paul Teitgen— Secrétaire de la préfecture de police d'Alger [Secretary of the Police Authority in Algiers]—was present and confirmed to them the daily use of torture in Algeria.[19] It was a terrible irony for Paul Teitgen to discover that the French were torturing in Algeria in ways similar to what he had personally experienced at the hands of the Gestapo in Nancy during World War II.

Ostracized from his own political party, the SFIO, André Philip founded with Alain Savary, Daniel Mayer, and Edouard Depreux a new left party, the PSA (Parti Socialiste Autonome [Autonomous Socialist Party]), in September 1958, which became the PSU (Parti Socialiste Unifié [Unified Socialist Party]) in 1960. Christiane Philip followed in her father's footsteps and became a member of the PSU, but she hid from him her own involvement with the Jeanson Network because she knew that André Philip would not approve of it, which proved to be the case.[20]

Christiane Philip was not the only member of the Jeanson Network not to embrace the affiliation between the Resistance and the suitcase carriers. Robert Bonnaud, the leader of the Jeanson Network in the Marseille region, called upon another legacy in order to legitimize his direct help to the FLN. Robert Bonnaud was a history professor and a Communist. He was also a *rappelé* (a draftee called up from the reserves) in Algeria in 1956 and wrote about his traumatic experience in the Catholic left journal *Esprit*. He then confessed how he witnessed the use of torture by the French army.[21] Bitter and disillusioned by the role of the French Republic in the Algerian War, Robert Bonnaud decided to cross the line from legal opposition to the war to illegal opposition. He opted for the antiwar activism of the Jeanson Network. The historian argued that he did not find his inspiration in the French Resistance. He drew another historic parallel between the network and the resisters to Nazism, arguing that the militants of the Jeanson Network should be seen as the descendants of German rather than French resisters, for like their counterparts in Germany they were fighting against their fellow countrymen in the Algerian War.[22] Another suitcase carrier, under the pseudonym Richard, wrote in *Vérités Pour* that he felt that he was paying homage to the German Resistance against Hitler in working for the liberation of the French colony. He pledged allegiance to the memory of his "camarades antinazis allemands des camps de concentration"[23] [German anti-Nazi comrades in the concentration camps].

In cultivating a similar relationship to the memory of World War II, Bonnaud approached but was not identical to Francis Jeanson in his political take on the situation.

Francis Jeanson and the Resistance Paradigm

Jeanson did not invoke the historical precedent of the Resistance in order to justify his acts of treason during the Algerian War. Yet he had been one of the few members of his network to have been a resister during World War II. He carried during the Algerian War an emotional memory of the Resistance, and the particular nature of his experience as a resister was precisely what prevented him from drawing a parallel between the Resistance to Nazism and the new Resistance to the French presence in Algeria.

Was it because Jeanson was ten years older than the majority of the members of his network that he could nurture a dissenting view on the legacy of the Resistance? Was it a question of a generational gap between Jeanson and the younger militants of the network? This seems unlikely, for some resisters during World War II such as Vercors and André Mandouze, in their writings as well as in theirs lives, did legitimize the appropriation of the Resistance by the Jeanson Network. They took up the defense of those militants who deliberately embraced what they read as the message of the Resistance.

During the Algerian War, Jeanson did not see himself as an heir to the resisters because he did not perceive himself as a hero of the Resistance. His personal relationship with the anti-Nazi Resistance and with his own Resistance was tortuous. If the historian Jean-Pierre Azéma forged the term "vichysto-résistant"[24] [Vichyite resister] in order to qualify former President François Mitterrand's political journey during World War II, and the historian Pierre

Laborie characterized the attitude of the majority of the French under Vichy as "attentiste"[25] (attentiste, i.e., non-committal), let me argue that Francis Jeanson acted as an "attentiste-résistant" (attentiste resister) during the same period.

Jeanson was eighteen years old in 1940. He was a student in philosophy at the University of Bordeaux and got his B.A. in philosophy in 1943. Between 1940 and 1943, Jeanson was not politically active. In his own terms, he was just enjoying life.[26] During the first three years of the German Occupation of France, which was particularly harsh in Bordeaux, Jeanson did not concern himself with it.

Nevertheless, his de facto acceptance of the German presence in Bordeaux and of the politics of Marshal Pétain came to an end in 1943. An external event forced him to change his view on the situation: in 1943 Jeanson faced the prospect of civilian labor conscription, the STO (Service du Travail Obligatoire [Mandatory Labor Service]) which would have forced him to go to work in Germany. Jeanson refused to go and decided instead to disobey. He then became a deserter. He left France through the Pyrenees but was arrested in Spain, where he spent three months in a concentration camp and three more months in prison before joining the French armies in Algeria in 1944. From Algeria, Jeanson was sent to France, where for eight months, from January to August 1945, he was in charge of mine clearance in the Alsace region.

Since then, Francis Jeanson had cultivated a complex and convoluted relationship with his involvement in the Resistance, which he saw as marginal. The philosopher considered that having spent six months in the Spanish jails of the Franco dictatorship did not transform him into a hero of the Resistance (although he almost died from TB). His involvement in the Resistance came late and was a direct response to the threat of being sent to Germany. Jeanson argued that, during the Algerian War, he was not trying to redeem his past as a minor resister during World War II. For someone like him, who had experienced the dark hours of the Nazi presence in France, there was an indecency in claiming that the suitcase carriers were the heirs of the resisters: precisely because the members of the Jeanson Network did not face the same dangers as the resisters. Jeanson did not put his life in harm's way during the Algerian War, whereas, during World War II, many French resisters died because they were resisters.[27] Jeanson did receive some threats from the extreme right wing OAS (Organisation Armée Secrète [Secret Army Organization]) and from the Main Rouge (Red Hand), an anti-FLN undercover organization run by the French secret services, but the ones who were the true heirs to the Resistance during the Algerian War, according to Jeanson, were the Algerians who fought against the French army for the independence of Algeria.[28]

Unlike some of his colleagues (for example, Jean-Louis Hurst and Hélène Cuénat) Jeanson did not worship the memory of the Resistance, as a golden age to be emulated, because he felt that he had too much respect and admiration for what he called the true resisters. To draw a connection between them and the Jeanson Network would have meant to diminish the intensity of the symbolic paradigm of the Resistance. Jeanson did not want to usurp the uniqueness of the Resistance to Nazism and to Vichy France. In a way, Jeanson re-mystified the unique courage of the resisters but, in the pose of the contrarian, he also demystified the after-war meaning of the Resistance message and legacy. Jeanson did not cultivate a blind adulation of the Resistance because, according to his judgment, if the Resistance achieved greatness during World War II, it failed to hold onto it after the war. Ultimately Jeanson was disappointed by the Resistance, which did not manage to transform France ideologically at the end of the war. For Jeanson, the legacy of the Resistance vanished as soon as the War ended because the Resistance's political claims were not realized at the Liberation of France. There was no political translation of the Resistance into the frame of the democratic structure of the Fourth Republic. The aspirations of the Resistance vanished in 1945-1946. In his attempt to analyze the failure of the Resistance, Jeanson shared the same view as the one remembered by history as the first resister, General de Gaulle, who retired from the political sphere in 1946 specifically because he did not see the ideals of the Resistance he praised being implemented at the Liberation. The Resistance was by no means a unified force; it embodied different aspirations of French political life.[29]

During and right after the war, Jeanson was a fervent admirer of de Gaulle, and he was chosen to be the spokesperson for the prisoners who fled France through Spain. Jeanson delivered a political speech in 1944, on the fourth anniversary of de Gaulle's "Appel du 18 Juin" (Appeal of 18 June), and declared: "Le gaullisme est l'âme même de la France renaissante"[30] (Gaullism is the very soul of France re-finding herself).

However, in 1958, when de Gaulle returned to power, Jeanson had lost his faith in him. Jeanson supported de Gaulle's political agenda during World War II but disrespectfully dissented in 1958. In adopting this subversive political posture, Jeanson shared the views of his comrades in the network. Even though he did not share their deference toward the Resistance model, Jeanson did share their opposition to the Gaullist handling of the Algerian War. For them as for him, de Gaulle in 1958 remained at best a shadow of the de Gaulle of 1940, and perhaps even a negation of that once great figure.

Conclusion

The legacy of the Resistance during World War II was at stake during the colonialist war conducted by the French government in Algeria between 1954 and 1962. The Algerian War may have been the "war without a name" but was not at all a war without a past. Indeed, the Resistance spawned a disputed and controversial legacy during the Algerian War. Not only was the memory of the Resistance a controversial memory within the Jeanson Network, between those who invoked it and those who did not want to plagiarize it, but the memory of the Resistance was also manipulated by political adversaries of the Jeanson Network. The opposite side of the political spectrum, the OAS, brandished the memory of the Resistance in order to legitimize its own political path during the Algerian War. The extreme right as well as the extreme left, the supporters of French Algeria as well as the partisans of Algerian Algeria, all drew on the "sacred" memory of the Resistance in order to justify their commitment. It is ironic that two great symbols of the Resistance, André Mandouze and Georges Bidault, who took radically antagonistic paths during the Algerian War, used the same emblematic title for their memoirs: Georges Bidault, in 1965, wrote *D'une Résistance à l'autre* (From one Resistance to another) and André Mandouze, in 1998, wrote *Mémoires d'outre-siècle. D'une Résistance à l'autre*[31] (Memoirs From a Past Century: From One Resistance to Another). The two works start from the same premises and end with opposite conclusions.

In Georges Bidault's historical analogy, Jeanson symbolized not the reactivated figure of the resister but the despicable figure of the collaborator, whereas Bidault saw himself as continuing to embody the spirit of the Resistance.[32] Bidault wrote of the Jeanson Network: "Le réseau qui travaille pour l'ennemi est en somme une sorte de milice au service du FLN."[33] (The network which works for the enemy is in sum a kind of militia at the service of the FLN.)

To conclude, I would suggest that the suitcase carriers were also carriers of memory and that there were as many colors and shades of the memory of the Resistance during the Algerian War as there were resisters against colonialism.

The memory was an elastic and buoyant force rather than a constraining one. It passed through distorting mirrors, hijacked and twisted by different political actors in order to serve their own specific and antagonistic aspirations. The memory of Resistance, far from being repressed—unlike the memory of the Algerian War—was overused and trivialized. It was taken hostage, but in the end, who is the true holder of its message? Is there one?

Perhaps General de Gaulle—who came to power in 1958 promising to keep Algeria French and then reluctantly brought the "war without a name" to an end, granting Algeria its independence in 1962—began to answer that question.

Notes

1. Paul Aussaresses, *Services Spéciaux. Algérie 1955-1957* (Paris: Perrin, 2001).

2. Suzanne Daley, "France Fines General, 83, for Memoir Justifying Algerian War," *New York Times*, 26 January 2002.

3. Raphaëlle Branche, *La Torture et l'armée pendant la guerre d'Algérie 1954-1962* (Paris: Gallimard, 2001), 418.

4. Martin Evans, *The Memory of Resistance: French Opposition to the Algerian War, 1954-1962* (Oxford: Berg, 1997); Marie-Pierre Ulloa, *Francis Jeanson, un intellectuel en dissidence. De la Résistance à la guerre d'Algérie* (Paris: Berg International, 2001); Sylvain Pattieu, "'Le Camarade' Pablo, la IVème Internationale et la guerre d'Algérie," in *Revue historique* 619 (juillet-septembre 2001): 696-729; Jacques Charby, *Les Porteurs d'espoir* (Paris: La Découverte, 2004).

5. Francis Jeanson, *Notre Guerre* (Paris: Éditions de Minuit, 1960), 54.

6. Hélène Cuénat, *Les Frères des frères* (France 3: 1992). See also Martin Evans, *The Memory of Resistance: French Opposition to the Algerian War, 1954-1962*, 41.

7. Jean-Louis Hurst, *Les Frères des frères* (France 3: 1992).

8. *Vérités Pour* 18, 26 September 1960.

9. Vercors, *Le Silence de la mer* (Paris: Éditions de Minuit, 1942).

10. *Vérités Pour* 8, May 1959.

11. Hervé Hamon and Patrick Rotman, *Les Porteurs de valises, la résistance française à la guerre d'Algérie* (Paris: Albin Michel, 1979).

12. Marcel Péju, *Le Procès du réseau Jeanson* (Paris: Maspéro, 1961; rpt. Paris: La Découverte, 2002), 114.

13. Péju, *Le Procès*, 121.

14. Péju, *Le Procès*, 118.

15. Péju, *Le Procès*, 122.

16. Jean-Pierre Azéma, *Jean Moulin. Le Politique, le rebelle, le résistant* (Paris: Perrin, 2003), 254, 264.

17. Christiane Philip, interview by author, 30 January 2003; Jacques Charby, *Les Porteurs d'espoir* (Paris: La Découverte, 2004), 220-222.

18. André Philip, *Le Socialisme trahi*, (Paris: Plon, 1957).

19. Christiane Philip, interview by author, 5 May 1996.

20. André Philip, *André Philip par lui-même ou les voies de la liberté* (Paris: Aubier-Montaigne, 1971).

21. Robert Bonnaud, "La Paix des Nétmenchas," *Esprit*, April 1957.

22. Robert Bonnaud, Interview by author, 28 May 1996 in Marie-Pierre Ulloa, *Francis Jeanson, un intellectuel en dissidence. De la Résistance à la guerre d'Algérie* (Paris: Berg International, 2001), 216.

23. *Vérités Pour*, August 1960, 5.

24. Jean-Pierre Azéma, *Jean Moulin. Le Politique, le rebelle, le résistant* (Paris: Perrin, 2003), 451.

25. Pierre Laborie, *L'Opinion française sous Vichy* (Paris: Le Seuil, 1990; rpt. Paris, 2001), 295-302.

26. Francis Jeanson, interview by author, 12 February 1996 in Marie-Pierre Ulloa, *Francis Jeanson, un intellectuel en dissidence*, 24-30.

27. Jeanson saw one of his comrades explode on a mine and die in front of him in Alsace. See Marie-Pierre Ulloa, *Francis Jeanson, un intellectuel en dissidence*, 52.

28. Francis Jeanson, "Du FLN à la Révolution," in *Les Temps modernes*, November 1962.

29. Pierre Laborie, *Les Français des années troubles. De la guerre d'Espagne à la libération* (Paris: Le Seuil, 2001), 245-269.

30. For the complete speech, see Robert Belot, *Paroles de résistants* (Paris: Berg International, 2001), 289-294.

31. Georges Bidault, *D'une Résistance à l'autre* (Paris: Les Presses du Siècle, 1965); André Mandouze, *Mémoires d'outre-siècle. D'une Résistance à l'autre* (Paris: Éditions Viviane Hamy, 1998).

32. Georges Bidault established a parallel between the CNR (Conseil National de la Résistance), which he directed after Jean Moulin's death in 1943, and the new CNR of the OAS, which he created in direct analogy.

33. Georges Bidault, "La Liberté d'expression et la liberté de trahison," *Carrefour*, 27 April 1960.

8

Intimate Acts and Unspeakable Relations

Remembering Torture and the War for Algerian Independence

Joshua Cole

The Torture Debate in France

STUDIES OF VIOLENCE AND MEMORY have undergone such explosive growth lately that it is probably dangerous to generalize too much about the various tendencies and methods employed to make sense of these two complex subjects of research. One might ask, however, if historians have been sufficiently clear about the relationship between histories of violence and histories of cultural memory. Histories of memory often focus on moments of intense violence, and it is no accident that much historical work on memory has focused on particularly traumatic episodes of conflict, such as the Holocaust and the First and Second World Wars.[1] Since histories of violence often become embroiled in the controversies that accompany the memories of trauma and victimization, one might have thought that it would be relatively clear by now what the relationship between historical writing about violence and research on memory should be. Nothing could be further from the truth. Historians working on the problem of violence have avoided treading in the murky waters of memory and cultural meaning, as if such complicated and messy subjects might contaminate an otherwise tidier realm of historical explanation.[2] Likewise, many historians working on the problem of memory have excluded violence from their analytic framework, as if the history of violent acts could be treated separately from the cultural memories generated by such acts.[3]

Historians and commentators on the French-Algerian war have been better than most in acknowledging the importance of violence itself as a necessary departure point in understanding the history of the conflict. The fact that the French government resisted labeling the conflict a "war" for so long may have something to do with this.[4] Those who sought to understand this struggle had to begin by talking about its violence, about the routine practice of torture and resettlement practiced by the French military, about the bombing campaigns against civilians undertaken by both the FLN (Front de Libération Nationale) and the OAS (a militant terrorist organization), and about the ruthless methods that all parties used against their perceived enemies, both French and Muslim. Frantz Fanon was only the first and the most explicit of commentators to find a departure point in a discussion of violence—in his case in the opening chapter of his 1961 book, Les Damnés de la terre, "Concerning Violence." Fanon sought to place the violence of decolonization—massacres, resettlement, torture, and mutilation—in its proper context, that is, by portraying it as an extension and natural result of the violence of colonialism itself.[5] For Fanon, the essential distinction was that which divided colonizer from colonized—and the virtue of his analysis was to show that maintaining this distinction, by violence if necessary, was a necessary part of the colonial enterprise itself.

After Fanon, however, sustained analysis of the violence of the French-Algerian war often receded into the background of arguments that focused elsewhere. Military commentators tended to focus on the new tactics of guerrilla warfare faced by the French in Algeria, and the counterinsurgency methods that they developed in response. This focus on tactics often resulted in a sanitized, even clinical, image of the conflict itself, in which rape, torture, and resettlement disappeared behind euphemisms such as "opération policière," "action psychologique," and "action sociale."[6] Diplomatic historians, meanwhile, have asserted that the real essence of the conflict lay not in the struggles on the ground in Algeria and in mainland France, but in the international arena, where the FLN shrewdly managed to defeat French efforts to prevent the conflict from taking on more than a local significance.[7] Only recently have historians begun to interrogate in a systematic fashion the specific history of the violent acts that are associated with this conflict, and this discussion has focused above all on one practice in particular: torture.[8]

The French army's use of torture had been the focus of public controversy since the war years, and the horrific details that emerged from survivors' accounts later became inescapable reference points for an entire generation in France.[9] Nevertheless, because the official response to specific allegations had always been to deny or minimize the extent to which torture was used, much of the discussion, both during and after the war, focused simply on establishing the fact that torture occurred. Furthermore, because of a general amnesty pushed through by Charles de Gaulle's government in 1968, no military or police official in France ever faced charges of torture in court. No historians were allowed into the relevant military archives until very recently. The result of this situation was that for nearly forty years after the fact, public debate about the military's use of torture in the Algerian war could never go beyond the most preliminary questions: Did it really happen? Who was responsible? And to what extent were higher authorities in the military and government aware of the practice?

This situation changed, however, following a renewed debate that began in the summer of 2000. In June of that year a former FLN militant, Louisette Ighilahriz, published an autobiographical account of her rape and torture at the hands of French paratroopers during ten weeks of detention in 1957.[10] The public outcry was immediate, all the more so because General Jacques Massu—92 years old in 2000 and perhaps the most celebrated of de Gaulle's generals in Algeria—admitted that her story was probably true. Following Ighilahriz's and Massu's public statements, a committee of twelve prominent intellectuals known for their public stands in favor of human rights publicly called for an official state apology in late October.[11] Meanwhile, an unrepentant former French intelligence officer, Paul Aussaresses, challenged both Ighilahriz and Massu, not by denying torture, but by defending its use and refusing to apologize for having been a torturer himself.[12] In response, many commentators called for Aussaresses to stand trial for crimes against humanity, though the committee of intellectuals who had published the October appeal warned against the dangers of attempting to settle complicated historical injustices in a trial that would necessarily focus on only one individual. On 5 December 2000, while the debates surrounding Ighilahriz, Massu, and Aussaresses were still very much in the public eye, historian Raphaëlle Branche defended the first doctoral thesis written in France on torture and the French army during the war years.[13]

Together, Ighilahriz and Branche—an Algerian woman who lived through the war years and a French woman who grew to adulthood in the 1980s—transformed the debate about torture in France. They did so, however, in very different ways. Ighilahriz's personal account of her experiences came in the form of testimony, an act of historical witnessing that had many precedents for the French public. Such accounts have the advantage of immediacy, and they are filled with the kinds of details that only a person who actually experienced this violence can provide. Testimony possesses an inherent weakness, however; an inherent subjectivity, which makes it easier for those who do not wish to accept the account to dismiss it as inherently partisan or even deceitful. Ighilahriz's autobiography benefited, therefore, from the appearance of Raphaëlle Branche's path-breaking book, for the latter provided precisely the detached tone and scholarly apparatus that Ighilahriz's autobiography, by definition, could not contain. The reception of Branche's work, in turn, was

largely predetermined by the emotions raised by the public airing given Ighilahriz's horrifying story, because it gave a face to the numbing succession of
countless victims who made their appearance in Branche's study. The reception of Branche's book, which appeared in the early weeks of 2001, also benefited from the continuing controversy over Massu's and Aussaresses's public
statements.

Even if this focus on torture is understandable, given the drama of these
revelations, the fact remains that the timing of this controversy in France had
more to do with the contingencies of public debate—the coincidence of
Branche's and Ighilahriz's nearly simultaneous publications, Massu's aston-
ishing confession, and Aussaresses's notorious acceptance of "responsibility"
for acts of murder—than it did with any systematic thinking through of what
it was that made torture the central focus of France's work of collective memory. In his account of this controversy, historian Neil MacMaster justified this
focus because "the issue of torture had been central to the debate on the Algerian war from the very beginning and continues to serve this function, not
only because it represented the fundamental moral dilemma, 'le mal absolu,'
but also because its exposure threw a penetrating light into the darkest cor-
ners of 'la raison d'état,' the overall structures of military, administrative, and
judicial power."[14] It is difficult to quarrel with MacMaster's assessment of torture's significance for the French, but his statement also sidesteps the question
of *why* torture has been so central "from the very beginning." What makes
these acts, among all the other acts of violence that took place in the war years,
the most problematic and charged for both victims and perpetrators, as well
as for the larger French public? Asserting that torture is a "fundamental moral
dilemma" or an "absolute evil" is not really an answer to this question, and
neither is the suggestion that torture is a particularly useful subject for laying
bare the logic of state power during this period. This may have been something that historian Raphaëlle Branche was interested in, but Louisette Ighilahriz had other things in mind in publishing her autobiography, and the
French newspaper-reading public's appetite for stories of torture certainly has
other origins than this project. In fact, an unspoken consensus seems to have
been established in France in recent years, one that includes many of the journalists, historians, and public figures who have written or commented on the
subject. This tacit consensus holds that all of the most controversial questions
about what France's colonial past means for contemporary French society—
the possibility of integrating Muslims into the polity, the meaning of national
citizenship in a postcolonial world, the treatment of people of North African
descent by police and other government officials—refer ultimately back to a
primal scene established by acts of torture during the war years. What is it
about torture that makes it so central to all of these questions?

Historians and Violence

In order to make sense of this question, one must first tackle the historical problem of violence itself, or more specifically, the problem of what violence *means*. Unfortunately, however, a great deal of historical research on violence focuses less on the meaning of violence than on what violence *does*. Those who seek to understand violence by focusing on what it accomplishes—that is, those who see violence as primarily a means to a more or less rational end—are usually either functionalist or instrumentalist in their focus. Functionalists look for ways in which violent acts serve certain structural needs of the social order.[15] In such accounts, society itself is held to contain certain logics of tension, confrontation, and competing interest, and it is the historian's task to reveal these often hidden logics in order to explain outbreaks of violence. These competing interests can be conceived of in many different ways—as characteristics of rival social classes or ethnic groups, for example, or as a part of the structural relations between the state and certain sectors of civil society. Regardless of the ways that the social structure is conceived, however, functionalist accounts tend to take the existence of such structures for granted. Their goal is not to examine how such social groups are constituted, but rather how their violent interactions tend to serve the needs of the system as a whole.

Instrumentalist approaches to violence share the functionalist emphasis on seeing violence primarily as a means to certain identifiable ends, but instead of focusing on the impersonal level of social structures, such accounts look to explain violent acts in terms of the intentions, ideologies, and will of the perpetrators—a typical example of such work might be Martha Crenshaw's essay on the causes of terrorism.[16] Such accounts tend to be political in their focus, rather than social, because instrumentalists are interested in the intentions and actions of individuals and on the institutions, procedures, capacities, or technologies that allow them to achieve their ends. Outside the realm of scholarly study, of course, instrumental accounts of violence are ubiquitous. The instrumental application of violence is the focus of the so-called military sciences, and one of the reasons that modern warfare has become such an arena of technological fantasy is the apparently irrefutable idea that violence is inescapably useful, and that these uses can be refined and elaborated in a myriad of different ways.

The assumptions behind these approaches—the instrumental and the functionalist—are so widespread both within and outside of the scholarly community precisely because they are reductive. They make something complicated—violence—easier to understand. It should not be necessary to point out that something is lost in this reduction, but in fact it is. Much of the recent debate about the use of force in Iraq, for example, has been structured by the assumption that one can and should separate out the U.S. army's idea of the tactical usefulness of violence from the meaning of this violence to Iraqis. Many people have pointed out the disconnect fostered by the clean computer-generated simulations of "smart bombs" hitting their targets that appeared on American news networks and the actual carnage caused by American weapons, images of which almost never reached the American public. The whisper campaign that one heard in certain quarters after 11 September 2001 about the need for torture in the arsenal against terror is another example of what happens when an instrumental approach to violence is divorced from an attention to the meaning of violence for the parties involved in the act. Once the initial photographs of torture at Abu Ghraib prison began appearing on the Internet, however, it became clear that such acts could never be reduced to a purely rational set of procedures. Defenders of the administration's "war on terrorism" thus stopped talking in veiled terms about the necessity of torture and instead concentrated on portraying the treatment of prisoners at Abu Ghraib as the anomalous acts of a few out-of-control soldiers. Instrumental explanations of violence ignore some of the most powerful meanings attached to violent acts, meanings that are quick to spin out of control as awareness of violence spreads.

The problem with functionalist explanations, on the other hand, is that they are themselves prisoners of the vocabulary and categories that emerge from the conflict under investigation. A functionalist account of the so-called French-Algerian war must assume that the conflict took place between groups constituted as "French" and "Algerian" and ignore the difficult fact that it was precisely these categories that were up for grabs in the war. Contrary to appearances, this is not a trivial point. Functionalist accounts are prone to a necessary literalism in laying out the categories that are subject to dispute, because parsing these categories and subjecting them to careful analysis makes the clear attribution of interest, motives, and strategy far more difficult than functionalists would wish. This was especially clear in much of the media coverage in the 1990s of the violence in the former Yugoslavia and in Rwanda. "Serb" and "Bosnian" or "Hutu" and "Tutsi" lend themselves to functionalist accounts only if one accepts an inevitable and obviously reified homogenization of historical reality within these categories and a disturbingly strict separation dividing them from one another. In other words, functionalism requires meeting Slobodan Milošević on his own terms.

There is good reason, therefore, to turn from purely functionalist or instrumental approaches to violence and look at the alternative—studies that seek to explore more subtly the meaning of violence, rather than its accomplishments. These studies are primarily ethnographic or cultural in their approach, and they focus less on the specific social or political circumstances of individual acts of violence than on the constellation of meanings that are at play in violent confrontations. Focusing on the complexities of meaning allows one to do several things: first, since meanings are both produced and consumed, an ethnographic or cultural approach to violence allows one to approach a violent event or act from a variety of subject positions—and to see precisely how these subjectivities are themselves made possible and transformed by the act of violence. Secondly, a cultural approach can do much more to explain the form that violence takes, since it is less concerned with the specific rationality of the violent act in a strictly functional or instrumental sense. Finally, a cultural approach can provide us with a clearer vehicle for linking histories of violence to the history of memory, because it is precisely the play of meanings that is at stake in contested memories of violent events.

The study of colonial violence is an especially charged arena for exploring these questions. Here, as elsewhere, violence should not be seen simply as a tool, as one means among many for achieving political or social ends. Rather, colonial violence should be examined as a form of communication whose meaning both arises out of a specific historical relationship and transforms this relationship in powerful and irrevocable ways. What is important in understanding such violence, therefore, is not only what it accomplishes in a realm outside of that defined by the violent act—material benefit, political advantage, territory, etc. Colonial violence also creates a specific space in which the violent relationship can be reenacted and exploited as a kind of existential condition; it is what gives meaning to the social and political relationships that emerge from this violence. In the long run, the colonial enterprise depends more on the perpetuation of such relationships than it does on any specific material or territorial goals. For this reason, violence in the colonial situation should not always be seen as simply the unfortunate cost of an otherwise more or less defensible goal—sometimes, at least, *it is the goal itself.*

Torture's Family Romance

The recent debates in France about the French military's use of torture in the Algerian war provide a good example for exploring this dynamic, because the army's use of torture was an open secret at the time, and its defenders, although never acknowledging its extent, publicly defended its use with an essentially instrumental account. According to General Jacques Massu's memoirs, the problem faced by the French army during the Battle of Algiers was essentially one of information: when the army arrested a suspected militant, they had twenty-four hours to get what they needed to know. After twenty-four hours, any information would be worthless because any associates of the arrested prisoner would have had time to find new safe houses, and any plans that he or she may have been privy to would have changed. The logic of this situation, said Massu, meant that interrogation "had to hurt a little" ("il fallait qu 'ça cogne' un peu").[17] Massu's account of torture made it seem like a rational procedure—he and his men tried the electricity out on themselves first, so they would know exactly how to calibrate the application of pain, and in their mind this scientific procedure distinguished him and his paratroopers from the sadistic torturers of the Gestapo, for example.[18]

The reception given to Louisette Ighilahriz's story in 2000, however, demonstrated that what is now most disturbing to both the French and Algerians about this history of torture is not the status of perpetrators and victims (i.e., the question of who did what to whom, or even the ostensible purpose used at the time to justify these acts). What needs to be explained is the terribly intimate and disturbing relations *between* perpetrators and victims fostered by torture.[19] Ighilahriz was severely wounded in an ambush and taken as a prisoner to the headquarters of General Massu's 10th Parachute Division. Held naked and tied to a bed in a cell for over two months, she was repeatedly tortured and raped. In her account she identified Generals Jacques Massu and Marcel Bigeard as having been present during some of her "interrogations." She was saved from execution when a military doctor discovered her in her cell and removed her to a hospital to treat her wounds. He later supervised her transfer to an ordinary prison. Louisette Ighilahriz was not even sure of the spelling of this doctor's name, but she overheard him addressed as "Commandant Richaud." She tried to contact him after the war to thank him but was not able to find him.

When Massu corroborated Ighilahriz's account, he explicitly invalidated all the justifications for torture that he had given in his memoirs—nothing he said there could have justified the continuous torture that Louisette Ighilahriz faced for a period of over ten weeks. Massu did not remember her case specifically—there were apparently so many others—but he agreed that the details sounded accurate and he apologized for the use of torture during the war years: "No," he said, "torture is not indispensable in wartime, we could have very well done without it. When I think of Algeria, it makes me sorry, because that [torture] was part of a certain atmosphere [*cela faisait partie d'une certaine ambiance*]; we could have done things differently."[20] Massu identified the mysterious Commandant Richaud, who had rescued Ighilahriz from her torturers, and said that he had remained in close contact with him until his death a year and a half earlier.

Other former military officers were shocked at Massu's apparent change of heart. General Marcel Bigeard, whom Massu said he had seen using electricity on a suspect in 1955, denied Ighilahriz's entire story and said that it was a "tissue of lies" from start to finish. He had never heard of Commandant Richaud, and was offended at the suggestion that he had been present while somebody was being tortured. What was odd, though, is that Bigeard denied something that Ighilahriz never actually accused him of—characteristically speaking of himself in the third person, he exclaimed to *Le Monde*'s interviewer "Bigeard practically raping a woman with Massu, it's unimaginable!"[21]

Bigeard's outburst got to the heart of the matter. By bringing rape and torture together in the same breath, the former general's denial concentrated all of the anxieties that the French felt in listening over the years to stories of torture and the army's justifications for its use in the struggle against the FLN. In fact, it is clear by now to anybody in France who is paying the least amount of attention to this discussion that torture and rape were never only about getting information about the FLN; these practices were not a regrettable but necessary tactic in a difficult and unpleasant war, or even a way of simply punishing suspected terrorists. Torture and rape were about establishing a particular relationship between French soldiers and Algerian Muslims, one in which the most essential parts of victim's personality—the integrity of their bodies, their relations with their families, their connection to a religion, a cause— were annihilated. When Massu said that this was the product of a certain atmosphere at the time he is not far from the truth: the French military—in both its conscript forces and its elite units such as the paratroopers—was determined to use the trauma of torture and rape as a kind of primal scene, that would forever define the relationship between the state and its colonial subjects, between the torture-ers and the torture-able.

Torture is an intimate violation of one person's body by another—it possesses the same sweaty closeness and proximity of an act of love, the same casual familiarity with the most private recesses of the body, its fluids, and smells. It is precisely because of this similarity to other intimate acts that torture has such powerful psychological effects on its victims and such apparent attractions for those who come to commit such acts. Of course, what distinguishes torture from other forms of intimacy, and makes even the use of the word in such a context seem perverse, is the absolute wall or separation that is constructed between the two individuals who are brought together so closely by the act. Elaine Scarry has written that there is nothing so difficult for a mind to comprehend as the pain felt by somebody else's body—and that there is nothing so difficult for that person to express than that pain.[22] The paradox at the heart of torture is that the two individuals involved are bound together by the enormity of what separates them.

The terror campaign that the FLN led against the French settler population of Algiers was, of course, the mirror image of this primal relation established by the intimacy of torture. In contrast to the unbearable violations exacted by the *parachutistes* in their interrogation centers, the FLN offered the horrifying anonymity of the café and office bombing. Even so, however, the FLN could not escape the fact that this violence was the product not of irrevocable difference or separation, but of close proximity. The bombing campaign was possible because these two populations knew each other, lived and moved among each other, and understood one another, in ways that nationalists on both sides were at pains to deny. This fact was well understood by Gillo Pontecorvo in his film, *The Battle of Algiers*, in his depiction of the young Muslim woman who flirts with a French soldier on her way to bomb a bar in the European quarter. This woman has dyed her hair and put on a short dress and summer blouse, so that she may pass for "French" and cross the barricade that separates the French part of the city from the Muslim quarter. Her moment of feigned interest in the young soldier is no less compelling for being insincere, since it is precisely her ability to mimic the French codes of courtship that illustrate Pontecorvo's point about the intimacies of civil wars, and the anxieties that arise from the unexpected human relations produced by such intimacy.[23]

In recent discussions about the torture and rape that accompanied French military action in the wars of decolonization, one can detect an underlying theme—what one might call the "family romance" of decolonization—a tendency to speak about the relations between French and former colonized peoples in terms of familial relationships that somehow have gone awry.[24] There is of course a history to this trope—the paternalist language of French colonialism in which the peoples of Africa were infantilized—but it also appears in the descriptions of French Algerian households, many of which had Muslim servants and laborers who were "part of the family" and whose betrayal during the war was described in the tones of horrified parents who can't explain why their children have forsaken them. Massu's 1972 memoirs are filled with this kind of language, and even Louisette Ighilahriz's account of her ordeal makes reference to this kind of relationship, in her description of her initial encounter with the Commandant Richaud, who discovered her in her cell and rescued her from almost certain execution. "I remember," said Ighilahriz, "he told me: 'I haven't seen my daughter for six months, you remind me terribly of her.'" Ighilahriz recounted that she now wanted to find Richaud's daughter, to tell her "how much her father loved her, over there, in Algeria."[25]

This family romance of decolonization lies at the heart of the controversy over torture in France today, and it is a preoccupation with the unfinished business of this perverse and terrifying intimacy that will not allow the issue to go away. A sign, however, that both sides are finally beginning to acknowledge what continues to tie French and Algerians together in the memory of this war came in the fall of 2001 in the case of Mohamed Garne. He was born on 19 April 1960 in a resettlement camp in Algeria to a sixteen-year-old married woman, Kheïra Garne, who had been repeatedly raped by French soldiers and subsequently repudiated by her husband. The husband was later killed fighting the French. Given up to a nurse immediately at birth, Mohamed Garne ended up in the hospital soon afterwards, with signs of beatings and malnutrition. He grew up in Algiers in a foster home that fell apart when he was fifteen and he was sent back to an orphanage. When he was seventeen his foster father told him in a rage that he was the son of a prostitute, and in despair Garne tried to commit suicide soon after. After getting out of the orphanage when he was twenty-five, he ended up spending several months in a psychiatric clinic and three years in prison for stealing from his adoptive mother. He later married, had a child and became a nurse. Obsessed with finding the truth of his origins, he embarked upon a three-year search to find his mother. He finally found her in 1988, living in a cemetery in Hydra, in the hills above Algiers. *Le Monde*'s reporter depicted the emotional meeting:

> . . . il tombait des trombes d'eau, ce jour-là. Les gens regardaient avec méfiance ce type qui cherchait Kheïra Garne, on a fini par lui dire qu'elle habitait tout près, dans le cimetière. Elle était là, devant une sorte de grotte, aménagée entre deux tombes, une hache à la main. Mais quand il lui dit qu'il était son fils, elle l'a embrassé.[26]

> . . . it was raining buckets that day. People looked with suspicion on this man who was looking for Kheïra Garne, but eventually someone told him that she lived nearby, in the cemetery. She was there, in front of a sort of cave, hollowed out between two tombs, a hatchet in her hand. But when he told her that he was her son, she embraced him.

Kheïra Garne eventually told Mohamed the name of her dead husband, Abdelkader Bengoucha, but she refused to undertake the necessary steps to have her son adopt her husband's name, and their relationship turned conflictual. When Mohamed Garne took his mother to court to insist on his paternity, her family provided evidence that Abdelkader Bengoucha had been sterile. Kheïra Garne testified that she had been raped and tortured over a period of weeks by French soldiers, who beat her and shocked her with electricity when she became pregnant. While telling this story in court, she collapsed on the stand.

According to the French journalist who recounted this story in the pages of *Le Monde*, Mohamed Garne left Algeria and came to France in 1998, "with one fixed idea: to make his story known to the one father he had left: the French state."[27] In 2000 his request for a military pension was turned down, but his lawyers continued to press his case. They argued that Mohamed Garne had suffered permanent effects from beatings his pregnant mother had received during her detention, and a court-appointed expert concurred, saying that his infirmities were "all attributable to the responsibility of the French state."[28] In

November 2001, a French court agreed with most of these arguments, and awarded Garne a 30 percent pension as a "victime de guerre" [war victim].

The court never actually recognized Mohamed Garne's paternity, but the decision to offer him a pension seems to be a much more significant act of remembrance than anything else the French government has done to commemorate the Algerian war. Prior to Garne's suit, his relationship to the French state was filled with ambiguity. Labeled by the French press "français par le crime" [French by crime], he was in fact French by birth, even without taking the story of his presumed father into account, because he was born in Algeria before 1962. Furthermore, since French nationality was a prerequisite to receiving this type of pension, the court's decision represented much more than a simple statement of responsibility for a "victime de guerre" [war victim]. It was also a victory for Garne's quest to resolve the painful story of his own origins, and an open recognition of the tacit and disturbing familial order that continues to structure conceptions of French-Algerian relations.

A functionalist account of torture during the Algerian war can do little to explore themes such as these, and such accounts cannot therefore explain the practice's continued relevance to contemporary French political debate. The French use of torture in the Algerian war, like other kinds of violence that take place in the colonial situation, was the product of intense and even intimate historical relationships, and it became the crucible for transforming these relationships into powerful linkages whose singular effects could not be effaced by the political dissaggregation that we call decolonization. The reception of Louisette Ighilahriz's autobiography in France, as well as the wide attention given to the story of Mohamed Garne, are only two examples that show the powerful resonances of a language that invokes familial connections and resemblances across the French-Algerian divide. It remains to be seen, however, if such a vocabulary has the same resonance in contemporary Algeria. As Neil MacMaster pointed out, representatives of the government in Algeria have been noticeably silent on the torture controversies raging in France, because some of their military leaders actually served in the French army during the war years and were thus implicated in the French army's repressive policies, and also because the Algerian government has itself resorted to torture in its recent struggles with oppositional groups and Islamic movements.[29] The work of memory in Algeria will necessarily begin with a different set of concerns, and it will play out against the background of a very different political situation. It seems significant, however, that it was "Algerian" voices which allowed the French to confront the family romance of their colonial war. The stories told by individuals such as Mohamed Garne—"français par le crime"—and Louisette Ighilahriz, a militant nationalist who took up arms against the French, received such close attention by journalists and the wider public in France because they spoke not only for themselves but for all those whose complicated family history was linked to the experience of colonial subjecthood. The French do not keep official statistics of citizens who are of Algerian descent—or Senegalese, or Ivoirian, or Vietnamese, or Malagasy, for that matter—because their laws do not allow them to make distinctions between different kinds of citizens. No one doubts, however, that these stories resonated differently for those French citizens who in their daily lives face the contradictions between a universal definition of citizenship and a colonial past that has made France a multicultural society in fact if not in name. In this sense, Garne's and Ighilahriz's stories provide a sincere refutation to Renan's suggestion that forgetting past conflicts is a necessary task for those who wish to forge a sense of national identity. At a minimum, such stories show the limits to any sense of national identity based on the suppression of past atrocities, and suggest that if those who consider themselves French are to fully come to grips with the lasting effects of their colonial history, they will have to learn to speak openly about the relationships engendered by decolonization and its violence.

Notes

1. Some of the most important work on memory in France has focused on World War I; see especially Stéphane Audoin-Rouzeau and Annette Becker, *14-18: Understanding the Great War* (New York: Hill and Wang, 2002), 233-62; Annette Becker, *War and Faith: The Religious Imagination in France, 1914-1930* (Oxford: Berg, 1998); Daniel J. Sherman, *The Construction of Memory in Interwar France* (Chicago: University of Chicago Press, 1999). For the memory of World War I in Europe more generally, see Jay Winter, *Sites of Memory, Sites of Mourning: The Great War in European Cultural Memory* (Cambridge: Cambridge University Press, 1995).

The literature on the memory of World War II and Vichy in France is long and well-documented elsewhere—the following are merely some of the most important: Jean-Pierre Azéma, "Vichy et la mémoire savante," in *Vichy et les Français,* eds. Jean-Pierre Azéma and François Bédarida (Paris: Fayard, 1992); Sarah Farmer, *Martyred Village: Commemorating the 1944 Massacre at Oradour-sur-Glane* (Berkeley: University of California Press, 1999); Sarah Fishman et al., *France at War: Vichy and the Historians* (New York: Berg, 2000); Richard J. Golsan, *Vichy's Afterlife: History and Counterhistory in Postwar France* (Lincoln: University of Nebraska Press, 2000); Henry Rousso, *La Hantise du passé* (Paris: Textuel, 1998); Henry Rousso, *The Vichy Syndrome: History and Memory in France since 1944* (Cambridge, Mass.: Harvard University Press, 1991); Henry Rousso and Eric Conan, *Vichy: An Ever-Present Past* (Hanover, N.H.: University Press of New England, 1998); Tzvetan Todorov, *A French Tragedy: Scenes of Civil War, Summer 1944* (Hanover, N.H.: University Press of New England, 1996); Nancy Wood, *Vectors of Memory: Legacies of Trauma in Postwar Europe* (New York: Berg, 2000).

Historical work on the memory of the French-Algerian war is also growing rapidly. See especially articles by Neil MacMaster, Benjamin Stora, Azouz Begag, Charles Bonn, James Le Sueur, and Philip Dine in the special issue of *Modern & Contemporary France* edited by Alec G. Hargreaves and entitled *France and Algeria, 1962-2002: Turning the Page?* 10, no. 4 (2002). See also Martin Evans, *The Memory of Resistance: French Opposition to the Algerian War (1954-1962)* (Providence, R.I.: Berg, 1997); Claire Mauss-Copeaux, *Les Appelés en Algérie: la parole confisquée* (Paris: Hachette Littératures, 1998); Patrick Rotman and Bertrand Tavernier, *La Guerre sans nom: Les appelés d'Algérie 54-62* (Paris: Seuil, 1992); Benjamin Stora, *La Gangrène et l'oubli. La mémoire de la guerre d'Algérie* (Paris: La Découverte, 1991); Benjamin Stora and Mohammed Harbi, eds., *La Guerre d'Algérie, 1959-2004, la fin de l'amnésie* (Paris: Robert Laffont, 2004).

2. An example of such work is the otherwise extraordinarily helpful book by Charles Tilly, *The Politics of Collective Violence* (Cambridge: Cambridge University Press, 2003). Tilly's book does not set out to analyze the causes of collective violence in general. Rather, he compared many different episodes of collective violence and noted patterns of variation in the comparison—in levels of coordination among the parties to the violence, and the salience of destruction, for example, or in the capacity of the existing regime to prescribe or prohibit violent interactions of particular kinds. Armed with these points of comparison, Tilly suggested a typology of different kinds of collective violence, ranging from "brawls" and "opportunism" at one end of the spectrum of organization to "coordinated destruction" and "violent ritual" at the other. Tilly's work is remarkable in its ability to account for the ways that certain kinds of nonviolent interactions can suddenly turn violent, and vice versa, and he also has many plausible arguments for explaining how one kind of violent interaction can turn into another, spiraling up and down the spectrum of his useful typology. Tilly's work is a useful antidote to older idealist or behaviorist explanatory models that see violence purely as the result of ideology or human nature, and he also allows us, once and for all, to dispense with the "pressure cooker" analogy in accounting for episodes of collective violence, in favor of an approach that focuses on social relations. The book is less helpful, however, in exploring the ways that violence shapes the realm of the political imaginary in a given society after the violence has subsided, or how it determines the space in which individuals negotiate their identities at the intersection of the local and more global forces that produce violent events. To answer these questions, the approach sketched out by Venita Das and Arthur Kleinman is more helpful. See, for example, the essays in Veena Das et al., eds., *Violence and Subjectivity* (Berkeley: University of California Press, 2000).

3. A recent exception to this that deals with World War I is Audoin-Rouzeau and Becker, *14-18: Understanding the Great War*, 15-90. Audoin-Rouzeau and Becker argue that military histories of World War I often appear to sidestep the violence of the conflict, preferring instead to dwell on tactical or strategic issues, as if the clash of bodies and weapons were somehow indecent or at least a distraction from more important matters.

4. Between 1954 and 1962 the French government insisted that its military operations were nothing more than police actions aimed at keeping the peace in the face of criminal elements. Not until 10 June 1999 did the National Assembly accept official

use of the term "guerre d'Algérie," in response to a law proposed by Jacques Floch, a socialist deputy and a veteran of the war himself. The law was aimed at providing benefits to widows and families of veterans who were denied assistance before the change in vocabulary. See Raphaëlle Bacque, "La Guerre d'Algérie n'est plus une guerre sans nom," *Le Monde*, 11 June 1999.

5. Fanon wrote: "When in 1956, after the capitulation of Monseiur Guy Mollet to the settlers in Algeria, the Front de Libération Nationale, in a famous leaflet, stated that colonialism only loosens its hold when the knife is at its throat, no Algerian really found these terms too violent. The leaflet only expressed what every Algerian felt at heart: colonialism is not a thinking machine, nor a body endowed with reasoning faculties. It is violence in its natural state, and it will only yield when confronted with greater violence." Frantz Fanon, *The Wretched of the Earth* (New York: Grove Press, 1963), 61.

6. The classic work of this type is Roger Trinquier, *La Guerre moderne* (Paris: La Table Ronde, 1961). See also Alf Andrew Heggoy, *Insurgency and Counterinsurgency in Algeria* (Bloomington: Indiana University Press, 1972). For a military account that tries harder to go beyond the reductionist and euphemistic language of Trinquier, see the essays in Martin S. Alexander, Martin Evans, and J. F. V. Keiger, eds., *The Algerian War and the French Army, 1954-1962: Experiences, Images, Testimonies* (New York: Palgrave McMillan, 2002).

7. The diplomatic history of the wars of decolonization has recently been a particularly rich area of suggestive research. On Algeria, see especially Matthew Connelly, *A Diplomatic Revolution: Algeria's Fight for Independence and the Origins of the Post-Cold War Era* (New York: Oxford University Press, 2002); Irwin Wall, *France, the United States, and the Algerian War* (Berkeley: University of California Press, 2001). On Indochina, see Irwin Wall, *The United States and the Making of Postwar France, 1945-1954* (Cambridge: Cambridge University Press, 1991), 233-262. Matthew Connelly's work on the international history of the Algerian war in particular has done a great deal to clarify the place of Algeria at the vortex of powerful global forces of aggregation—the emergence of a bipolar world order during the Cold War—and fragmentation—the highly varied effects of the spread of consumer markets, which bound some parts of the world tighter to the developed world, and left others increasingly on the margins. According to Connelly, these "fault lines" as he calls them, ran right through Algeria, making the international context of the war the essential focus of his work. Because of this focus, however, his book contains no sustained attention to the violence of the conflict.

8. A useful and timely guide to this debate is Neil MacMaster, "The Torture Controversy (1998-2002): Towards a 'New History' of the Algerian War," *Modern & Contemporary France* 10 (2002). For a more comprehensive look at the war's violence against the background of North Africa's *longue durée*, see Omar Carlier, "Violence(s)," in *La Guerre d'Algérie, 1954-2004: la fin de l'amnésie*, eds. Mohammed Harbi and Benjamin Stora (Paris: Robert Laffont, 2004), 347-379.

9. Books and pamphlets on torture that appeared during the war years include Henri Alleg, *La Question* (Paris: Minuit, 1958); Laurent Schwartz, *Le Problème de la torture dans la France d'aujourd'hui* (Paris: Comité Audin, 1961); Pierre-Henri Simon,

Contre la torture (Paris: Seuil, 1957); Pierre Vidal-Naquet, *La Raison d'État* (Paris: Éditions de Minuit, 1962). The cases of Maurice Audin, Djamila Boupacha, and Djamila Bouhired received a great deal of attention in the French press, and Kristin Ross has argued that the memory of violence against Algerians played an important role in the political awakening of the generation of May 1968. Kristin Ross, *May '68 and its Afterlives* (Chicago: University of Chicago Press, 2002), 40-64.

10. Ighilahriz's story was first published in *Le Monde* in June 2000 (see "Torturée par l'armée française en Algérie, Lila recherche l'homme qui l'a sauvée," *Le Monde*, 20 June 2000). She later published a fuller account of her detention in Louisette Ighilahriz, *Algérienne* (Paris: Fayard/Calmann-Lévy, 2001).

11. The appeal of the twelve intellectuals was published in *L'Humanité*, 31 October 2000. The signatories were Henri Alleg, Josette Audin, Simone de Bollardière, Nicole Dreyfus, Noel Favrelière, Gisèle Halimi, Alban Liechti, Madeleine Rebérioux, Laurent Schwartz, Germaine Tillion, Jean-Pierre Vernant, and Pierre Vidal-Naquet.

12. "Torture et exécutions sommaires pendant la guerre d'Algérie. Deux généraux s'opposent sur une repentance," *Le Monde*, 22 November 2000.

13. A published version of the thesis appeared shortly thereafter as Raphaëlle Branche, *La Torture et l'armée pendant la guerre d'Algérie, 1954-1962* (Paris: Éditions Gallimard, 2001). On the scene at Branche's dissertation defense, see Jean-Dominique Merchet, "Torture en Algérie: 1211 pages d'histoire," *Le Monde*, 6 December 2000.

14. MacMaster, "The Torture Controversy," 449-50.

15. This work is primarily sociological in character, in a line that is traceable from Max Weber to Charles Tilly, via Hannah Arendt. See Hannah Arendt, *On Violence* (New York: Harcourt Brace, 1969); Tilly, *The Politics of Collective Violence* (Cambridge: Cambridge University Press, 2003), Max Weber, "Politics as a Vocation," in *From Max Weber: Essays in Sociology*, eds. H. H. Gerth and C. Wright Mills (Oxford: Oxford University Press, 1946), 77-128.

16. Martha Crenshaw, "The Causes of Terrorism," in *Violence: A Reader*, ed. Catherine Besteman (New York: New York University Press, 2002), 99-117.

17. Jacques Massu, *La* Vraie *bataille d'Alger* (Paris: Plon, 1971), 177.

18. Branche, *La Torture*, 51-56.

19. Branche mentioned the intimate nature of the conflict during the Algerian war, but she does not develop a consideration of this intimacy as it specifically related to acts of torture. Branche, *La Torture*, 15.

20. "Non, la torture n'est pas indispensable en temps de guerre, on pourrait très bien s'en passer. Quand je repense à l'Algérie, cela me désole, car cela faisait partie d'une certaine ambiance, on aurait pu faire les choses différemment." Philippe Bernard, "La Gangrène au cœur de la République," *Le Monde*, 22 June 2000.

21. "Bigeard en train de pratiquement violer une femme avec Massu, c'est inimaginable!" Bernard, "La Gangrène au cœur," *Le Monde*, 22 June 2000.

22. Elaine Scarry, *The Body in Pain: The Making and Unmaking of the World* (New York: Oxford University Press, 1985), 3-19, 36.

23. In another context, Ann Laura Stoler has emphasized the importance of the intimate sphere in the maintenance of colonial relations, and my argument here owes much to her conception of the problem. See Ann Laura Stoler, *Carnal Knowledge and*

Imperial Power: Race and the Intimate in Colonial Rule (Berkeley: University of California Press, 2002).

24. In a provocative rereading of the French Revolution, Lynn Hunt argued that "the French had a kind of collective political unconscious that was structured by narratives of family relations" and she used the term "family romance" to refer to "the collective, unconscious images of the familial order that underlie revolutionary politics." Lynn Hunt, *The Family Romance of the French Revolution* (Berkeley: University of California Press, 1992), xiii. I am using the term even more loosely here, to refer to a tendency of both historians and contemporaries to speak of the unexpected relations produced by the Algerian war in familial terms. For an argument that develops the notion of family romance in a colonial context, see also Françoise Vergès, *Monsters and Revolutionaries: Colonial Family Romance and Métissage* (Durham, N.C.: Duke University Press, 1999).

25. "Je me souviens qu'il m'avait dit: 'Je n'ai pas vu ma fille depuis six mois, vous me faites terriblement penser à elle.' Alors, je la cherche, elle aussi. Je voudrais lui dire combien son père l'aimait et à quel point il pensait à elle, là-bas, en Algérie." Cited in Florence Beaugé, "Torturée par l'armée française en Algérie, Lila recherche l'homme qui l'a sauvée," *Le Monde*, 20 June 2000. Contrast these words with the account given by General Massu of a situation that developed between his landlady on the outskirts of Algiers, and a local Muslim woman with whom she had long had close relations. "Bouleversée, elle me raconte un jour qu'une vieille femme, Fatma-Zohra, qu'elle a souvent aidée et qui l'aime beaucoup, a tenu à lui exprimer l'étendue de son affection et de sa reconnaissance. Elle lui a dit: 'Il paraît qu'on va tuer tous les Européens. Nous aurons leurs maisons et leurs frigidaires. Mais j'ai demandé à te tuer moi-même parce que je ne veux pas que tu souffres. Je ferai cela vite et bien, je te le jure, car je t'aime." Massu, *La Vraie Bataille d'Alger*, 23. [Very upset, she told me one day that an old woman, Fatma-Zohra, whom she had often helped and whom she loved very much, had come to her to express the extent of her affection and gratitude. She [Fatma-Zohra] told her: "It looks like we are going to kill all the Europeans. We will have their houses and their refrigerators. But I asked to kill you myself because I don't want you to suffer. I will do it quickly and well, I swear to you, because I love you."] The two quotations mirror one another in a curious way. In the one, a combatant taken prisoner and subjected to horrifying atrocity becomes the focus of paternal concern by an officer serving in the opposing army. In the other, a family friend who is the object of much affection reveals herself to be an enemy, capable of the most frightful crime, which she would perform with love.

26. Johannes Franck, "Mohamed Garne, né d'un viol collectif dans un camp, demande réparation à l'État français," *Le Monde*, 11 October 2001.

27. Franck, "Mohamed Garne," *Le Monde*, 11 October 2001.

28. Franck, "Mohamed Garne," *Le Monde*, 11 October 2001.

29. MacMaster, "The Torture Controversy," 456.

9

Revisiting Ghosts

Louisette Ighilahriz and the Remembering of Torture

Sylvie Durmelat

I dare to assert that torture is the most horrible event a human being can retain within himself. . . . Whoever was tortured stays tortured.

—Jean Améry[1]

Face à ces ombres, s'approcher à tâtons, ou faire détours, cercles, méandres et rosaces, pour enfin regarder la source noire, maculée de boue, de cris gelés, de pleurs non taris.

—Assia Djebar[2]

In the face of these shadows, one has to feel one's way, make detours, circles, meanderings, cloverleafs, to finally look into the black spring spattered with mud, frozen cries, tears that won't dry.[3]

THE DEBATE ON TORTURE HAS LONG SERVED as a non-consensual public site of memory where individual, collective, group, and national memories of the Algerian war of independence have opposed and exposed one another. In the previous chapter, Joshua Cole examines the significance of these debates in the work of historians. My purpose here is to focus on the textual forms taken by testimonies of torture, in particular that of Louisette Ighilahriz,[4] and on the ways in which these have been shaped by and have in turn impacted upon a variety of social milieux ranging from the judicial and the journalistic to the commercial and the political. All testimonies result from a complex process of construction and representation through language. In addition, testimonies such as those of Ighilahriz (an Algerian nationalist and torture victim during the war of independence) and Paul Aussaresses (a French intelligence officer and avowed perpetrator of torture during the Algerian conflict) were made possible with the help of professional writers and were in part the products of editorial negotiation and mediations in a highly charged political context. They clearly are commercial as well as memorial commodities. The testimonies of Ighilahriz and Aussaresses have also been deeply enmeshed with judicial processes. For historians such as Henry Rousso,[5] this interface is potentially dangerous because the legal norms that preside over the judicial arena impose constraints upon the witnesses that do not necessarily foster free speech. For Antoine Garapon,[6] on the contrary, the very configuration of a trial can be therapeutic and salutary rather than muzzling: "La scène de la justice, par sa procédure et ses rites offre à la cité le pouvoir de maîtriser son histoire."[7] [The Judicial scene, through its procedures and its rituals, gives the city the power to master its history.] However, Garapon does recognize a risk inherent in judicial approaches to testimony. While victims are recognized as such and are allowed to enter history by testifying in court, they also run the risk of being trapped in the status of victims[8] and thereby of being robbed of their own power to narrate.

While they stood on opposing sides historically and politically, Aussaresses and Ighilahriz were both caught up in the testimonial inflation of the memory business. Aussaresses had initially written a very thick manuscript of memoirs. After an interview he had given to *Le Monde*[9] provoked a heated controversy over his open acknowledgment of having personally tortured prisoners during the Algerian war, he was asked by the publisher to prune his 1,200-page-long memoirs and concentrate only on his activities during the Algerian conflict. The revised text, written with the help of ghostwriter Claude Ribbes, appeared in book form in February 2001.[10] During his subsequent trial on charges of *apologies de crime de guerre* [justifying war crimes], these editorial and marketing choices became the target of intense questioning aimed at proving or disproving the intent to vindicate war crimes. Key elements in this were the number of pages devoted to the war in the original manuscript and the level of assistance provided by Claude Ribbes.[11]

In a similar way, Louisette's public testimonies reflect not only the personal and deeply painful process that brought her to finally tell her story, but also social interactions with and pressures from the media and publishing industry. Florence Beaugé, recently hired by *Le Monde*, had met Ighilahriz in Algiers in 1999, because one of Ighilahriz's sisters had been in touch with Beaugé's father-in-law, a former officer, who was trying to help them find Commandant Richaud, a French military doctor who had saved Ighilahriz from her torturers by arranging for her to be transferred to a hospital. Little by little, Florence Beaugé convinced Ighilahriz to tell her story: "Il lui fallait beaucoup d'effort pour sortir les mots de sa souffrance. Surtout, elle n'avait pas encore la force de parler du viol dont elle a été victime et moi-même je ne savais pas comment l'écrire."[12] [It cost her a lot of effort to utter her suffering out. Above all, she did not yet have the strength to talk about her rape, and I myself did not know how to go about writing it.]

When a first version of Ighilahriz's testimony appeared in an article written by Beaugé in *Le Monde*,[13] Beaugé said she was surprised to see it on the front page. Journalists Cécile Plet and Pierre-Yves Schneider (writing for *Tocsin*, an online journal on the media) imply that Edwy Plenel, editor-in-chief of *Le Monde*, took control of the story out of her hands. Limitations on Ighilahriz's own control over the text of *Algérienne*,[14] her published autobiography written by war journalist Anne Nivat, were revealed during a legal action for slander which Ighilahriz and the MRAP (Movement Against Racism and for the Friendship Among Peoples) brought against General Maurice Schmitt, former Army Chief of staff and a lieutenant during the war, who had dismissed Ighilahriz's book as being "un soi-disant témoignage, ... un tissu d'affabulations"[15] [so-called testimony, ... a tissue of fabrications]. Schmitt had himself been accused of torturing prisoners by Malika Koriche, another nationalist militant who, in the wake of Ighilahriz's testimony, told *Le Monde* that she had been one of his victims.[16] In October 2003, Schmitt was found guilty of defamation and sentenced to pay token damages, but not before he had detailed seeming inconsistencies and inaccuracies in Ighilahriz's testimony in the hope of undermining her credibility. In recounting the torture she suffered at the hands of the French military, Ighilahriz had accused French Generals Massu and Bigeard of giving the orders, and Captain Graziani of executing them. According to Schmitt, Bigeard did not wear a red beret, as claimed by Ighilahriz, but a famous cap; her torturer Graziani did not have "beautiful green eyes," as stated by Louisette, but black eyes; and Bigeard's regiment was never garrisoned at the Paradou-Hydra, so he could not have been present when Ighilahriz was imprisoned there. Ighilahriz was forced to acknowledge: "On m'a donné très peu de temps pour relire le manuscrit et je me suis plantée dans les dates. Mais sur le fond tout est vrai."[17] [I was given very little time to reread the manuscript and I got the dates wrong. But everything is essentially true.] Going through the painful experience of having to retell and relive once again her torture in front of French officers who had fought during the war, looked down upon her and denied the validity of her testimony, Ighilahriz disclosed that Graziani raped her not only with objects, as previously stated in her autobiography (2001), but with his penis (2003). This additional revelation provides us with a window into the way her traumatic experience was locked and unlocked.

Through a closer analysis of Ighilahriz's testimony, I would like to focus on the dynamics and strategies of one individual's quest to inscribe her story and hence rewrite history. For as Susan Crane states: "Collective memory is itself an expression of historical consciousness that derives from individuals . . . [and] ultimately is located not in sites but in individuals."[18] Torture attempted to turn Ighilahriz's body into an insignia of the torturers' power, and she in turn transformed it into a site of memory. During the Algerian war, testimonies by European victims or witnesses of torture elicited considerable attention and outcry. *La Question* by Henri Alleg[19] is the most well known instance of such testimony and it had the most profound impact on public opinion and on the course of the war. The case of Maurice Audin was also widely publicized because of its tragic and still unresolved end to this day.[20] Torture suffered by Algerians provoked in general less public interest and discussion. Ighilahriz is the first Algerian woman to bring to the fore the use of torture and rape during the war. Her words allowed other Algerian women and men to speak up and to start their own process of anamnesia despite the reluctance or the blunt refusal of the Algerian governing elite to support them in this. Ighilahriz's modest if powerful testimony gave visibility and leverage to the witnesses and upholders of a counter-history often at odds with the official, authorized national histories, both in France and in Algeria. Ighilahriz did not tell her story once and for all, either. She repeated it in different fora and for various publics. She made it come to life again and again. It is still amazing that the voice of a tiny old woman could bring about such a national conversation. Her testimony took a life of its own and attested to the power of personal remembering and retelling in the contested construction of any shared memory.

While it is indispensable to describe the larger constellation of historical, political, and cultural conditions that made the emergence of this debate possible, it tends to efface the role individual persons and witnesses do play in the process of remembering. Paul Ricœur's critique of Maurice Halbwachs's *Collective Memory* stresses that recollecting is an act performed by individuals whom it turns into "acting subjects."[21] To overlook the self-generating characteristic of the memory-making process risks dispossessing Ighilahriz of her reclaimed agency as storyteller of her experience of subjection. As Paul Ricœur asserts, "suffering, trauma or extreme experience might be in part incommunicable but it does not make them unspeakable."[22] As a narrative object, Ighilahriz's testimony begs the question of whether and/or how a written trace or an oral account relates to an extreme experience in which the very ability of the witness to utter words is crushed. My objective here will be to analyze how Ighilahriz managed to make her voice heard in a highly politicized context, and how in turn, public controversies affected the way she retold and represented her experience of torture, as well as the strategies she deployed to cope with the painful retelling of her story in attempting to recompose her self. The aesthetics of testimonial narration, centering on the formal modalities of the witness's expression are here intertwined with the construction of memory as well as the therapeutic power of such utterances (or lack thereof). For instance, in Ighilahriz's case, the public revelation of her rape and the seeming inconsistencies between her written and oral accounts bring to the fore the repressions, ellipses, and silences that accompany any testimonial account. They also give us an uneasy purview into the ambiguous relationships fostered by colonial history.

The torture controversy often turned into a trial of colonization. As many commentators, from Ighilahriz to Henri Alleg and Pierre Vidal-Naquet, have stressed, torture did not only occur during the war of independence, even though it became quasi-systematic during the war. It was used by the army as a means to conquer, submit, and dominate Algerians throughout the colonial era. Because the Algerian war has been read as the ultimate episode of a war of conquest that never really ended,[23] it cannot be dissociated from a reassessment of colonization as a system of domination. However, Henry Rousso cautions against examining the long-range consequences of "colonization as an oppressive system and as a phenomenon of acculturation" as crime alone. Such an analysis would be insufficient, for it would not take into account the contradictions that have to be accepted as inherent in colonization. Despite her strong and unequivocal condemnation of colonization, Ighilahriz's own testimony reflects some of these contradictions and gives us a more contrasted portrait of the inner tensions typical of the colonial relationship and its avatars. With their contradictions, ambiguities, subtleties, irregularities, and unintended consequences, Ighilahriz's testimonies demonstrate that the history between France and its ex-colony, Algeria, cannot be limited to a confrontation between enemies.

Recollecting Through Others and Revisiting Ghosts

The June 2000 article by Florence Beaugé in which Ighilahriz first speaks out begins: "J'étais allongée nue, toujours nue. Ils pouvaient venir une, deux ou trois fois par jour. Dès que j'entendais le bruit de leurs bottes dans le couloir, je me mettais à trembler." [I was lying down naked, always naked. They could come one, two, or three times a day. As soon as I would hear the sound of their boots in the corridors, I would begin trembling.] Beaugé's rendition of Ighilahriz's oral testimony underlines simultaneously the violent dehumanization, the utter sense of vulnerability caused by the nudity, and the violence of the account itself in which Ighilahriz at once separates herself from this image of her naked self and becomes one with herself by sharing her account with the public.

Beaugé's presentation of the body in its most powerless and dehumanizing nakedness, in its permeability, endows the claims of the sufferer with incontestable reality and a certain shock value. By displaying the body through writing, this testimony reverses what state-sponsored torture is trying to achieve according to Elaine Scarry.[24] According to her, "torture aspires to the totality of pain"[25] and relies on its indisputable reality to the sufferer and its unreal quality for others, to better deny it. Torture transfers the attributes of pain ("its incontestable reality, its totality, its ability to eclipse all else, its power to dramatic alteration and world dissolution")[26] to the (torturing) regime in an attempt to consolidate its illegitimate and failing power. In Ighilahriz's first published testimony, the use of the first-person account and the use of the past tense can be interpreted in various ways. On the one hand, her testimony helps her recover and restore her suffering body by representing her past experience and making it public. The testimony has the power to finally remove the suffering naked body from under the voodoo politics of torture by exposing its very suffering and exposing the torturers. Her testimony reassigns the attributes of pain to her very body, whose nakedness is now brandished and publicly revealed in the media, instead of being made to remain an invisible, suffering, all-encompassing body, hidden for the mere use and abuse of the torturer. Describing her naked body allows Ighilahriz to set its boundaries again. On the other hand, in recounting her testimony to Florence Beaugé, Ighilahriz is looking into the past at her own suffering young body from a perspective that could well be that of the torturers glancing at her. This perspective confirms Roberta Culbertson's observation that "to recall this nearly-lost self in its bodily presence is the essence of tortured memory."[27] We are faced here with one of the major paradoxes of trauma testimonies. While they enable the witness and victim to become the agent and subject of the retelling (instead of the victim and the object of the violation being told), they can concurrently alienate this very self by concatenating it to the ever-present traumatic experience.

In her testimony, Ighilahriz reduces the power and the presence of her torturers to that of their boots which she can hear as they come to her room. The stark contrast with her own nakedness is thus underlined. Boots are not only a piece of clothing but also a symbol of domination, and as a part of military uniforms, they establish a direct hierarchy between dehumanized detainee and empowered abusers. The noise boots make also suggests the torture of the sufferer. Their noise announces the beginning and marks the end of a torture session. As such they punctuate the passing of time in the torture chambers,

where the seemingly simple succession of days and nights, sleep and wakeful-
ness, has been overturned. The noise of boots confirms that for the tortured,
sounds and cries are the first signal that they have entered a different world.
The characterization of her abusers by their boots can also be read as the resort to another survival strategy delineated by Roberta Culbertson as "leaving
the body."[28] Reducing the torturer's body to the instrument inflicting harm,
hence reifying it, allows Ighilahriz to distance herself from her experience of
subjection. Ighilahriz also uses this strategy in her subsequent accounts of
rape.

Ighilahriz relies on two women who write, two journalists, Florence Beaugé
from Le Monde and Anne Nivat, a war reporter, to (re)compose her self. They
become the recipients of her story. During a series of visits to France, including a visit to the grave of the man who rescued her from her torturers, Commandant Richaud, depicted at the beginning of Nivat's book, Ighilahriz also
relies on the support and companionship of her sister, Ouardia, who witnessed her torture as a young child. Ouardia represents the whole family[29]
while Ighilahriz is in France and plays the role of an antique choir as Ighilahriz
relives her tragedy while searching for Richaud's grave. She documents her sister's search for Richaud's resting place in a cemetery in southern France and
she holds the digital still and video cameras to engrave this very moment for
the whole family back home in Algiers.

Ighilahriz puts her trust in these three women, among others (one thinks,
for example, of the solidarity between Ighilahriz and Josette Audin demonstrated during the Fête de l'Humanité in September 2000),[30] to help her
"reweave her body, mind, and cultural context from a point of unraveling or
rupture"[31]so that she can move "to reintegration with a community of others."[32] Ighilahriz needs their words and their body in her attempt to gather the
truncated pieces of her experience into a more coherent and also socially ac-
ceptable sense of self. This demonstrates that memory making is not solely an
individual process of recollection but also an intersubjective construction.
Similarly, Ighilahriz's public testimony triggers that of Malika Koriche, a Mou-
jahida and FLN fighter, who testified in Le Monde in Spring 2001 that she had
been tortured by the then Lieutenant Schmitt.[33] As Roberta Culbertson writes:
"Narrative requires a narrator, but the destruction of the self at the root of
much violence makes this narrative nearly impossible by definition."[34] Hence,
Ighilahriz entrusts surrogates and intermediaries with the oral pieces of her
story for them to recompose and recombine them. She seems to be more interested in the process of making her story come to life than in the task of putting it down on paper or inscribing it. This problem of agency in the retelling
of one's story is typical, as Culbertson suggests, of any testimony about a traumatic experience. However, in Ighilahriz's case, her lack of control over her

written texts[35] led to Schmitt's accusations against her, which in turn led to her legal action for slander against him. But, this apparent disinterest might mean other things as well, as examined further down.

In Beaugé's article and in Anne Nivat's *Algérienne*, Richaud is another guardian figure (he is the second dedicatee of the book), one that allows crossings and passages from the hell of torture to safety and, when Ighilahriz visits his grave, between past and present. Commandant Richaud is the military doctor who found Ighilahriz on the premises of the 10th parachutist division. Ighilahriz had been shot during an ambush with the French army before she was taken prisoner. She had her waist and a leg in plaster casts and could not move. Her abuser, Graziani, kept trying to destroy them, and raped her with various objects. While at the Paradou Hydra, she was forced to defecate and urinate on herself. Horrified to find that she had been tortured, Richaud looked after her and sent her to the hospital. Once she was taken back to Paradou-Hydra, Commandant Richaud visited Ighilahriz again to ensure that she was well cared for. He carried out his pledge to transfer Ighilahriz to a regular prison, thereby removing her from the grasp of her torturers. Ighilahriz recounts: "Je me souviens qu'il m'avait dit: 'Je n'ai pas vu ma fille depuis six mois, vous me faites terriblement penser à elle.' Alors je la cherche elle aussi. Je voudrais lui dire combien son père l'aimait et à quel point il pensait à elle, là-bas, en Algérie."[36] [I remembered he told me: 'I haven't seen my daughter in six months, you make me miss her terribly.' Thus, I am also looking for her. I would like to tell her how her father loved her and how much he thought of her, there in Algeria.] Ighilahriz never expressed her gratitude to Richaud in part because she thought she would see him again and in part because she was still suspicious of his motives. And indeed, the paternal figure of Richaud complicates the image of the army's role by showing the complicity and also the disconnection between its different missions: protection and destruction, healing and wounding (and sometimes healing to better continue the torture). Ighilahriz's desire to express her gratitude to Commandant Richaud borders on obsession and it is presented as one of the main motivations behind her speaking out. Her previous attempts to find Richaud have been unsuccessful until she meets with Florence Beaugé through the latter's father-in-law. After Beaugé's article came out, General Massu, who knew Richaud well, informed Ighilahriz that he had passed away in 1997. A meeting between Richaud's daughter and Ighilahriz was subsequently arranged during *La Fête de l'Humanité*.

Algérienne begins with a short chapter entitled "With All My Gratitude," which is set in the cemetery where Commandant Richaud is buried. Told in the third person,[37] this passage recounts the train trip Ighilahriz and her sister, Ouardia, make to visit Richaud's (not so) final resting place in order to finally thank him. Anne Nivat describes the two women in exhausting detail, as would a ubiquitous narrator in the hope of touching the reader and making it possible for him or her to relate to her characters. This visit to the cemetery had taken place in September 2000, a month before Nivat's first meeting with Ighilahriz. One assumes Nivat may have watched the video or seen the pictures taken by Ouardia, and that she has in turn memorialized them. The passage presents Ighilahriz's trip to the cemetery as an intense catharsis: "After forty years, it's taken forty years for Louisette, the militant Algerian nationalist, to find her savior. She knew that in going to reminisce by his tomb, she would feel relieved of an enormous debt of recognition." (16-17) Ighilahriz symbolically pays her debt to her savior by inscribing a commemorative graffiti "With all my gratitude. . . Louisette" (15) with a black pen on his marble tombstone that reads simply: "*Francis Richaud: 1917-1997*" (14). The two sisters then decide to have a plaque made to honor Richaud's memory and to replace Ighilahriz's spontaneous memorial graffiti. On the following day, they find themselves in a store selling funeral articles in Créteil. There, they choose a little rectangle of gray brass on which they have the words inscribed: "Wherever you are, you will always be among us. Louisette." (16) It is adorned with a dove carrying an olive branch. Symbolically, the passage ends with Ouardia's trip back to the cemetery to lay down the brass plaque, without Ighilahriz who has gone back to Algeria. This scene plays the role of a *captatio benevolentiae* for the reader because it introduces Ighilahriz as a moving character in search of her savior, driven to tell her story by gratitude and not revenge.[38]

Alive, Richaud rescued Ighilahriz from her abusers. After his death and following Ighilahriz's visit to his grave, conjuring up Richaud's memory also helps Ighilahriz in her recollection of the events as she revisits her past abuse and struggles to find a way to re-present it. Richaud cared for her and compared her to his daughter whom, he says, is the same age as Louisette. As such, he considers himself and is considered as a surrogate protective father figure. Ouardia, Ighilahriz's sister, "considers him a relative and regrets not having met him" (15). The memory of Dr. Richaud has become a family memory for Ighilahriz's kinfolk. The formulation of Ighilahriz's quasi-filial quest in reassuring terms that draw from the vocabulary of the family and her insistence on Richaud as a paternal figure helped to make her claim and testimony less threatening and more easily palatable to the public. But there is more to it. Richaud is a metaphor for wholeness and for an elusive and never completed healing. He was the one who restored Ighilahriz to life and made her feel whole. He liberated her from her all-encompassing suffering body and his intervention broke her corporeal engulfment. Her gratitude toward Richaud, the good doctor, is a protective factor in many a way. First, looking for Richaud protects her somewhat from the potential attacks of those who might question her motives for speaking out about her torture so late after the fact. Her self-avowed aim is to express gratitude and not to get revenge or claim reparations or repayment. Then, invoking Richaud and her obsession to thank him forty years later works as a self-narrating and self-protective device, for it allows Ighilahriz to recount her torture and the fragmentation that it once inflicted upon her without losing herself again in its dissolving effects. It is less threatening for Ighilahriz herself to start her quest as a search forward for someone rather than as a journey deep into an agonizing and horrific past. Richaud, who once healed her body, is conjured up as a healing presence and principle that holds her together through the filial sentiment she feels for him, as she revisits the past in the hope of resolving the half-repressed and conflicted memories of torture. Finally, by expressing her feelings of gratitude, Ighilahriz asserts her human dignity and her trust in the world, which her torturers unsuccessfully attempted to crush.

By visiting Richaud in his final resting place and by having her picture taken by his grave, Ighilahriz also stages her own death: the very death she escaped thanks to Richaud's intervention, but also the death she is preparing herself for by finally daring to speak up and by making this trip before it is too late. In Richaud, she has lost the one person who brought her back to life and allowed her to be reborn. By paying him a visit now that he is dead, Ighilahriz brings him back to life. She brings back to life some of his actions that were unknown to his own daughters[39] and that his gravestone leaves unsaid. With this visit, Ighilahriz also hopes for a second rebirth. Richaud delivered her from her broken body by healing it and he may also allow her to mend her broken self since her gratitude for him is the one factor and principle that holds her together and justifies her testimony. In this respect Richaud is a key figure, the one that opens up the book, and for Ighilahriz he is also an intercessor with the past, with her own body and her suffering.

Richaud functions as a double of Ighilahriz's father. By comparing her to his daughter back home, Richaud puts himself in this position. By visiting his grave, Ighilahriz reclaims this filiation. Since he brought her back to life, she is Richaud's daughter, as much as her own father's. This double filiation has fascinating implications for what it means to be an *Algerian* (as the title of her book puts it).

This passage also invites us to consider the following notion: testimony as social graffiti. Ighilahriz's last-minute impulse to write her gratitude on Richaud's tombstone and to sign her name could well be illegal, even desecrating. It acts as an ephemeral form of enunciation that puts into question the inscriptions written on the gravestone, as well as time-honored and ritualized forms of remembrance and commemoration. Ighilahriz's graffiti, like her testimony, opposes the official version and the dominant representations of the war, represented by the cross of the Legion of Honor and by the plaques laid down on Richaud's grave by veterans' associations. These decorations and representations, like the gravestone, exorcise the past and traumatic events by commemorating them into silence and oblivion. Conversely, Ighilahriz's graffiti and testimony metaphorically reopen Richaud's grave by recalling his forgotten (and somewhat illegal) good deeds and by inscribing her own name on this official and petrified version of history. In the same vein, Ighilahriz's sister symbolically brings Richaud back to life and invites him to haunt the living by drinking "with him" the coffee she had brought for her sister and herself: "Ouardia tient à prendre un café 'avec le docteur Richaud,' et extirpe le Thermos de son cabas." (15) [Ouardia wants to have coffee 'with Doctor Richaud,' she roots around in her shopping bag and pulls out the Thermos.]

However, the two sisters are fully aware that they are themselves engaged in a personal commemoration. The cameras they brought, as well as their decision to have a plaque made to replace the initial graffiti, point to their own historical consciousness. The small metal plaque is their contribution to rewriting the history of the war and amending the official memory of Richaud. It also plays the role of a mini gravestone. After having conjured up Richaud's memory and his ghost, Ouardia performs a burial of sorts on behalf of her sister when she goes back to the cemetery to place the plaque there. Anne Nivat's narrative ensures that the initial graffiti becomes part of the new official version. However, Ighilahriz leaves it to her sister to attend to this burial, just as she lets other women write down her testimonies. She is not interested in commemoration and in burial but in bringing to life her near-death experience and by inviting ghosts to haunt us.

Locking and Unlocking the Memory of Rape

Ighilahriz entrusts other women with pieces of her testimony and with the task of inscribing it. It may be because, despite (or due to) her efforts to achieve a sense of closure, as the repetition of words like "relieved," or "liberated" indicates in her testimonies, her suffering is not yet past and the wound is still gaping. One may find some similarities between Ighilahriz's narrative devices and Assia Djebar's novel, *La Femme sans sépulture*. In Djebar's novel,[40] the life and death of Zoulikha, a nationalist tortured and killed by the French army, is retold through the many voices and songs of a choir of women, daughters, friends, neighbors, and female witnesses whose narratives are woven into a eulogizing and lyrical narrative. Similarly, Ighilahriz's story is told by female relatives or women she has befriended. In each case, victims of torture and their relatives enlist the help of others, listeners or writers, when they tell their story, to avoid having to face the horror alone again.

This is reflected in Ighilahriz's representations of her rape. Her testimonies about her rape form a complex text, characterized by inconsistencies, semi-truths, and partial statements. They give a conflicting and conflicted depiction of her painful experience, while making visible for us how such a trauma is locked and unlocked, repressed and expressed, and how it can only come out as fragments and only later reassembled as a cogent, presentable whole. Beaugé's article does not spell out the rape, since both Ighilahriz and the journalist have trouble finding the words to say it. However, by underlining her nakedness from the very start, it suggests what happened. We are made to suspect it. Later on during her intervention at the *Fête de l'Humanité*, Ighilahriz revealed publicly in front of a supportive and attentive crowd the fact that she was raped. However, in *Algérienne* (2001), she explains that Graziani "ne pouvait pas non plus me violer, j'étais trop dégueulasse! En revanche, il m'enfonçait toutes sortes d'accessoires dans le vagin." (113) ([Graziani] could not rape me either, I was too disgusting! However, he would stick all kinds of instruments in my vagina.) When Ighilahriz was reunited with her mother in the prison where Richaud had her transferred, according to her wishes, her mother admonished her against talking about her undescribed rape:

—Ma fille, ils t'ont violée! Les salauds, ils t'ont violée?!
Je l'ai immédiatement rassurée en lui affirmant que cela ne s'était pas produit. Elle en a été soulagée. En lui disant que je n'avais pas été violée je ne mentais pas, mais Maman a néanmoins compris le genre de sévices auxquels j'avais eu droit. Jusqu'à aujourd'hui elle n'en connaît pourtant pas le détail. Je tenais à minimiser les violences que j'avais subies.
—Bon, tu gardes tout pour toi, m'a-t-elle dit. Surtout, ne raconte rien à personne. Tu me promets? (128-129)

—My daughter, they raped you! These bastards raped you?!
I immediately reassured her that it hadn't happened. She was relieved. I was not lying when saying I hadn't been raped, but Mother understood nonetheless the type of abuses I got. To this day though, she does not know the details. I wanted to underplay the abuses I had undergone.
—Fine, keep everything to yourself. And most of all, don't say a word about it to anyone. Promised?

When Ighilahriz says that she was not lying to her mother when she said she was not raped, she seems to suggest that she was not raped by a penis (as distinct from the various objects used by Graziani). But during her oral testimony at the trial against General Schmitt in June 2003, Ighilahriz testified again that she was raped by Graziani with various objects and this time added that he also "raped me with his penis."[41] Ighilahriz's characterization of Graziani's penis as an instrument is a defense mechanism that allows her to once again disown and separate herself from her experience of violation, because it is still too difficult to face and admit that this is what happened to her. The sense of alienation that persists intertwined in an ultimate liberating statement is also a way of refusing the intimacy imposed by rape.

Ighilahriz's mother was still alive in 2000 when the debate broke out and when Ighilahriz's book came out in 2001. She died before the court hearing in June 2003 in which Ighilahriz accused Graziani of raping her with his penis. Soon after her court victory over Schmitt, Ighilahriz told the Algerian paper *Le Soir d'Algérie*: "Moi j'ai prêté serment à ma défunte mère pour prendre ma revanche sur ceux qui m'ont fait vivre ces atrocités."[42] [I swore to my late mother that I would get my revenge from those who put me through these atrocities.] As attested by Ighilahriz's written and oral declarations, her mother seems to have alternately locked and unlocked her testimony about her rape.

The rapes had dire consequences for Ighilahriz. Her pregnancies in 1963 and 1964 were the source of great psychological distress as she was under the impression that she would give birth to monsters. She had to terminate a third pregnancy because she slipped into a deep depression. Later on, when Ighilahriz had to choose a field as a student of psychology, she decided to work on female juvenile delinquency and prostitution partly because, while in French prisons, she had met a number of prostitutes, jailed with her at Les Beaumettes, la Roquette, and Fresnes.[43] Her research involved meeting and discussing with young women in difficult situations. To win their trust, Ighilahriz would disclose parts of her own experience. Because of political pressure, she never finished her thesis and was advised to stop working on this topic.[44]

Ighilahriz's reluctance to fully acknowledge her rape reflects her resistance and emotional turmoil faced with the perverse yet pervasive eroticization of torture performed by her torturers. Breaking cultural taboos and disturbing the borders between rape and consensual sexual intercourse[45] are integral parts of the victim's subjugating process destined to trigger self-censorship, repression, and silence, and hence further isolate the victim.[46] It is paradoxical, and yet not unusual, that the repression elicited by the torturers is reinforced by Ighilahriz's family,[47] by her former comrades,[48] and by the institutions and governments in place.

Years later, her testimony prompted some Algerian women who had been raped during the war by French soldiers to come out and publicly tell their stories, despite the taboo and stigma associated in Muslim culture with the loss of female virginity before marriage. But, as stated by Khaoula Taleb Ibrahimi, the majority of the *moudjahidate*, or former women nationalist combatants, remained silent,[49] a point previously made by Algerian historian Mahfoud Kaddache. In 2002, Kaddache had stressed that testimonies would remain individual instead of paving the way for collective recognition. This topic was still too painful in Algeria, and the women and men who both had been tortured and sexually abused would refuse to talk out of modesty and shame.[50]

Conclusion

General Schmitt was onto something when he picked out the inconsistencies in Ighilahriz's narrative and its lack of precision. It is in the nature of a traumatic event that it interrupts the apparent continuity and coherence of H/histories. It manifests itself as fragments and "irregularities" in narratives whose authenticity, reliability, and representativeness it puts into question. However, Schmitt willingly misinterprets as lies what is a manifestation of memory at work. Schmitt relied on inconsistencies on dates and colors, on small mistakes and memory lapses, to deny the validity of Ighilahriz's testimony. During the trial, two different definitions of memory work as well as two versions of historical truth conflicted with each other. On the one hand, the cohesion and self-coherence of a narrative were deemed to guarantee the veracity and the verifiability of any account of the past; on the other hand, forgetting, silences, and inconsistencies were understood as significant and inherent parts of the representation of the past. Ighilahriz is more interested in retelling her experiences and in sharing them than in recording, documenting, and commemorating them. So much so that her testimony during the 2003 trial competed with her previous testimonies as recorded by Anne Nivat and Florence Beaugé. The discordance and dissonance she created translate the fragmentation of her traumatic experience more clearly than any single reconstructed narrative.

Notes

1. Jean Améry, *At the Mind's Limits: Contemplations by a Survivor on Auschwitz and Its Realities*, trans. Jenseits von Schuld und Sühne (Bloomington and Indianapolis: Indiana University Press, 1980), 22-34.

2. Assia Djebar, *La Femme sans sépulture*, (Paris: Albin Michel), 31-32.

3. All translations from French into English are my own.

4. Florence Beaugé's first article in *Le Monde*, "Torturée par l'armée française en Algérie, Lila cherche l'homme qui l'a sauvée," 20 June 2000, refers to Louisette Ighilahriz as Lila, her *nom de guerre*, and thereafter as Louisette Ighilahriz. Some articles in *Le Monde* and *L'Humanité*, the newspapers responsible for bringing out her story, referred to her by her first name, Louisette. This familiar and friendly address demonstrates that Ighilahriz was able to touch numerous people who felt a personal connection to her story and showed their support that way. The use of her first name might also be read as the persistence of the paternalistic relationship produced by colonization; however, Ighilahriz herself helped foster that family pattern by the way she described Richaud, her savior, as a father figure.

5. Henry Rousso, "UTLS—Conférence du jeudi 21 mars 2002—Henry Rousso: La guerre d'Algérie dans la mémoire des Français," *Le Monde*, www.lemonde.fr/web/article/0,1-0@2-3328,36-267206,0.html (24 April 2003).

6. Antoine Garapon, *Des crimes qu'on ne peut ni punir ni pardonner: pour une justice internationale*, (Paris: Odile Jacob, 2002).

7. Garapon, *Des crimes*, 237.

8. Garapon, *Des crimes*, 164-170.

9. Florence Beaugé, "Je me suis résolu à la torture. . . . J'ai moi-même procédé à des exécutions sommaires. . . ," *Le Monde*, 23 November 2000.

10. Paul Aussaresses, *Services Spéciaux: Algérie 1955-1957* (Paris: Perrin, 2001).

11. Arnaud Grellier, "Le Général Aussaresses dans le box des accusées," *Diplomatie Judiciaire*, www.diplomatiejudiciaire.com/France/Aussaresses2.htm (29 Oct. 2003).

12. Cécile Plet and Pierres Yves Schneider, "La Torture à la Une: Quand *Le Monde* va tout va," *Tocsin: le journal en ligne des média*, 7 December 2000, www.tocsin.net/dossier/4_algerie/1/index.htm (14 Sept. 2002).

13. Florence Beaugé, "Torturée par l'armée française en Algérie, Lila recherche l'homme qui l'a sauvée," *Le Monde*, 20 June 2000.

14. Louisette Ighilahriz, *Algérienne*, récit recueilli par Anne Nivat, (Paris: Fayard/Calmann-Lévy, 2001). References to this work hereafter are cited as page numbers in the main body of this chapter.

15. Laurent Mouloud, "Torture—Schmitt après Aussaresses," *L'Humanité*, 25 June 2003.

16. Philippe Bernard, "Tortures en Algérie: Une ancienne combattante du FLN met en cause le général Maurice Schmitt," *Le Monde*, 15 June 2001, 40.

17. Alexandre Garcia, "Attaqué en diffamation, le général Schmitt met à mal le témoignage d'une femme torturée en Algérie," *Le Monde*, 6-7 July 2003, 9.

18. Susan Crane, "Writing the Individual Back into Collective Memory," *American Historical Review* (December 1997): 1372-1385; this quotation, 1381.

19. Henri Alleg, *La Question*, (Paris: Minuit, 1961).

20. A Ph.D candidate in Mathematics at the University of Algiers, and married father of three, Maurice Audin was an active member of the Algerian Communist Party. He was arrested, tortured, and killed on 21 June 1957. The Army alleged that he was killed as he was trying to escape; however his body was never recovered. Because he

was the first European to be killed under torture by the French army, his death provoked a public outcry. The circumstances of his death and the identity of his killer(s) were kept secret despite his widow's continuous efforts and questions to military and public officials. A "Comité Audin" was founded by intellectuals and chaired by historian and activist Pierre Vidal-Naquet to elucidate his death; this led to a trial, to no avail. The secret of Audin's death remains well kept by the surviving Army officials, Aussaresses included, despite his "revelations" (see also Florence Beaugé's fascinating interview with General Massu in *Le Monde* on the taboo that the Audin Affair still represents within the army: Jean Planchais and Florence Beaugé, "Jacques Massu le général repenti," *Le Monde*, 28 October 2002). In May 2004, Paris Mayor Bernard Delanoe and historian Pierre Vidal-Naquet dedicated a square to Maurice Audin at the instigation of elected communist municipal officials.

21. Paul Ricœur, *La Mémoire, l'histoire, l'oubli* (Seuil: Paris, 2000), 151.

22. Ricœur, *La Mémoire*, 584.

23. Raphaëlle Branche, *La Torture et l'armée pendant la guerre d'Algérie* (Paris: Gallimard, 2001), 423.

24. Elaine Scarry, *The Body in Pain*, (New York: Oxford University Press, 1985).

25. Scarry, *The Body*, 4.

26. Scarry, *The Body*, 56.

27. Roberta Culbertson, "Embodied Memory, Transcendence, and Telling: Recounting Trauma, Re-establishing the Self," *New Literary History* 26, no. 3 (1995): 169-195; this quotation, 171.

28. Culbertson, "Embodied Memory," 191.

29. In *Algérienne*, Ighilahriz describes the sacrifices her whole family went through and their unwavering support and commitment for the independence of Algeria. In one way or another, the whole family participated in the war, following the example set by the father. The book is dedicated in part to Ighilahriz's parents.

30. Josette Audin is Maurice Audin's widow. In September 2000, she attended the *Fête de l'Humanité*, a cultural, musical, and political event organized every year by the Communist Party newspaper *L'Humanité*. The following month she was among the twelve signatories of an appeal by prominent intellectuals published by *L'Humanité* calling for an official state apology for the crimes described by Ighilahriz.

31. Culbertson, "Embodied Memory," 174.

32. Culbertson, "Embodied Memory," 179.

33. Philippe Bernard, "Tortures en Algérie: Une ancienne combattante du FLN met en cause le général Maurice Schmitt; L'ancien chef d'état-major des armées entre 1987 et 1991 dénonce le témoignage d'une terroriste," *Le Monde*, 15 June 2001.

34. Culbertson, "Embodied Memory," 191.

35. Anne Nivat does not include any metatextual information regarding the nature and the extent of the work she did with her interviews and conversations with Ighilahriz. How much is mere transcription? How much is reworked? The cover only mentions that Anne Nivat has taken down and recorded Ighilahriz's story. Except from the beginning and the epilogue where she describes her relationship and her trips with Ighilahriz, the rest of the text is presented as an "unreconstructed" first-person narrative.

36. Florence Beaugé, "Torturée par l'armée française en Algérie, Lila recherche l'homme qui l'a sauvée," *Le Monde*, 20 June 2000.

37. The rest of Nivat's book is told in the first person, as if Ighilahriz was talking directly. The only exception is the epilogue in which Nivat and Ighilahriz revisit important places of Ighilahriz's story.

38. Ighilahriz declares: ". . . je vois la France non pas à travers Massu et Bigeard, comme on nous a souvent, nous les Algériens exhortés à le faire, mais à travers Richaud, le médecin plus que le militaire, un homme qui avait un profond respect du serment d'Hippocrate." [I do not see France through Massu and Bigeard as we Algerians were often exhorted to do, but through Richaud, the doctor more so than the soldier, a man who deeply respected the Hippocratic oath.] (Florence Beaugé, "J'obtiens la vérité par la justice, je ne demandais rien d'autre," *Le Monde*, 26 June 2000).

39. Philippe Bernard, "Le Témoignage de Ighilahriz rouvre le débat sur la torture en Algérie; *Le Monde* a retrouvé la famille du médecin français qui a sauvé la militante," *Le Monde*, 23 June 2000.

40. Djebar, *La Femme sans sépulture*.

41. Laurent Mouloud, "Torture et suffisance," *L'Humanité*, 7 July 2003.

42. "Torture en Algérie: Le général Schmitt condamné pour diffamation et soulagement pour la moudjahida plaignante," *Elkechfa* 14 October 2003, www.elkechfa.com/modules.php?name=News&file=article&sid=294 (20 Oct. 2003).

43. Florence Beaugé, "J'obtiens la justice par la vérité, je ne demandais rien d'autre," *Le Monde*, 26 June 2000.

44. Ighilahriz, *Algérienne*, 204-210.

45. See Françoise Sironi's book, *Bourreaux et victimes: Psychologie de la torture* (Paris: Odile Jacob, 1999), especially chapter III "Clinique de la destruction" (51-61) and chapter IV "L'Influence du tortionnaire" (63-77).

46. In *La Femme sans sépulture*, Zoulikha's last postmortem monologue courageously describes how, in her body and mind, torture and sexual pleasure start to get "gruesomely" blurred and confused (198). She also stresses that her exposed female dead body, a body that has born many children, is a subject of fear and unease for both the French soldiers and the young nationalist combatant who fought by her side. His decision to bury her according to Muslim rites, against her wish to remain without a grave, is motivated, as Zoulikha suggests, by his desire to hide her body and to lock it away (210-212).

47. See Khaoula Taleb Ibrahimi's article, "Les Algériennes et la guerre de libération nationale. L'émergence des femmes dans l'espace public et politique au cours de la guerre et l'après-guerre," in *La Guerre d'Algérie 1954-2004: La fin de l'amnésie*, eds. Mohammed Harbi and Benjamin Stora (Paris: Seuil, 2004), 197-225. In a footnote (225), the author mentions that Ighilahriz talked about her rape despite her son's reluctance. This is the only mention of Ighilahriz's son regarding the issue of censorship and no sources are provided.

48. In her autobiography, *Algérienne*, Ighilahriz explains that the Paradou Hydra, the barracks where she was tortured, were transformed into a villa for the well-off with a landscaped garden and a swimming pool. A government official she knew asked her to come and visit the place. "He was very proud that no traces of my martyrdom were

left. And then he added: 'Whatever you do, Louisette, if you ever meet my wife, never tell her that you were tortured here. . .'" (111).

49. Ibrahimi, "Les Algériennes et la guerre de libération nationale, 197-225; this quotation, 225.

50. Florence Beaugé, "Le Débat qui a eu lieu en France a passionné l'Algérie," *Le Monde*, 19 March 2002.

10

The Poetics of Memory in
Assia Djebar's *La Femme sans sépulture*
A Study in Paradoxes

Florence Martin

Djebar in Georgetown

IN A LECTURE DELIVERED AT GEORGETOWN UNIVERSITY in the fall of 2002, Assia Djebar described *La Femme sans sépulture* as a way to meet her pressing need to "écrire la mémoire des femmes ... en Algérie"[1] [write the memory of women ... in Algeria]. The French word "mémoire" is already steeped in semantic ambiguity,[2] and since then, my own silent questions have been: how can we conceptualize the singular "mémoire" of a plural entity (women) in Algeria—or, for that matter, anywhere else? And how can we write it? Djebar responds with new poetics of memory in *La Femme sans sépulture*, as she transcribes and directs, in the cinematographic sense of the term, a polyphony of remembering voices ("la mémoire des femmes") in order to (re)create the narrative of one woman in particular, Zoulikha, a heroine of the Algerian resistance, with nothing left to her name—not even a tomb. I wish to examine how Djebar's specific conjuring of anamnesis in this novel sheds light on the rest of her work, and further inscribes Djebar in an ancient literary and mythical tradition of women's memory poetics.

That day in Georgetown, Djebar delineated her poetics of memory as follows:

1. "The memory of women is subject to ellipses." And so is the narrator's. Djebar confessed to having "forgotten" Zoulikha, in spite of two important public recollections of her: Djebar's 1977 film, *The Nuba of the Women on Mount Chenoua* is dedicated to her—even if her narrative is

one of many, and covers only seven minutes out of the film's 115; Djebar also started writing a short story on her in 1981, "forgot" about it, and found the manuscript twenty years later in her attic. Hence, the narrative born after these two ellipses points to a delayed memory, a memory retrieved piece by piece from the oblivion of the authorities of Independent Algeria (busy erecting statues for the male heroes of the Algerian revolution, although willing to subsidize Djebar's film made for TV in the 1970s) as well as from the oblivion of the narrator Djebar (in her various incarnations: historian, novelist, journalist, friend).

2. The visible can be written whereas "le caché du désastre" [the hidden face of disaster] still needs to be urgently expressed. Djebar cited 11 September 2001 as a disaster whose visible face was amply described, but whose hidden, terrifying face resists words. To tell a story, one has to circle around the "hidden face of disaster," the impossible to show, the always/already secret or intimate: the obscene face of memory, the face one needs to temporarily repress before being able to face it.

3. Quoting the opening line of her second film, *La Zerda ou les chants de l'oubli* (1982): "Memory is a veiled woman's body." Here I am reminded of Dominique Fisher's study of Djebar's anamnesis as "a scriptural practice relying on the corporeal dimension of memory (both individual and collective)" which she links to the "constant conjuring of muted voices, and forbidden gazes."[3]

Another way of articulating these questions on memory is to ask: how can a narrator (a distracted narrator, liable to forget) write out that which is the (definitely) hidden side of Zoulikha's body? And, more urgently: how can she tell the tale after having filmed and aired seven minutes of it on Algerian TV? Djebar chooses to retell this memory-history in a framed narrative, on several levels: she retells the stories of Zoulikha's women friends (a literary re-make of the *Nuba*); she retells the memory of the women who preceded Zoulikha, and she ends up exploring the memory of story-telling women all the way back to mythical Shahrazad.[4]

Retelling the Story of Zoulikha

Telling Zoulikha's story a second time means listening to the silence surrounding it, heeding the voices of all the women who knew her, circling around the "hidden face of disaster" and recording the latter's refractions and most minute echoes. The narrator seems to favor the perspective of a documentary as she proceeds through a metonymic approach of memory-history: she lets the inner and outer voices of Zoulikha's past female entourage speak out. Hence, the narrator transcribes in French the thoughts of Mina, Zoulikha's youngest daughter:

> Ces souvenirs me sont une pelote de laine emmêlée dans la paume! Face à ces ombres, s'approcher à tâtons, ou faire détours, cercles, méandres et rosaces, pour enfin regarder la source noire, maculée de boue, de cris gelés, de pleurs non taris . . .[5]

> These memories are a ball of entangled yarn in the palm of my hand! In the face of these shadows, feeling one's way toward them, or fingering detours, circles, meanders, and rose windows, in order to eventually face the black, mud-stained source of frozen cries, of tears that have yet to dry . . .

Such a gradual approach to disentangle the knots of memory reminds us of the double dimension of Pierre Nora's *templum* of memory:[6] memory resides in a *locus* that is both closed and open to an infinity of possible meanings. In order to grasp a few of these meanings, "la quêteuse" (the inquirer) has to be willing to go off on tangents, to follow narrative tentacles, seemingly pushing away from the main body of the tale. For instance, the narrator weaves in the story of Mina's hurt love, which Mina confided to her. Why? Because framed narratives are the only possible points of entry through the thick walls of Zoulikha's *templum* into the site of memory—an imaginary one, since nothing remains of Zoulikha, not even a tomb on which to pay one's respect.

> Une histoire dans l'histoire, et ainsi de suite, se dit l'invitée. N'est-ce pas une stratégie inconsciente pour, au bout de la chaîne, nous retrouver, nous qui écoutons, qui voyons précisément le fil de la narration se nouer, puis se dénouer, se tourner et se retourner . . . n'est-ce pas pour, à la fin, nous découvrir . . . libérées? De quoi, sinon de l'ombre même du passé muet, immobile, une falaise au-dessus de notre tête . . . Une façon de ruser avec la mémoire . . . (129)

> A tale within the tale, and so on, the guest thought. Isn't this an unconscious strategy for us to, at the end of the line, find one another, we who are listening, we who are carefully watching the thread of the narrative tie itself in a knot, and untie itself, twist and untwist itself . . . isn't all of this, in the end, done for us to discover ourselves . . . liberated? From what, if not from the shadow of the motionless, mute past, a cliff over our heads. . . . A way to trick memory . . .

The first part of this quotation refers to a specific narrative mode: the story is framed in another one, even a widely diverging one, but both shed light on each other. The secondary narrative retells the primary one, while pretending to focus on a different matter altogether. Hence the main narrative, the story of Zoulikha, contains another one: the narrative of the remembering, the piecing together of Zoulikha's recalled story. Each secondary narrative thus reshapes a "member" of the body of the story, of body Zoulikha. Take Lla Lbia— or Dame Lionne—for instance: she is an enabling source of memory to (re)construct the story of Zoulikha. Lla Lbia holds a unique, privileged position as a trusted narrator because she was an adult when Zoulikha was alive, and her memory is therefore more "trustworthy" than Mina's for instance, and also because she used to be a corpse washer and a seer (she gave up predicting the future when her Muslim faith eventually convinced her that it was a sinful practice). In a formidable ironic reversal, this woman who, in the old days, could both tell the future *and* prepare dead bodies for their last resting place, is now the one who both reenacts the past she grieves and mourns the absence of the body. "Elle souffle, Lla Lbia: long halètement. Vingt ans plus tard, tout revit, le tranchant du temps, et la peine, et son impatience . . ." (36) [Lla Lbia gasps for air: a long panting. Twenty years later, everything is alive again: the blade of time, and the sorrow, and her impatience . . .] Yet retelling the memory no longer suffices: Mina and her "new friend," haunted by Dame Lionne's voice, feel the need to retell her story themselves. Why? Mina evokes the pleasure of childhood narratives: "je m'aperçois que le plaisir est plus grand d'écouter une histoire dont on sait pourtant tout à l'avance!" [I realize how much more pleasurable it is to listen to a story even if you know everything about it ahead of time!] Her friend thinks: "L'histoire, contée la première fois, c'est pour la curiosité, les autres fois, c'est pour . . . pour la délivrance !" (156) [The first telling is to satisfy curiosity; the following ones are . . . for relief!] Hence, retelling memory could also mean shedding its weight, laying down its burden of pain, purging it, dulling its "blade."

The narrator thus conducts a *nuba* of female narrative voices: each tells her story of Zoulikha in turn—one of the meanings of the Arabic term.[7] This polyphonic mode of narration differs from the narrative in the Derridian sense of the term: the narrative is enunciated at point X in space and time, and its various signifiers are differed in time (Zoulikha dies in 1958; her story is told on film in 1977; a skeleton of her narrative is written in 1981, before it is fully written out in a "novel with a documentary approach" in 2002), in space (Zoulikha dies near Cherchell—or Césarée; her story is first broadcast on Algerian television; it is published in book form in Paris); in languages (Zoulikha speaks French, Arabic, Berber; her friends and daughters express themselves in Arabic and Berber; Djebar writes in French); in audiences (Cherchell's inhabitants; the Algerian nation; the francophone readers of *La Femme sans sépulture*). In this maze of signifiers and signified, it is becoming more urgent to see not so much how the book is a remake of the film, but rather to whom the book speaks.

Retelling the Filmic Tale

The *Nuba of the Women of Mount Chenoua* was therefore one of the first Djebarian inscriptions of the plural memory of the women of Cherchell (a.k.a.
Césarée). Although the film director is preoccupied with retrieving the past
of women, she generally refrains from using the cinematographic narrative
technique of flashbacks (with one exception toward the end of the film) since
the narrator, Lila, is not recalling that period of time herself—she is an outsider, an empathetic one, but an outsider nonetheless. Instead of projecting a
fictitious visual rendition of the women's past, Djebar chooses to film a series
of interviews with women who narrate their revolution, and tell in their own
words, whether Berber or Arabic, how they and their mothers and sisters became *mudjahidat* (freedom fighters); how they, as women, fought and resisted against the French. The interviewer is a fictitious character, although reminiscent of Djebar herself: she returns to her country, has a Berber
grandmother who tells the oral history of the community, does not speak
Berber fluently, and needs translations, etc. Filmmaker Djebar intervenes in
the filmic narrative by splicing images from newsreels from the period,
adding sound effects (explosions and other war sounds), and by punctuating
the film with several recurring shots. One of them shows a solitary tree on
which teenager Chérifa is perched. At first, the shot has no immediate meaning, other than connoting a sense of waiting. Gradually, as the viewer learns
about the history of the young girl, and starts to grasp the various issues at
stake (the role of women freedom fighters in a patriarchal world; the way to
tell or not tell their stories; the various degrees to which each woman was able
to participate in the movement, depending on social and/or religious codes),
the shot starts to gather meaning. At some point, Chérifa, who has witnessed
her own brother's execution, will jump off the tree, where she has taken refuge
for two days away from the French, and run to her brother's corpse to perform the ritual of purification; at some point, then, she dives in and joins the
resistance. The vignette thus simultaneously illustrates both the sister's need
to honor the body of the departed, and the woman's need to participate in the
resistance to the occupier.

Similarly, the absence of Zoulikha's corpse, a visible blank in the film, a clear
void around which Djebar's camera at first—and later her pen—circles, makes
sense only gradually, almost unwillingly, against the grain of the women's
eager revelations of their own narratives of freedom-fighting.

In her film, Djebar already employs the same "re-membering" technique of
mise-en-abyme she uses in her book: she pieces together secondary narratives
in order to approach the main one. Hence, as narrator Lila searches for the
women's tales of their pasts, she starts digging through a larger past, and pays

a visit to the ancient mosaics of Césarée, thus fusing the recent past with the ancient one. Djebar starts to film the visible remains of the Roman history of Cherchell, and evokes it again in her book. In both, the air is "full" of the past, Djebar writes (88), whether full of something or of the absence of something. Zoulikha's body, robbed away from her daughters, is not the only absent embodiment of the past: what about the Greco-roman statues of the ancient town of Césarée now residing at the Louvre museum in Paris (88)? Fortunately for the narrator of *Une femme*, there remains a mosaic titled *Ulysses and the Sirens*, the latter half-women/half-birds:

> De longues pattes d'oiseaux prêts à s'envoler au-dessus de la mer—c'est une scène marine, elles sur le rivage, contemplant un grand vaisseau au centre de la scène, flottant au dessus des vagues. (106)

> The long legs of birds ready to take off above the sea—it is a seascape: the sirens are on the shore, watching a large ship at the center of the scene, floating above the waves.

And the narrator adds: "L'une des trois femmes-oiseaux a un corps à demi-effacé. Mais les couleurs, elles, persistent." (108-109) [One of the three bird-women's bodies is half-erased. But the colors endure.] The narrator provides an unexpected reading of the mosaic:

> Je me disais, en venant jusque-là: Elles vont s'envoler, c'est sûr, ces femmes de la ville: avec leur chant et leur légèreté! Or (et je m'attriste, tout haut) la torpeur, depuis 1962, s'est réinstallée, écrasante: on la sent dans les rues, dans les patios, mais pas là-haut, ni dans les montagnes, ni dans les collines où flotte comme une réserve désabusée des gens, une poussière de cendres en suspens, après le feu d'autrefois! . . . Une seule femme s'est vraiment envolée: et c'est ta mère, ô Mina, c'est Zoulikha! (109)

> On the way here, I was telling myself: these city women, I am sure, are going to take off. What with their songs and lightness! Yet (and I grow sad, aloud), since 1962, inertia has settled in again, and crushingly so: you can feel it on the streets, in the patios, but not up there, not in the mountains, nor on the hills where there hovers something akin to a disenchanted reserve emanating from the people, a dust of suspended ash after the fire of yore! . . . Only one woman has really flown away, O Mina: your mother, Zoulikha!

The retelling of Zoulikha's story now merges with the telling of a myth. And the myth in turn sheds light on the post-Zoulikha history. The *mise-en-abyme* technique deploys itself in the text, as it were, along dynamics of its own: the evocation of the past is framed by the representation of the myth, and the

myth by history in a forward and backward movement in time. The apathy
that has come back to haunt the town since Independence is the inertia of
women who have gone from freedom and fighting in the mountains to oppressive homes in the city, women who remain silent except in two spaces: the
kitchen (loud with womanly speak), and the historical sites of resistance—
Mount Chenoua, the famous "historical" site of resistance of 1871. The latter
constitutes a recurring, sacred date in Djebar's writing whose terms are never
elucidated: an almost fetishized point of anamnesis, both evoked and never
thoroughly articulated.

The film celebrates the insurrection through a specific memory of Lila's,
staged in its only flashback: suddenly we hear the resounding voice of her
grandmother tell the feats of her own grandmother and of Sidi Malek Shraoui
of the Berber Berkani tribe. Djebar is the great-granddaughter of Malek, and
intervenes directly (via the character of Lila) in the film narrative. Her intru-
sion highlights what Donadey has analyzed as the "palimpsestic" quality of
Djebar's text[8] that weaves together literature, history, and autobiography on
several levels: it highlights Djebar's own inherited memory as well as the
memory of the women before her, whose narratives have been hushed by the
French and the Algerian authorities.

> As the images of the 1871 insurrection unfold on the screen, the soundtrack is
> filled with whispers, emphasizing the creation of a muted but living counter his-
> tory, a subterranean memory, transmitted by the female ancestors. The film thus
> highlights the process of female transmission.[9]

The 1871 call for revolt is heard by the women of Mount Chenoua, and relayed and acted out in their *nuba* performed in the cave of the Dahra mountains. The grandmother explains to the child that the enemy killed Sidi
Malek, and then erased all traces of his corpse in order to make the tribe believe that he was a coward who had fled from the French army. But the tale-
telling grandmother never fell for the ruse. Hence it is in the wake of this
story of a nineteenth-century disappeared body that new whispering
women tell the story of Zoulikha's body, a body also taken and disposed of
by French occupants.

Finally, the female narrator in the film, Lila (or Layla, i.e., "night" in Arabic)
lights up the candles illuminating the historical cave where women can perform the 1871 *nuba*. She is the one who revives the Mount Chenoua women's
memory, triggers their performance of history. She reappears in the book as a
woman who is called alternatively "the guest," "the stranger," "the new friend,"
or "the inquirer," according to her relationship to this or that interlocutor (and
even according to the various stages of her relationship to the same interlocu-

tor). Here again, her role is to trigger the remembrance of Zoulikha among the latter's companions, daughters, neighbors, aunts. In both cases, she listens to women, and, in the film at least, invites them to look at themselves.

Fin des années 70 dans les villes d'Algérie, dans les salles obscures, c'était un public presque exclusivement masculin. Or, les femmes de tous âges, de tous niveaux regardaient en majorité la télévision. Ainsi "La Nouba des femmes du Mont Chenoua" fut une production de la télévision algérienne, originellement . . .

[Je voulais] que les femmes qui n'avaient pas le droit d'être regardées, puissent vraiment se regarder, elles. L'effet miroir est pratiquement impossible dans une société islamiste qui dissimule les femmes, et qui donc les aveugle, à elles-mêmes d'abord, hélas![10]

At the end of the 1970s, in Algerian cities, movie theaters were frequented by almost exclusively male audiences. At the same time most women of all ages, of all levels, would watch television. This is why "The Nuba of the Women of Mount Chenoua" was produced, originally, by Algerian television . . .

[I wanted] women who did not have the right to be looked at, to be able to really gaze at themselves. Mirror effects are practically impossible in a fundamentalist society that hides women, and therefore blinds them to first and foremost themselves, alas!

Hence, through her various retellings of Zoulikha's memory-narrative, Djebar reaches two distinct audiences: women in Algeria—and women of Cherchell in particular—and Djebar's francophone readers on either side of the Mediterranean. Here, Djebar succeeds where Benjamin Stora thinks historians have failed: for once, audiences on both sides of the sea have access to the same story. That very story, once articulated in specific ways for one or the other audience, becomes not a *lieu de mémoire* ["memory site"] but, rather, the fertile meeting ground for several memories: the memory of the Cherchell women and of the Algerian nation, then the memory of the Cherchell women and the French nation (the novel was published on the eve of the year of Algeria in France). Perhaps Djebar wanted to target, first and foremost, the women who have been the victims of French colonialism and then of independent patriarchal Algeria.[11] This is why, although the starting point of this retelling resembles a Foucauldian expedition in archeological memory focused on a particular character, its end point is multiple, diffuse, and resonates differently depending on who is listening. But that's not all. . . . Our novelist-cinematographer-historian explores the ultimate depth of the art of retelling, and *mise-en-abyme*: her novel is, in itself, an echo of a "tale" written by Djebar, itself a reimagining of Shahrazad's "Tale of the Three Apples" from *The Arabian Nights*.[12]

Retelling the Tale of the Three Apples/Retelling Shahrazad

In the 1990s, Djebar wrote a collection of short stories published under the title *Oran, Langue morte.*[13] One of them, "La Femme en morceaux,"[14] (The Woman Cut Up in Pieces) is a variation on Shahrazad's *Tale of the Three Apples*, featuring the protagonist as Atyka, a young teacher of French in 1994 Algiers, teaching some of *A Thousand and One Nights* in a French translation in her seventh-grade class.[15] The opening of the 1994 tale is an actual rewriting of the opening description in the old one, rendered in a quasi-filmic zoom technique. The detailed description ends on a close-up view of the cut-up body of a woman, lying under several layers (a white city woman's veil, a precious carpet from Kurdistan, a basket of woven palm leaves, a wooden chest) at the bottom of the Tigris river, a stone's throw away from the Caliph's palace in Baghdad. The discovery of the mutilated body constitutes the starting point of the original story. Shahrazad then goes against the grain of time (in flashback mode), and stages various voices (all of them male), in order to clear the mystery of the murder. We learn that the victim's husband, blinded with jealousy caused by an unfounded rumor, killed her. However, the investigation, replete with twists and turns, and told a-chronologically, frames several narratives (the Caliph and his Vizir discovering the coffer; the murderous widower's account; the story of the boastful slave; the Vizir's predicament) and has several narrating characters intervene each in turn. What remains unsolved in the investigation is why the corpse of the woman is carefully staged in such a gruesome way and surrounded with such luxurious accessories, and above all, who the woman is: we learn the husband's name, but the dead wife remains anonymous. Atyka, who is glossing over the tale, is not surprised: "comment prénommer un personnage qui se présente d'abord en morceaux?" [how can you name a character who is introduced in pieces?][16] In both instances, a woman narrator (Shahrazad in the first; Atyka in the second) tells a story of male protagonists, and frames their narratives. In Djebar's "La Femme en morceaux," while Atyka is wondering whether she will have enough time to go through all the possible levels of reading with her students, agents from the FIS (Front Islamique du Salut) (Islamic Salvation Front) also called "Fous de Dieu" (the madmen of God), barge into the classroom, kill and behead the woman who "apparently tells obscene stories to young people" (209). But the tale does not stop with the death of the narrating protagonist. Omar, one of her students, takes the narration over, and reports on listening to Atyka's head—set on the desk by her killer, dripping with blood on the desk—finish the tale, and conclude: "La nuit, c'est chacun de nos jours, mille et un jours, ici, chez nous, à . . ." [Night is all of our days, a thousand and one days, here, at home, in . . .][17]

Hence, the three intertextually linked tales open on the discovery of a woman who has been tortured and killed by one or several male agents. The starting point of the three tales resurrects the violence done to woman's body, to woman's memory. Djebar seems to focus on that violence which has attempted to erase the woman's body/memory (the narrative of the woman's execution, of her "disappearance") in order to activate the narrative of that memory, a narrative that can only be polyphonic (a single narrator may be unable to find the words for such ferocious cruelty). Hence, in the three cases, a *nuba* of various narrative voices is conveyed, and framed by a female main narrator, and then relayed by a narrative voice located outside the original narrative: a "stranger" in one case, Shahrazad in another, Omar in the last one. Perhaps the most striking retelling is the (re)writing of a dead woman's speech: in the Djebarian tales, the dead woman keeps on talking after her own physical death. Atyka keeps on talking to Omar; similarly, Zoulikha has four monologues in the book in which she addresses her daughter Mina. It is not the first time Djebar uses literature as "the language of the dead" in order to recall the dead from Hades, and give them their voices back. The act of writing then becomes a generous offering of a new "vital space" as Calle-Gruber wrote,[18] which Djebar constantly opens to her Algerian dead. The novel ends on: "L'image de Zoulikha certes, disparaît à demi de la mosaïque. Mais sa voix subsiste, en souffle vivace: elle n'est pas magie, mais vérité nue, d'un éclat aussi pur que tel ou tel marbre de déesse, ressorti des ruines, ou qui y reste enfoui." (220) [True, Zoulikha's image half disappears from the mosaic. But her voice endures in a vivid breath: it is not magic but naked truth, of a brightness as pure as this or that marmorean goddess, coming out of the ruins, or remaining buried in them.] Hence, the erasure of the womanly body, the nonlocus of her absent tomb, and the reiterated attempt to ruin the body-memory of woman, all of these violent attempts at annihilating woman, are for naught: her voice keeps on resonating.

It is on this idea of erasure that I wish to conclude. It seems to be playing a crucial role in Djebar's writing. She ceaselessly returns to it, when evoking the forgotten past, whether the latter be the Berber language she cannot speak, the name of a woman whose body was mutilated in the old city of Baghdad, the story of Zoulikha *in abstentia* of her body, or the forgetting of her story and multiple other stories.

Il y a deux sortes de perte: il y a la perte qui vous hante et la perte que vous oubliez, l'oubli de la perte. . . . Le terrible, c'est l'oubli de la perte. Vous avez oublié que vous n'avez pas. Donc, vous avez l'ombre de ce que vous avez perdu. C'est cette ombre-là que vous ramenez dans la chair de la langue.[19]

There are two types of losses: the loss that haunts you and the loss that you forget about, the forgetting of the loss. . . . The awful one is the forgetting of the loss. You have forgotten that you do not have. Hence, you have the shadow of what you have lost. It is this shadow that you bring back in the flesh of the language.

The sudden awareness of a framed forgetting (forgetting to have forgotten Zoulikha), while triggering the writing of the novel, also poses the question of memory in a totally new light. One erasure is not enough to condemn to oblivion, Djebar might be saying: it can be compensated, even reversed by the sounding of a voice. The really terrible sin would be to forget to heed voices. How, then, do we interpret the "half-erased" mosaics of Césarée? Should we see the negative imprint (in the photographic sense of the term) of another mode of inscription of memory? Assia Djebar tells of her lessons in Arabic in the following terms:

J'ai appris avec un roseau et de l'encre. On écrivait sur une planche et après on apprenait par cœur. Le maître tapait sur les doigts des récalcitrants—nous les filles, nous étions quand même un peu préservées—et ma mère faisait la fête quand j'avais appris une sourate. Et ce qui m'est resté de frappant, c'est qu'il fallait qu'on lave chacun sa planche et laver la planche, cela voulait dire qu'on avait tout dans la tête, donc qu'on pouvait l'effacer.[20]

I learned with a reed and some ink. We would write on a plank of wood and then learn by heart. The master would rap the knuckles of the stubborn ones—we girls were somewhat protected, however—and my mother would celebrate when I had learned a *sura*. What struck me and remained with me, is that we each had to clean our plank; and washing out the plank meant we had it all in our head, so we could erase it all.

Erasing written words, erasing the trace of what we now have "in memory," would then participate in an economy of recycling—perhaps even of preventing.[21] I am erasing because the inscription is henceforth useless to me. However, forgetting the gesture of erasure itself would condemn me to the loss of memory dynamics.

Hence a first paradox: in order to better listen to the voice of memory in me, I need to first erase its written trace. Yet, once I have heeded the voice of memory, I have to write it in a book—or a film (i.e., give it a permanent trace).

Second paradox: this vision of memory can appear solid from one angle and can be decomposed from another much like a prism of light, or like Zoulikha's or Djebar's mother's shimmering veils. This vision of memory that reverberates from one tale to the next, intertextual and polyphonic beyond the initial anamnesis, strikes me as the novel expression of an ancient Mediterranean invention. Remember Echo, the poor nymph, condemned, says Ovid, to the "briefest use of her voice," who mourns the indifference of Narcissus (a male voyeur of himself), and ends up gradually dissolving into a pile of rocks, then erasing herself completely from Narcissus's landscape, and reducing herself to voice. A voice. . . . A voice that carries from one rock to the next, the aural image of enduring memory, with no fixed memory site. And yet, the female voice of Echo still haunts us.

Last paradox—actually the one opening this essay: Djebar's forgetfulness. In her acceptance speech of the 2000 "Prix de la Paix," the author equates "le désir sauvage de ne pas oublier" [the wild desire to not forget] with "l'acier de la résistance" [the steel of resistance].[22] In short: to remember = to resist, that is, to resist the powers that be (French in the old days, FIS today). One could therefore read the silence between the *Nuba* and *La Femme sans sépulture* not as a sign of oblivion but as a sign of a time when the necessity of writing about Zoulikha is not crucial. However, as violence against people—and women in particular—swells in Algeria, the recall of Zoulikha becomes urgent. At this point, Djebar posits herself as a resister (her weapon is writing—and in French, to boot!). While she is clear on why and how she writes in French, she is busy placing herself in the line of women freedom fighters, and less clear on her silence (hence the myth of the distracted narrator). In the end, *La Femme sans sépulture* is as much about Zoulikha as about myth-making around Djebar, eager to claim her space in the ancestral tradition of resistance among story-telling Arab women: Shahrazad, Zoulikha, Atyka, and finally Assia.

Notes

1. Unpublished comments by Assia Djebar in a public lecture given at Georgetown University, Washington, D.C., on 26 September 2002, titled "Écrire la mémoire des femmes . . . en Algérie" (Writing the memory of women . . . in Algeria).

2. In its masculine singular form ("le mémoire"), it refers to a textual signified (an essay on what is remembered); in its masculine plural form ("les mémoires"), it refers to a written recollection, or confession, a revelation born out of autobiographical data, such as the Cardinal de Retz's own version of the Fronde, his take on a past history in which he was an actor; in its feminine singular form ("la mémoire"), it points to the ability to remember, to the remembered, and to the form of the remembered. Hence writing "la mémoire" encompasses the process of conjuring up individual narratives, the form they may take, and what, from the past, percolates through the text.

3. "L'anamnèse . . . définit une pratique scripturale qui prend appui sur la dimension corporelle de la mémoire (individuelle et collective) d'où les appels constants à la mobilité, à l'écoute des voix tues, et, aux regards interdits." Dominique Fisher, "L'Anamnèse, histoire ou littérature en état d'urgence," in *Expressions maghrébines* 2, no. 1 (Summer 2003): 113-123. All translations are mine unless otherwise noted.

4. Here I am using Sir Richard Burton's spelling of the famous narrator, as appeared in his canonical translation of the text (*The Arabian Nights: Tales from a Thousand and One Nights*, New York: The Modern Library, 2001).

5. Assia Djebar, *La Femme sans sépulture* (Paris: Albin Michel, 2002), 31-32. Henceforth cited by page references in the main body of this chapter.

6. "*Templum*: découpage dans l'indéterminé du profane—espace ou temps, espace et temps—d'un cercle à l'intérieur duquel tout compte, tout symbolise, tout signifie. En ce sens, le lieu de mémoire est un lieu double; un lieu d'excès clos sur lui-même, fermé sur son identité et ramassé sur son nom, mais constamment ouvert sur l'étendue de ses significations." [*Templum*: the cut out, in the indeterminable of the secular—its space or time, or its space and time—of a circle within which everything is important, symbolizes, signifies. In that sense, the place of memory is double; a place of excess closed unto itself, unto its identity and name, but always open to the expanse of its meanings.] Pierre Nora, *Les Lieux de mémoire*, tome 1, (Paris: Gallimard, 1997), 43.

7. نوبه (*nuba*) refers to an Andalusian musical form structured along specific movements (*touchiya*, instrumental overture; *m'ssadar*, lento with singing; *b'tayhi*, allegro; *darj*, lento; *khoulass*, finale), using specific rhythms, and involving musicians playing "in turn." Borrowed from the Arabic, the term *la nouba* in French means a feast, a party.

8. Anne Donadey, *Recasting Postcolonialism: Women Writing Between Worlds*, (Portsmouth, N.H.: Heinemann, 2001), 45-51.

9. Donadey, *Recasting Postcolonialism*, 55.

10. Kamal Salhi, "Assia Djebar Speaking: An Interview with Assia Djebar," *International Journal of Francophone Studies* 2, no. 3 (1999), 177.

11. See Touria Khannous, "The Subaltern Speaks: Assia Djebar's *La Nouba*," *Film Criticism* 26, no. 2 (Winter 2001-2002), 41-61.

12. Sir Richard F. Burton, trans., *The Arabian Nights: Tales from a Thousand and One Nights* (New York: The Modern Library, 2001), 124-131.

13. Assia Djebar, *Oran, Langue morte* (Arles: Actes Sud, 1997).

14. Assia Djebar, "La Femme en morceaux," in *Oran, Langue morte* (Arles: Actes Sud, 1997) 163-215.

15. This is not the first time Djebar refers to the classic text of the Middle Eastern tradition. She had opened up an intertextual relationship between her own text and *A Thousand and One Nights* in *Ombre Sultane* (Paris: Lattès, 1987) and *Vaste est la prison* (Paris: Albin Michel, 1995).

16. Djebar, "La Femme en morceaux," 209.

17. Djebar, "La Femme en morceaux," 213.

18. "Parler 'la langue des morts' n'est pas, ici, parti pris funèbre, tout au contraire. C'est exercer le pouvoir magique de la littérature qui est pouvoir de revenance et de survivance. C'est la chance de ne pas oublier l'oubli." [Speaking "the language of the dead" reflects no particular funeral bias, quite the opposite. It means exercising the magic power of literature: the power of return and survival; the opportunity to not forget oblivion.] Mireille Calle-Gruber, *Assia Djebar ou la résistance de l'écriture* (Paris: Maisonneuve et Larose, 2001), 256.

19. Lise Gauvin, "Territoires des langues. Assia Djebar," in *L'Écrivain francophone à la croisée des langues. Entretien,* ed. Lise Gauvin (Paris: Karthala, 1997), 17-34; this quotation, 30.

20. Gauvin, "Territoires des langues," 27.

21. In her most recent novel, Djebar describes the return of her protagonist Berkane to Algeria and his reminiscence of the same learning procedure this way: "Enfant, j'inscrivais les bribes du texte sacré même sur du papier de soie, sans savoir que cette calligraphie ne servait pas pour guérir mais pour bénir seulement et prévenir tout malheur!" [As a child, I used to write snippets of the sacred text even on tissue paper, not knowing that this calligraphy served not to heal but only to bless and ward off all misfortune!] *La Disparition de la langue française* (Paris: Albin Michel, 2003), 169.

22. Djebar, Assia. "Idiome de l'exil et langue de l'irréductibilité" (acceptance speech for the *Prix de la Paix* 2000, www.remue.net/cont/Djebar.DOC), 12.

11

A Literature without a Name
René-Nicolas Ehni's *Algérie roman*

Mireille Rosello

RENÉ-NICOLAS EHNI IS NOT AN ALGERIAN, nor a *pied-noir* (European settler), he was never a *fellagha* (Algerian insurgent) nor one of the French *porteurs de valises* (carriers of funds for the Algerian insurgents). He is not a *harki* (a Muslim soldier who sided with the French), or the son of Algerian immigrants. In other words, critics interested in the cultural memory of the Algerian war may easily overlook his recent *Algérie roman* simply because the author does not belong to the communities that we perceive as the main actors of the French-Algerian tragedy.[1] Who, then, is this prolific and multifaceted artist whose name does not belong to our postcolonial canon? The author of provocative novels and plays, his literary career started in the 1960s with *La Gloire du vaurien*[2] and has hardly slowed down until *Algérie roman*, a generically ambiguous text published in 2002 and that I propose to analyze in this chapter.[3] Ehni now resides in Crete, but in the 1970s his circle of friends included Jean-Paul Sartre and Simone de Beauvoir, Pier Pasolini and Elsa Morante. Ten years later, at the beginning of the Mitterrand years, he worked with Gisèle Halimi (another public figure whom we associate more closely with the Algerian war) during her campaign for the legislative elections.[4]

Ehni discovered Algeria as a soldier and *Algérie roman* is obviously inspired by his experience. The story speaks of traumatic memories and shocking inner conflicts. Although the author had a solid reputation as a dissident and a marginal, he was an *appelé* (draftee) rather than as a defaulter or an antiwar activist.[5] But his book does not read like the few autobiographies recently published by men who remember the months or years they spent in Algeria in the colonial army.[6] As one of the soldiers sent to uphold the law of the Republic at a time when its government claimed that no boundary existed between Dunkerque and Tamanrasset, Ehni did have a first-hand experience of what "pacification" meant. But he never insists that he was a credible, legitimate witness or that what he says is the truth. Instead, as the title of his book indicates, he focuses on what is constructed as a fiction. In spite of Ehni's metropolitan origin, his style has much in common with Jacques Derrida's or Hélène Cixous's dense and poetic texts about their Algerian experience.[7]

I suggest that *Algérie roman* ambitiously yet humbly proposes to experiment with a genre of fictive history, adding a new color to the palette available to writers seeking to remember the Algerian war. The novel does not make sensational revelations. Most of what Ehni talks about is already known. Factually, the book does not add much substance to the highly publicized stories told by unrepentant or remorseful generals such as Paul Aussaresses or Jacques Massu.[8] After years of denial, France has been paying attention to the memory of the Franco-Algerian conflict and since the end of the 1990s, it has been the object of increasing attention. Today, some cultural historians even suggest that the war explains much of what happened on the French intellectual scene during the second part of the twentieth century, including such supposedly hexagonal movements as poststructuralism.[9] In that context, Ehni's contribution is to think about the meaningfulness of textual testifying by drawing our attention to the ever-changing quality of what we call cultural memory.

To this often disparate and self-contradictory monument he adds a strikingly self-referential testimony that reflects on the genre of testimony and on the definition of collective memory. More specifically, *Algérie roman* looks for the tenuous links that might be woven between the traumatizing narrativization of one's guilt and the definition of hope and forgiveness. This "novel," as the title calls it, constantly reminds us that the story is made of words and that the author is an experienced storyteller.

Ehni's primary goal is not to add to the chorus of voices that have exposed the thick layers of euphemism hiding the reality of a full-blown war and the atrocities that were committed in Algeria. The book clearly starts from the premise that the case has already been made. Ehni does not need to demonstrate that violence reigned; instead, he asks whether his own story has a point, who are its addressees, and who may benefit from what he calls "le livre du crime"[10] (book of the crime). Remarkably, Ehni's narrator seems convinced that testimonies are not a useful narrative genre. His doubts are not, however, a version of the theories of memory according to which some degree of horror is unspeakable.[11] Typically, when such arguments are presented, the implied consequence is that testifying is impossible and yet all the more necessary if we at least want to make sure that the murderers, who wanted to cover their tracks, do not get away with their crime. In addition, the imperative to remember and testify seeks to protect us from future barbarity.

Instead, the first-person narrator of *Algérie roman* implies that the Algerian war renders his testimony both absolutely indispensable (he must tell, it is possible to tell) but also utterly useless (his story will not change anything nor can he hope to formulate even the beginning of a rational historical or personal explanation). The pain of living with the belief that testifying is both necessary and pointless is part of the narrator's traumatic syndrome. To make his point, he adopts very specific narrative techniques, three of which are spectacular textual performances that I propose to analyze in some detail. The first one is the textualization of an obsession, namely the representation, throughout the novel, of the same tragic encounter between the "I" and the (murdered) Algerian rebel. The constant retelling of the same episode is like the beating heart of the narrative. The second remarkable technique is used several times in the novel, but one of the most representative examples can be found in a self-contained passage in which the narrator superimposes a description of a photograph taken during the war onto the analysis of his own description of the picture. The story allows the narrator to show *how* his own testimony is constructed and it clearly exposes the limits of his endeavor. The third narrative experiment has to do with the invention of what the narrator calls a "paramyth," that is, a new type of historical storytelling activity that enables a new "I" to take responsibility for the past. The witness, who has come to terms with the fact that the past is both unforgivable and inexplicable, replaces himself with a voice that can imagine the preconditions of responsibility and meaningfulness.

The Fall of Aïssa-Jesus

At the beginning of this story, the worst has already occurred and the crime has been confessed. The episode that serves as the equivalent of a primal scene slowly emerges as if we were observing a pointillist painting. At first, the allusions to what happened are like disconnected dots but they progressively add up, until a horrific image slowly forms in front of the reader's eye. A ghost who haunts the narrator—a murdered *fellagha*—constantly interrupts the narrative by presenting himself from different angles and at different moments of his story. The narrator participated in his arrest and torture and in the end pushed him out of a helicopter. At the same time, in an almost impossible exercise of simultaneity, certain passages of the novel describe the relationship between the victim and the narrator as characterized by mutual respect, almost a friendship. On the very first page, we learn that the two men were "like friends."[12]

In his own eyes, the first-person narrator is even worse than a murderer. He admits not simply to having killed a man but to having committed the ultimate murder, a deicide. This orthodox and almost mystical Christian confesses that he is guilty of a crime for which there can be no statute of limitations. He killed his God, who came to him as a *fellagha*: "La rencontre avec mon Dieu eut donc lieu pendant cette terrible guerre appelée pacification"[13] [The encounter with my God took place during this horrible war called pacification]. When asked what his name is, the *fellagha* answers: "Aïssa! . . . Jésus comme vous dites!"[14] [Aïssa! . . . Jesus as you say!] *Algérie roman* does not describe the symbolic death of a brother nor the divorce between a couple of passionate lovers—two of the topoi that have haunted Franco-Magrebi literature.[15] In Ehni's book, we are not expected to view the prisoner as the victim of an act of war but as a divine figure who is sacrificed by the narrator. Before dying, Aïssa gives his torturer his sacred Book, the Koran: "Il fouilla dans sa poche et en sortit son saint livre Coran. Il me le donna après l'avoir vénéré. C'était si beau, entre nous aucun schisme. J'ai conservé le Coran comme on garde près de soi un corps angélique"[16] [He reached into his pocket and pulled out his Holy Koran. He gave it to me after venerating it. It was so beautiful, no schism between us. I kept the Koran as one keeps an angelic body close by]. The Koran-relic is the ultimate witness and legacy. The murder of the Arab as intimate friend is not an event among others,[17] a crime that human tribunals can judge. The act that symbolizes the war can only be ritually commemorated like a religious sacrifice.

Consequently, *Algérie roman* is neither about memory nor about the duty to remember. It is a quest for a sort of textual prayer that would allow the narrator to properly ask for forgiveness. Ehni wants to define the relationship between forgiveness and storytelling and looks for a specific literary genre, made necessary by the ways in which literature and history have dealt with the Algerian war. No legal system ever asked the young soldier to take responsibility for his actions. The novel is the only space where he can testify against himself and refuse the poisonous gift that the State imposed upon him: a blanket amnesty and systematic non-imputation. No relief or genuine pacifying ever occurred because memories got stuck in what the French call a "non-lieu," literally a non-place, a vacuum from which the judicial system withdrew. *Algérie roman* is not a confession to the extent that the narrator does not address someone who can press charges or absolve him but it is a quest for the type of narration that would performatively ask for forgiveness in the (definitive) absence of the man who could grant it: the man killed by the narrator.

> À qui peut-on demander pardon pour ses crimes, je vous le demande? . . . On demande pardon aux témoins. Ils sont morts. Ils ne sont plus de cette mort que nous appelons la vie. Mais ils croyaient dans l'au-delà. C'est donc à l'au-delà qu'on demande pardon, car ici que des masques, que des masques.[18]

I ask you, to whom do you ask forgiveness for your crimes? . . . To witnesses. They are dead. They are no longer of this death that we call life. But they believed in the afterlife. We must ask the afterlife to forgive, for down here, there are only masks, only masks.

The testimony does not have any addressee: "Si j'étais intelligent, je me jetterais dans le néant du vide (auquel je ne crois pas). Se tuer est la seule façon de dire l'Algérie. . . . Là est le seul devoir de tuer: se détruire. Autodestruction"[19] [If I were smart, I would throw myself into nothingness (I don't believe in it]. To kill oneself is the only way of talking about Algeria. . . . It is the only duty to kill: to kill oneself. Self-destruction).

Furthermore, it cannot be used to justify or even explain what happened. The narrator stages several possible explanations (which the reader will recognize as familiar arguments), quoting conversations between soldiers or dialogues that took place between witnesses after the war. He repeats comments that he overheard or read. Each attempt at rationalizing the soldiers' behavior is both proposed and immediately refuted as untenable. Each example is followed by a peremptory: "There is no explanation," repeated several times until the litany makes it clear that no exoneration can take place. One attempt at blaming the generals rather than the young soldiers is attributed to a so-called "ancien" (veteran). At first, it is presented as a plausible analysis of the situation, a version of the story that might partly absolve the narrator: "De ces jeunes citoyens sans expérience que nous étions, au lieu de nous éduquer comme des soldats de la République, ils ont fait des tortionnaires. Cela, je ne leur pardonnerai jamais. Nous n'étions au fond que des enfants malheureux"[20] (We were inexperienced young citizens and instead of training us as Republican soldiers, they turned us into torturers. I will never forgive them for that). But no sooner is the veteran quoted than the "I" immediately, quietly declares the hypothesis unacceptable. "Je n'accepte pas, bien entendu cette explication"[21] (Naturally, I do not accept that explanation).

The testimony, which neither explains nor justifies, which lacks a proper addressee, is a symptom of a malady of history that affects the meaning of words and the value of cultural memory. Even in the presence of the archive that is supposed to make the narrator remember, he can neither bring back complete memories nor erase them altogether. Both forgetting and remembering are impossible. When he tries to share the document with us, his own recollections remain hopelessly fragmented and incomplete.

The Rape of "Mother as a Child"

The narrator tells the story of a photograph taken during the war. He kept the picture that he must now transform into words for the reader. The narrative blends two elements: what is represented and what it means to testify from a photograph. The image that the narrator contemplates more than forty years after the war is all the more horrifying as it is a euphemism. It reminds him that even more paroxysmal excesses took place. At first, the narrator is in the position of the historian who studies a document in order to tell the truth. As Roland Barthes's terminology suggests, this posture of observation that he calls the "*studium*" has to do with studying, it is a studious approach linked to the calm pleasures of the intellect. But as the semiotician reminds us, the *studium* is often immediately interrupted by something in the photograph that interpolates us in spite of ourselves. The *studium* is then displaced by the "*punctum*," literally the arrow's point or more specifically the hole, the wound caused by the weapon. The *punctum* causes pain, it hurts and destabilizes the onlooker.[22] The *punctum* also points to another direction, inviting us to see what lies beyond the photograph, not what is unspeakable since the narrator is precisely about to put it into words, but what is even more poignant and frightening than the image:

> J'ai gardé une photo où l'on peut voir une toute petite fille, six ans à peine, s'avancer vers le photographe sous la menace du fusil de mon ami Guy, un alsaco du bled très indigénisé. Au dos de la photo: "Copain Guy et la petite fille qui ressemblait à Maman enfant." Ressemblait? Ressemblait? Est-ce que nous l'aurions tuée après l'avoir violée?[23]

> I kept a photograph of a very young little girl, she is barely six. She walks towards the photographer, she is held at gunpoint by my friend Guy, a fellow Alsacian gone very native. On the back of the photograph: "My buddy Guy and the little girl who looked like Mommy as a child." Looked like? Looked like? Did we kill her after raping her?

The passage reframes a familiar type of archive, the photograph of the Arab female, whose image is more or less stolen. It is a tradition whose political violence has been well documented.[24] Like his famous predecessors, Ehni knows that no archive is transparent and that even the document that historians look for as evidence may be disconnected from meaningfulness. The photograph cannot bear witness. It only demonstrates that it is impossible to tell the whole truth. Within the narrative written more than forty years after the photograph was taken, the *punctum* is not the image itself but another text, a bit of the caption written at the back of the picture. The narrator must look away from the little girl, averting his eyes in order to see what is literally behind the scene.

Even within the text, the words are less meaningful than the grammatical tense of the verb used to describe what was going on. Ehni focuses on the ominous past tense of "looked like," which reminds us that the little girl's youth belongs to the past. In the novel, in the absence of the narrator's explicit intervention, the past tense could have been read as the most self-evident choice since the whole story takes place in the past. But the narrator interrupts our reading by repeating the word and inserting a question mark that functions like a red light: "looked like?" We must now pay attention to the horror that the grammatical marker reveals and which the presence of the little girl on the picture masks. The photograph as archive is shrouded by allusions to what probably happened. Although what is represented is meant to testify to the crime, it is only a prelude to the worst that was, perhaps, yet to come: "Did we kill her . . . ?" For the reader, it is not clear whether the question mark refers only to the killing or to the raping or both. The ambiguous end of the sentence, "after raping her?" suggests that rapes were so systematic that the narrator thinks it may have happened not because he remembers, but because it is the type of action that you know took place regularly, as we "remember" taking the same itinerary every day.

Testifying to what would have been plausible forces us to envisage such acts as part of the soldiers' routine rather than as exceptions. Here, being a guardian of memory means alerting us to the fact that the worst is even beyond the archive. The narrator is directly implicated in the scene, up to the horrible "*my* mommy as a child" which puts him right at the center of the unbearable scene where a little girl is symbolically raped by her own son. He describes an insane combination of tenderness for one's own mother and of a type of violence that can annihilate the other as human being. The soldier makes the little girl disappear and replaces her with his own mother or rather, with a nostalgic image of his own mother at an age that she could only have when he did not exist either as body or consciousness. The strange return of that ghostly image robs the little girl of her identity. She is turned into a ghost too, losing all freedom of movement except that of accepting to take the pose that will lead to that abject metamorphosis. The powerless prey is ordered to take the place of the man's fantasized object of love and tenderness. The soldier suddenly says "my mommy" like those who are still kids themselves. He both regresses and forces his own mother to a sort of anachronistic disjuncture, back to a present from which he is absent and which he can only know through another photograph, another mediated portrait. He does take a picture of the war at the very moment when he pretends to turn his camera to another time and another place because this is the moment where he creates the "we" that the narrator will eventually denounce as systematically guilty of generic murder and rape: "Did we kill her after raping her?"[25] The tenderness for the "mommy" and the vulnerability conveyed by the phrase "maman-enfant" does not protect the child from the soldier's violence so that the reference to the filial love, far from inserting an element of peace into the gruesome encounter, contaminates the relationship between the soldier and his mother.

The reference to "my mommy" suggests that the "I" is guilty of violating and killing his own mother as well as the six-year-old girl that the war absurdly encodes as the dangerous enemy.

But the choice to describe this violence as incestuous and to bring together rape, murder, and filial tenderness is a deliberate narrative strategy because it can also be reversed. It becomes the ingredient of what Ehni calls a "paramyth," the unexpected beginning of a solution to his quest for a testimony that asks the dead for forgiveness. The "resemblance" that forces the narrator to invite his own mother into the circle of violence modifies the economy of the text and leads to a redefinition of genealogy and of cultural memory. The fact that children killed and raped other children who looked like their own mother gives the reader the impression that the war has created a mad family tree, a diseased genealogy. The narrativization of such imaginary filiations enables the narrator to talk about their madness without becoming mad himself.

The "Paramyth": The Son of the Grandfather's Killer

The most original element of this narrative is indeed the way in which the text slowly creates, in the reader's mind, a fusion between two types of cultural transmission that are normally treated as the two poles of a mutually exclusive binary pair: "filiation" and "affiliation." As defined by Edward Said, the terms describe the complex practices of migrants, orphans, and exiles who must reinterpret cultural memory.

> If a filial relationship was held together by natural bonds and natural forms of authority—involving obedience, fear, love, respect and instinctual conflict—the new affiliative relationship changes these bonds into what seem to be transpersonal forms—such as guild consciousness, consensus, collegiality, professional respect, class and the hegemony of a dominant culture. The filiative scheme belongs to the realms of nature and of "life," whereas affiliation belongs exclusively to culture and society.[26]

Ehni does not simply replace filiation with affiliation by proposing to adopt a sort of historical social contract that would replace one narrative with another. He suggests that catastrophic violence has turned words themselves into orphans. He must find a new type of story, and what he proposes is a narrative called a "paramyth." Unexpectedly, the suicidal narrator has become a father and when his son says "I," his self-portrait is the solution to the quest for a new genre. When "maman-enfant" is shown to be the victim of incestuous violence, every single relationship, including the father-son bond, is affected.

It is transformed into a horizontal relationship between two characters who say "I," one of whom is the other's child.

Here is how the novel starts:

C'était en Afrique, quand la patrie de papa était attaquée par les Arabes, et papa était soldat. Et voilà que papa et les Français attrapent un partisan arabe. Papa parle avec lui mais il ne lui permet pas de s'évader. Cet homme s'appelle Aïssa, ce qui veut dire Jésus. Ils se parlent et deviennent comme des amis. Aïssa fait cadeau à papa de l'Évangile des Ottomans. Et puis les Français et papa mettent Aïssa dans un hélicoptère, ils s'envolent et quand ils passent par la montagne ils poussent Aïssa hors de l'hélicoptère et Aïssa tombe sur un rocher. Il est mort. Aïssa c'est mon grand-père, le papa de Myriam ma maman. Comme papa il était allé à l'école en France où il avait pris pour femme une Polonaise, ma grand-mère Catherine. Grand-maman attendait maman quand grand-papa Aïssa est mort. Papa a fini par retrouver maman et, plus tard, papa a demandé à maman d'être sa femme. Je suis né et aussi ma sœur Makrine et ma sœur Catherine.[27]

It happened in Africa when Dad's country was attacked by Arabs and Dad was a soldier. And Dad and the French catch an Arab rebel. Dad talks to him but he does not let him escape. The man's name is Aïssa, which means Jesus. They talk and become like friends. Aïssa gives Dad the Ottomans' Testament. Then the French and Dad put Aïssa into a helicopter, they take off and when they are above the mountain, they push Aïssa out of the helicopter and Aïssa falls on a rock. He is dead. Aïssa is my grandfather, the father of my Mommy Myriam. Like Dad, he went to school in France and he married a Polish woman, my grandmother Catherine. Grandma was expecting Mommy when granddad Aïssa died. Dad found Mommy eventually and later, Dad asked her to marry him. I was born and also my sister Makrine and my sister Catherine.

In this "paramyth" as the narrator calls it, the child is the almost unimaginable nodal point where the victim and the torturer are one. But the imaginary construction of this figure where the victim and his murderer coexist is not a metaphor of the healing power of time that erases rather than builds. The novel does not claim that the years that separated the narrator from his acts have led to a beneficial alchemy of conciliation nor is the point that both people were equally cruel to each other and that violence, somehow, is cancelled out. Long and painful work was necessary to finally reach a delicate point at which forgiveness starts becoming possible although it must not "être trop vite assigné à quelqu'un qui en serait le sujet absolu"[28] (be attributed too hastily to an absolute subject). As Ricœur puts it then, in *Algérie roman*, "there is forgiveness."[29] No subject grants or asks for forgiveness. Instead, its existence is imagined through the (literary) invention of the "I-child-father."

Certain types of historical myths use the past to justify the present. Louis Bertrand's Algerianist novels wished to emphasize the Latin elements in Algeria's identity in order to legitimize the colonial regime. Instead, Ehni's opening "paramyth" views the past as a pathological family tree, with no clear legitimate genealogy. His goal is to look toward the future, to make it possible in spite, and not thanks to, the past that he wishes neither to forget nor to pardon. Ehni does not simply replace filiation with affiliation. Instead, he starts his book with a myth of continuity and rebirth that invents a sort of a-filiation: the filiation crisis leads to the rethinking of the difference but also points of intersection between filiation and affiliation. Through an unexpected and revolutionary reinvention of filiation (the presence of a textual son and new narrative voice), he imagines the possibility of an a-filiative genealogical network that fuses both principles.

Thus, the first pages of this autobiographical book introduce us to a first-person narrator who is not the same as the "I" who will tell us about his Algerian war. This former is directly connected to the latter who literally but also metaphorically engenders him. The character of the son apparently demonstrates that the principle of filiation has replaced the death drive of a narrator who thinks that his testimony is useless. Instead of yielding to the temptation of self-destruction that haunts survivors, the "I" becomes a father, and his son says "I," testifying to the possibility of survival.

Before the beginning of the father's confession, we know that the son knows everything. And the tone of his childish narrative suggests that he accepts, as the norm, a genealogy that could be described as completely pathological. His affiliation is to a type of filiation that the testimony recognizes as abominable. But the son is not mad. His story is sane and the character does not suffer from the father's traumatic syndrome. The author seems to test the hypothesis that a healthy text can talk about a mad history. In the scene, the (real or imaginary) son's storytelling activity is therapeutic for the grown-ups. The paramyth carefully adopts all the characteristics of a child's language, with its references to "mommy" and "daddy," its short sentences and sometimes borderline syntax ("Je suis né et aussi ma sœur"), the predominance of a technically impossible present tense ("Aïssa c'est mon grand-père"), the absence of subordination that seems to abolish causality at the very moment when the story talks about obviously and horrifyingly related stages of the same event ("Aïssa tombe sur un rocher. Il est mort"). In the child's "paramyth," the horror of a moment that the rest of the narrative always describes as an unforgivable and irreparable moment is transformed into a perfectly logical genealogy, a normal world where torturers and victims are now the members of the same family, ancestors to be loved and respected, moms and dads, grandmothers and grandfathers of the same little boys.

The ultimate point of fusion and confusion between all the stories is reached later on at the end of the "maman-enfant" episode. The passage where the narrator presents us with the picture of a child who was probably raped and killed by his patrol ends with a note that reuses the problematic notion "resemblance" to confirm the attempt at creating a revolutionary pattern of a-filiation. Resemblance, here, can be redefined as the gaze that agrees to recognize the other as the same, as a member of one's own tribe or even family. The narrator provides closure to the unbearable episode when he points out that the little girl of his memories looks like another "mother," the woman who since then became the mother of his own son but who is also Aïssa's granddaughter and his own wife. In *Algérie roman*, Myriam is another "maman-enfant" who plays a different role in this story: "je signale que j'ai montré la photo à mon épouse Myriam qui, lorsque je la retrouvai, avait l'âge de cette petite fille et lui ressemblait comme deux gouttes d'eau"[30] [let me mention that I showed this photograph to my spouse, Myriam, who, when I found her, had the same age as the little girl and looked exactly like her]. Like Fanon, Ehni knows that violence affects both victim and torturer but he can envisage the future of this shared cataclysm with a degree of lyrical and cautious optimism.[31] A-filiation is an atypical mixture of filiation and affiliation. It goes against the grain of solutions that privilege a principle of separation between two people, two nations, and also between culprits and innocents. Whereas state amnesty forever locks the victims in their position of helpless sufferers, and even an efficient intervention of human justice creates more differences and sometimes physical boundaries when it sends the torturers to prison, a-filiation favors chaotic fusion. It weaves the fabric of a myth capable of giving an identity and a place to this tragic yet sane "I" who knows that he is the son of his grandfather's murderer, and also the killer of (his) mother as child. The son is not the brain child but the physical and textual emanation of the union between myth and memory: "je veux pénétrer la mémoire, la connaître tel Zeus qui s'unit à elle pendant neuf nuits, en eut neuf filles."[32] [I want to penetrate memory, know it like Zeus who was with her for nine nights and had nine daughters with her].

The strange carnal and mythical relationship with memory is the solution to the "malady," that pathological type of memory caused by the incestuous and violent relationship between the *métropole* and its empires. The disease prevents him from turning his memories into a narrative that could be read as a meaningful testimony. Like an incurable and chronic infection, it never disappears and is transmitted to the next generation; but the difference is that the son does not develop symptoms of madness. The son is a healthy carrier of diseased past. Engendering the child could have been the creation of a monster and of a monstrous family. Instead, this is a one-generation solution to the father's unsolvable problem. The text believes in at least one form of continuity that is also a beneficent fracture: the father's testimony coincides with the staging of a new "I," which he literally and literarily created, without erasing a past of suffering and violence but without transmitting it as a burden.

In this carefully and precariously maintained distinction between violence inherited as a compulsion to perpetuate fury and insanity, and violence inherited as a paramyth of which our existence is a living testimony, flickers the glimmer of hope that we may be snuffing out if we insist that the Algerian war remains a unique, irrevocable, and still secret matrix of the end of the twentieth century. For Ehni's narrator, the "maman-enfant" is not killed twice because the second generation is not mad. The narrator does not marry Myriam in order to redeem himself or to reconcile two camps. Instead, his couple confirms something that already existed, the fact that two people, two generations, and two nations had always been inextricably intertwined. The promiscuous and almost incestuous imbrications are both the poison and the remedy. Not only was a child born of that union, but he is the subject of his own history. Both his body and mind are sane, and the past holds no secrets.

Notes

1. René-Nicolas Ehni, *Algérie roman* (Paris: Denoël, 2002).

2. René-Nicolas Ehni, *La Gloire du vaurien* (Paris: Julliard, 1964; Christian Bourgois, 1964; 2000).

3. See the texts cited in the reference lists and the bibliography provided at the end of Eric Dussert's review of Ehni's *Pintades* (Paris: Christian Bourgois, 1974; 2000): Eric Dussert, "*Pintades* de René-Nicolas Ehni," *Le Matricule des Anges* 30, March-May 2000, www.lelibraire.com/din/tit.php?Id=7115 (16 May 2004).

4. Gisèle Halimi, *Une embellie perdue* (Paris: Gallimard, 1995), 204.

5. Ehni tells the story of a man whose political convictions about imperialism were confirmed rather than modified by the war. About the French who actively helped the NLF, see Hervé Hamon and Patrick Rotman, *Les Porteurs de valises* (Paris: Albin Michel, 1979).

6. Pierre Olaïzola, *Algérie! Nous aurions dû tant nous aimer* (Anglet: Sauve Terre, 2002) and Henri Pouillot, *La Villa Susini: Tortures en Algérie, un appelé parle, juin 1961-mars 1962*, (Paris: Térésias, 2000).

7. Jacques Derrida, *Le Monolinguisme de l'autre* (Paris: Galilée, 1996); Hélène Cixous, *OR—Les Lettres de mon père* (Paris: Éditions des femmes, 1997); *Les Rêveries de la femme sauvage* (Paris: Galilée, 2000); and "Pieds nus," in *Une enfance algérienne*, ed. Leïla Sebbar (Paris: Gallimard, 1997), 53-63.

8. The year *Algérie roman* came out, Massu died after publicly disagreeing with Aussaresses (Paul Aussaresses, *Services spéciaux, Algérie 1955-1957* [Paris: Perrin, 2001]), although some believed that his "belated regrets" were too little too late (see

Olfa Lamloum, "La Mort de Massu vue par la presse algérienne," *Le Monde*, 13 October 2002, www.lemonde.fr (16 May 2004). See Jacques Massu's earlier *La Vraie Bataille d'Alger* (Paris: Plon, 1971) and Pierre Vidal-Naquet's response in *La Torture dans la République* (Paris: Minuit, 1972 and 1998).

9. Robert Young, *Postcolonialism: An Historical Introduction* (London: Blackwell, 2001).

10. Ehni, *Algérie*, 34.

11. These theories have been most convincingly developed by Holocaust studies specialists. These theses serve as an indirect point of reference when Ehni alludes to the Second World War throughout his novel. See Giorgio Agamben, *Remnants of Auschwitz: The Witness and the Archive*, trans. Daniel Heller-Roazen (New York: Zone Books, 1999) and George Didi-Huberman, *Mémoire des camps, photographies des camps de concentration et d'extermination* (Paris: Narval, 2001).

12. Ehni, *Algérie*, 9.

13. Ehni, *Algérie*, 155.

14. Ehni, *Algérie*, 155.

15. See Mouloud Feraoun, *Journal 1955-1962* (Paris: Seuil, 1962) and Jules Roy, *Étranger pour mes frères* (Paris: Stock, 1982).

16. Ehni, *Algérie*, 156.

17. So diametrically opposite to what happens in Albert Camus' *L'Étranger* (Paris: Gallimard, 1957) that one wonders if the counterpoint is intentional.

18. Ehni, *Algérie*, 36.

19. Ehni, *Algérie*, 72.

20. Ehni, *Algérie*, 69.

21. Ehni, *Algérie*, 72.

22. Roland Barthes, *La Chambre claire* (Paris: Gallimard, 1980), 69.

23. Ehni, *Algérie*, 35.

24. See Malek Alloula, *The Colonial Harem*, trans. Myrna Godzich and Wald Godzich (Minneapolis: University of Minnesota Press, 1986); Assia Djebar, *Femmes d'Alger dans leur appartement* (Paris: Albin Michel, 2002), 223-230; Jean-Michel Belorgey and Leïla Sebbar, *Femmes d'Afrique du Nord* (Paris: Bleu autour, 2002).

25. Ehni, *Algérie*, 35.

26. Edward Said, *The World, the Text, and the Critic* (Cambridge: Harvard University Press, 1983), 20.

27. Ehni, *Algérie*, 9.

28. Paul Ricœur, *La Mémoire, l'histoire, l'oubli* (Paris: Seuil, 2000), 604.

29. Ricœur, *Mémoire*, 604.

30. Ehni, *Algérie*, 35.

31. Frantz Fanon, *Les Damnés de la terre* (Paris: Maspero, 1962).

32. Ehni, *Algérie*, 129.

III

POSTCOLONIAL MIGRATION

12

Decolonizing the Past

Re-visions of History and Memory and the Evolution of a (Post)Colonial Heritage

Dayna Oscherwitz

IT HAS BECOME WIDELY ACCEPTED IN RECENT YEARS that France has found itself in the midst of a debate about what it means to be French. It is also well established that this debate, which centers on questions of immigration and "integration," is the result of a transformation of the French population by the (post)colonial immigration that helped to rebuild and reshape France during the latter part of the twentieth century.[1] Often, these debates have been understood as an ideological and political conflict between two opposing conceptions of Frenchness—a traditionally "Republican" (I would argue nationalist) vision of national identity that considers Frenchness a cultural identity belonging to those with historical ties and a shared sense of history and memory, and a multicultural vision that considers Frenchness a post-national, civic identity that coexists seamlessly with any number of cultural identities.[2] These conceptions have corresponding political positions, namely, an assimilitationist model of citizenship that requires immigrants to erase all differences between themselves and the dominant population and a multiculturalist model that refuses assimilation. While in many respects the characterization of these positions is accurate, I would call into question the classification of these conceptions of national identity as oppositional in nature. I would further challenge the assumption that the multicultural model of citizenship is a postnational model. Rather, it seems in many ways to be a national model, and in that regard, to accept many of the basic principles of the Republican model (most notably an insistence on the importance of the collective past and of collective memory). Moreover, I would suggest that where the two models actually differ is in what they consider to be the content of that collective past and of that collective memory. Where the nationalist model regards French national identity as essentially fixed and stable, and the content of national memory, therefore, established and closed, the multicultural model offers a more open and evolving vision of both the collective past and collective memory. Yet, the multicultural model is less a revision of the nationalist model than it is a reconception of the national past and therefore of the memory of that past. That is to say, the multicultural model sees national identity as still in process and the past, therefore, as still being constructed, whereas the nationalist model sees both as a fait accompli.

Collective Memory and National Identity Politics in France

Memory has a privileged place in the nationalist conception of French identity, primarily because integration as it is presently conceived presupposes the existence of a certain set of collective memories that the integrating subject is supposed to assume. Nowhere is the linking of collective memory and national identity more evident than in the landmark historical work, *Les Lieux de mémoire* (*Realms of Memory*), which seeks to document and classify the precise content of French national memory. Pierre Nora, who edited the work, drew attention to the place of memory in debates about identity in his introduction to the text, in which he posits a fundamental connection between memory and nation.[3] The nature of this connection is explored in Nora's essay "Entre histoire et mémoire" (Between History and Memory), included in *Les Lieux de mémoire*. In this essay, Nora asserts that there exists between history, memory, and nation "une circulation naturelle, une complémentarité circulaire, une symbiose à tous les niveaux"[4] [a natural circulation, a complementary circularity, a symbiosis at every level]. What is more, Nora follows this assertion with the claim that French national memory is disappearing; thus it is clear that Nora considers Frenchness itself to be disappearing.[5] David A. Bell has remarked that Nora attributes the loss of collective memory in France to the weakening of the French state and of those institutions—school, Church, family—that are seen to be the transmitters of both collective identity and collective memory.[6] In this regard, Nora's insistence on the breakdown of memory may be understood as one version of the widely held and often repeated idea that French culture is breaking down and that the French, therefore, are losing their identity. While Nora does not explicitly make the connection between collective memory and collective identity, and while he makes no direct reference to previous iterations of the idea of the breakdown of *francité* in his essay, a connection may be seen to exist between his affirmation of the breakdown of memory and, for example, the question "Will we still be French in thirty years?" posed by *Le Figaro Magazine* in 1985.[7]

To some extent both the October 1985 edition of *Le Figaro Magazine* and the entire text of *Les Lieux de mémoire* are informed by a general preoccupation with French identity in general and cultural memory in particular that might be traced as far back as François Mitterrand and his *grands travaux*. Mitterrand, like Nora after him, feared the decline of France and the French and sought, through these monuments to French culture, to restore France to what he saw as its proper place. One might argue that these monuments were Mitterrand's attempts to counter a loss of cultural cohesion on the part of the French, and particularly a loss of the sense of a common past.[8]

It is not insignificant that the preoccupation with memory and collective identity emerged in the early 1980s, at precisely the same moment as a parallel preoccupation with "immigration"—or more precisely, with demographic changes in France's population—brought about by (post)colonial immigration.[9] In fact, the focus on memory that emerged in the 1980s might be read as a retreat into the national past in an effort to bind national identity to heritage and to render *francité* a mental space that could not be overwritten by the changes of the present at precisely a moment when that present seemed uncertain. Moreover, the double emergence of anti-immigrant sentiment and nostalgia can also be directly tied to the rise of the assimilationist model of national identity, to which both are related, since, as Maxim Silverman has noted, it was precisely during the early 1980s that "citizenship was merged with the idea of cultural conformity."[10]

The linking of memory and *francité* constitutes in many ways a double "retour en arrière" (return to the past) in that the theoretical conception of national identity current in contemporary France bears a strong resemblance to nineteenth-century conceptions of *francité*. In fact, the first use of the word "nationalité" in French dates to the nineteenth century, and appeared for the first time in Mme de Staël's *Corinne* (1807). According to Gérard Noiriel, there then developed two strains of the national idea—a purely ethnic conception of nationality, in which being French is the result of a direct blood connection to mythical ancestors, and a more cultural conception, which views nationality as the product of a common history.[11] The dominant view of identity that ultimately emerged was based on common history and cultural distinction, and in both of these domains, memory plays a central role. Two of the most important figures in the formation of this version of French national identity were the historians Jules Michelet and Ernest Renan. Their writings on the nation (such as Michelet's *Le Peuple* [*The People*] and Renan's

"Qu'est-ce qu'une nation?" [What is a Nation?]) present the French as a blended people united by several hundred years of a common history, and both emphasize the necessity of a common remembering (and in the case of Renan, a common forgetting) of certain moments of the past. This insistence on the need for a common history and a common memory is evident elsewhere in the nineteenth century, particularly in the doctrine of the *mission civilisatrice* (civilizing mission), which was used to justify and define France's role as a colonial power. According to this doctrine, France, the bearer of a "superior" civilization, had the right and obligation to transmit this culture to those in other regions of the world, and so to "elevate" those peoples to the same level as the French. There is, moreover, a strong resemblance between the doctrine of the *mission civilisatrice* and current assimilationist models of national identity in France. First and foremost, both doctrines are rooted in a belief in the existence of a unified French culture or civilization, and both take for granted the superiority of that culture. What is more, both doctrines see this culture as transmissible. In fact the institutions and doctrines that were developed as forms of cultural intervention in the colonies led directly to Third Republic ideas about the existence of a unified French culture as well as to the creation of the institutions charged with transmitting that culture.[12] And these ideas and institutions are in turn closely linked to the current doctrine of assimilation.[13]

Cultural Memory and the Heritage Wave

A neo-nineteenth-century vision of *francité*, then, is recognizable in contemporary French political and cultural discourse. This same vision is also central to the heritage wave in literature and cinema that emerged in France in the 1980s. The term "heritage" has been applied primarily to cinema, and it describes films of various types—costume dramas, biopics, remakes, and literary adaptations.[14] Apart from a traditional, linear narrative structure, what unites such films is their tendency to center around what have been termed "heritage properties" such as culturally prestigious literary texts, historically significant buildings, or culturally resonant landscapes and interiors, and their tendency to generate heritage space rather than narrative space.[15] In the French context, in particular, Phil Powrie has remarked a tendency among such films to nostalgically recreate certain historical periods—among them, the Revolution and the Third Republic—to depend on high production values, and to privilege the past over the present.[16] Andrew Higson has argued that despite the various forms heritage films take, the function of heritage films is identical:

By turning their backs on the industrialized chaotic present, these films nostalgically . . . offer apparently more settled and visually splendid manifestations of an essentially pastoral national identity and authentic culture.[17]

Moreover, as Guy Austin has suggested, many heritage films involve "the artful and spectacular production of an elite, conservative vision of the national past" and function as "intimate epics of national identity played out in a historical context."[18] Films by French filmmakers such as Claude Berri, Bernard Tavernier, Jean-Paul Rappeneau, Patrice Leconte, and Régis Wargnier, among others, may be numbered among French heritage films. Such films posit a direct connection to the French past and a common memory of French historical experience as defining characteristics of *francité*, and in this respect they heighten what Susan Hayward has argued is French cinema's constant engagement with and participation in the construction of national identity. Hayward notes specifically that French national cinema is always "simultaneously constructing a historicity of the nation in that it is reconstructing myths already mobilized by the nation."[19] Moreover, she notes that in the early 1980s this engagement with national identity became characterized by a "backward reflecting."[20]

Le Retour de Martin Guerre (*The Return of Martin Guerre*) (1982) sometimes cited as the first French heritage film, offers insights into the French heritage genre. Based on folk tradition and history, the film anticipates the engagement with cultural heritage through a visually splendid recreation of life in sixteenth-century rural France. Thematically, the film represents the resurgence of the past in the present, as the narrative centers on the "return" of a husband, brother, and son (Martin) the family had believed dead. It is significant, however, that what returns is not really the past, but rather an idealized revision of that past, since Martin is not really Martin, but rather a brother in arms who has decided to "return" in Martin's place. In fact, this new Martin is the ideal husband, son, and brother that the family would have perhaps wished Martin to be.

Similarly, heritage films are less about the past than they are about valorizing and/or recreating that past potentially in order to counter or allay anxieties in the present. Some of the best examples of the French heritage film are Bernard Tavernier's *Un Dimanche à la campagne* (*A Sunday in the Country*) (1984), Claude Berri's *Jean de Florette* (1986) and *Manon des sources* (*Manon of the Spring*) (1986), Régis Wargnier's *Indochine* (1991), Jean-Paul Rappeneau's *Cyrano de Bergerac* (1990) and *Le Hussard sur le toit* (*The Horseman on the Roof*) (1995), Alain Corneau's *Tous les matins du monde* (*All the Mornings of the World*) (1991), Yves Angelo's *Le Colonel Chabert* (1995), Patrice Leconte's *Ridicule* (1996), and Edouard Molinaro's *Beaumarchais* (1997). All of these films are biopics, literary adaptations, or costume dramas, and nearly all of them have a connection to high cultural forms of art, literature, or music—the most obvious examples being *Un dimanche à la campagne*, which has a strong connection to painting, and *Tous les matins du monde*, which has a strong connection to classical music. The Berri films also have a strong connection to the golden age of French cinema, the so-called *tradition de qualité* (tradition of quality) since they are reworkings of previous films by Marcel Pagnol.[21] Moreover, all of these films represent privileged periods of French history—the *ancien régime*, the revolution, the Third Republic, or the *entre deux guerres*—critical moments in the creation or evolution of the nation. Finally, the majority of these films feature landscapes that privilege the pristine beauty of rural France and are set in recognizable provinces with strong regional identities—the Berri films, for example, are set in Provence as is *Le Hussard sur le toit*; *Beaumarchais* and *Ridicule* foreground Versailles. This emphasis on the rural is significant, since as Shanny Peer has observed, "images of peasants and provincial France remain key emblems of French national identity."[22]

In their content, it is clear that heritage films are closely tied to history, or quite often to an idealized version of history. Their connection to memory, however, lies more in their form. First and foremost, as Paul Connerton has suggested, film offers a unique link to memory, since it positions the spectator at one and the same time inside and outside of what it depicts.[23] This inside and outside effect in some ways replicates the experience of anamnesis—a memorial process—in which the past resurges upon the present, and a person feels as though they are in both places at the same time.

Maureen Turim's study of flashback in film is also insightful in understanding heritage cinema's relationship to collective memory. Turim argues, for example, that flashback as a cinematic device is linked directly to memory and specifically to historical memory. She goes on to explain that flashbacks consist of "images of memory, the personal archives of the past" but also "images of history, the shared and recorded past."[24] Turim further asserts that "flashbacks in film often merge the two levels of remembering the past, giving large-scale social and political history the subjective mode of a single, fictional individual's remembered experience."[25] While Turim refers to individual flashback sequences within a given film, her assertions are also true of heritage films as a whole. In heritage films, the entire narrative constitutes a long flashback sequence in which the viewer experiences the past through the subjectivity of a central character or characters. In many ways, heritage films are the quintessential flashback, in that their recreation of the past is so complete that the present is entirely effaced from the narrative space, an effect that forces a direct identification with the past through the present. In this respect, the memory of the past presented becomes not that of a character within the narrative, but rather the "memory" of the spectator, or more particularly, the spectator's participation in a collective remembering.

Literature in France has also seen the emergence of a heritage wave. Historical novels such as those by Pascal Quignard parallel historical costume dramas in their depiction of a disappeared but glorious past and in their success in providing the reader with a direct and lived connection to that past. In fact, Quignard's writing enjoys a particular connection to heritage film, since one of the best examples of heritage cinema, *Tous les matins du monde*, is an adaptation of a Quignard novel. Family history novels such as those by Annie Ernaux, Jean Rouaud, and Jean Delay are connected to the heritage wave.[26] In their narrative structure, these novels imitate the structure of flashback by mediating the past through the experiences of a single character, thereby bringing the reader into the past through the reminiscences of another. Moreover, like heritage films, the heritage novels privilege certain moments of history, link themselves directly to high cultural forms through literary, artistic, and musical references, and present a past that is for the most part quintessentially rural.

Heritage films and novels are both characterized by this "re-membering" of the past. In many of these texts, a significant function of this "re-membering" might be to counter anxieties about the disappearance of an idealized *francité*. For example, heritage texts frequently foreground regional identities. Regional identities are often closely linked to the agrarian, pre-industrial past, and are, as Shanny Peer has noted, highly evocative of an idealized national identity. In heritage works, this connection between the *paysan* and regional identity is emphasized such that it is directly linked to periods prior to the rural exodus and urbanization. One function of this may be to offer an alternative to the anxieties about crime, insecurity, and unemployment, all of which are closely associated with immigration and the urban space.

This retreat to a pre-urban, pre-immigrant past is interesting, given the attention the issue has received in the larger culture. Read through the filter of immigration and identity politics, heritage works would seem to exclude immigrants and their descendants from the space of collective memory, since many of them would have no direct familial or experiential connection to many of the events or spaces privileged by such texts. However, this is not necessarily the case. In privileging regional identities, heritage works point to a particular subset of identities within the national space—a subset of identities that were once seen as marginal and peripheral, but which are now central to that space. What is more, regional identities have become iconic within the national space despite the fact that they maintain certain specific characteristics of identity—languages, costumes, folklore—particular to them. That is to say, regional identities, by their very existence, challenge the traditionally Republican notion that there can be no subsets of identity or community within the national space, and in that regard, they also challenge much of the thinking regarding the ability or inability of France to assimilate its non-European immigrant populations.

Therefore, although the construction of nationality as memory that the heritage wave in many ways embodies would seem to reaffirm what is seen as the hardline nationalist vision of identity, I am not certain that this is the case. While it is true that these films and novels often do privilege the past over the present and tend to valorize a direct familial connection to the past, they also open the door for alternative means of identification. First of all, as noted above, some of the content of heritage works points directly to a process of integration, whereby former "outsiders" were brought into the national space and transformed into insiders. This seems to suggest that the same process might be repeated. Moreover, it would seem that simply by participating in the memorial reconstructions that heritage novels and films often embody, a person with no direct familial or experiential connection to the national past obtains access to it. In many ways, simply to participate in these remembrances is to take on this past and the identities it implies.

Multicultural Novels and Films and the Evolution of the National Past

Even if heritage novels and films could be read as an affirmation of the nationalist position on identity, they are not the only cultural response to debates about identity that French culture has produced. There emerged in the 1980s and 1990s a multicultural literature and cinema, in which questions of integration and of national identity are often quite central. Multicultural novels and multicultural cinema, one strand of which is sometimes referred to as the *cinéma de banlieue*, are closely tied to the antiracist movement and to multicultural paradigms of *francité*.[27] Many of the writers and filmmakers who have produced these novels and films have openly participated in the antiracist movement, and the messages and themes in the texts and films reflect the messages of antiracist groups such as *SOS Racisme*. Among these multicultural novels and films can be counted Leïla Sebbar's novels, such as *Shérazade: 17 ans, les yeux verts* and *La Seine était rouge*, as well as her edited volumes such as *Une enfance algérienne*, all of which foreground the ways in which the shared colonial history between France and Algeria have shaped the experiences of the French, the Algerians, and the French of Algerian descent. Another example is Azouz Begag's autobiographical novel *Le Gone du Chaâba*

(*The Little Kid from the Chaâba*) which might be seen as a Beur heritage novel, in that it chronicles the life of a second-generation Algerian boy in 1960s France. Mehdi Charef's *Le Thé au harem d'Archi Ahmed* (*Tea in the Harem of Archimedes*), and Nina Bouraoui's *La Voyeuse interdite* (*Forbidden Watcher*) are also novels that explore the coming of age of "second-generation" Algerians descended from immigrant parents. Films which may be included in the category of multicultural cinema are Mathieu Kassovitz's *Métisse* (1992) and *La Haine* (*Hate*) (1995), Malik Chibane's *Hexagone* (1994) and *Douce France* (1995), Mehdi Charef's *Le Thé au harem d'Archimède* (1985) and Karim Dridi's *Bye Bye* (1997), among others, all of which actively engage questions of immigration, integration and identity.

An important theme of these novels and films is the "Third Space"—that space which, according to Homi Bhabha, lies between and beyond the binary logic of insider/outsider that defines national and cultural identities.[28] Bhabha conceives of this "third space" as a "liminal space" wherein identity exists not as a subject position (French or Maghrebi, Muslim or Christian) but as an "in-between designation" that serves to displace the existing binary oppositions that characterize identity. Multicultural novels and films may be seen to articulate the need for such a "third space" by demonstrating the degree to which those descended from immigration are caught in the existing logic of identity in France. More than simply articulating the need for a hybrid space of identity, however, these narratives participate in the creation and/or the recognition of that space, by insisting on the Frenchness of those descended from immigration. At the same time, these narratives insist that immigrants and their descendants are and must be tied to their culture of origin. Moreover, in many cases, these narratives suggest that these cultures are not oppositional, as the dominant discourse on identity would suggest, but rather that they are intertwined as a result of colonial history. Multicultural novels and films may therefore read ultimately as an affirmation that the space of *francité* is already a "third" and hybrid space.

In some multicultural works, the focus seems to be the present, but the past is revealed as determinative in the present. In these texts, characters live and move in a contemporary setting, but their capacity for action or movement in the present is determined by their relationship to the past. Such is the case in the works of writer Leïla Sebbar, in which, quite often, knowledge of the past, or lack of such knowledge, directly determines a character's ability to move or act in the present. Another example is Mathieu Kassovitz's film *La Haine*, in which the film's protagonists, trapped in present-day Paris, move from situation to situation, unable to interpret or react to what is happening to them, arguably because of a distinct alienation from the past and from the dominant culture as a whole.

Other multicultural novels and films are more directly concerned with the past, and may be seen to take up the discussion of the past at a point where heritage novels and films leave it off. Gérard Noiriel has described in French culture as a whole a sort of historical amnesia with respect to immigration—what he calls a "non-lieu de mémoire"[29] (non-site of memory). By this he means that despite the enormous numbers of immigrants who have formed the French population, there has been, until very recently, no marking of such immigration in French history, in French culture, or in French national memory. This "amnesia" seems for the most part to have inscribed itself into heritage production. Of those moments and sites that are privileged in heritage films, very few point to immigration, to the presence of immigrants, or to the contributions of immigrants and their descendants to French history and culture. Multicultural novels and films, by contrast, tend to counter this "amnesia" by pointing back to a historical and experiential connection between the French and their former colonial subjects. In so doing, they seem to offer the argument that many of those immigrants whose children and grandchildren are now seen as "inassimilable" were the same colonial subjects that France once schooled in French culture as a part of the *mission civilisatrice*. What is more, such texts may even point directly or indirectly to some of the similarities that exist between that doctrine and the current doctrine of assimilation. One function of remembrance in these novels and films, then, may be to highlight certain commonalities of history and memory that unite France and its recent immigrants and in turn to call for the inclusion of those who are now so often excluded from the space of *francité*.

Beyond simply evoking the past, many multicultural novels and films point directly to the fact that immigrants, their descendants, and the so-called French of French roots are directly linked in experience and in memory by the French colonial past—a past that has shaped the present of the majority French population, those immigrants currently living in France, and the French of immigrant descent. Moreover, such texts foreground the relative absence of colonial history in dominant-culture reminiscences of the past. Two of the best known and most successful multicultural works, Azouz Begag's 1986 novel *Le Gone du Chaâba* and Yamina Benguigi's 1992 film, *Mémoires d'immigrés*, may even be read as multicultural heritage works, privileging and re-presenting key moments in the past of many of France's immigrants and their descendants.

Beyond pointing to gaps in the national memory, multicultural cinema and the multicultural novel also enlarge the space of *francité* by allowing for differences in both history and memory—that is, they emphasize both commonality and difference. Although they present French colonial history as having inscribed immigrants into the history of France, these novels and films also emphasize that this shared history was experienced differently by immigrants than by the majority population. Moreover, these novels and films seek not only to point to differences of experience, but also to inscribe those differences within the space of national memory. This, too, is a borrowing from the heritage wave, since multicultural novels and films, like heritage novels and films, accept that, at least to some degree, Frenchness is a product of pastness.

Conclusion

Ultimately, I would argue that the multiculturalist vision of Frenchness, which is often understood as a rejection of the very idea of a national identity and of a national memory, has not been properly understood. In many ways, the multiculturalist model seeks not so much to create a post-national paradigm for identity as it does to attempt to enlarge the space of national identity by challenging the content of *francité* and particularly of collective memory. In this respect the debates about identity that have shaped French politics, literature, and cinema of the past twenty years are less about whether or not there exists a French identity and a collective French memory than they are about the events and experiences that have shaped that culture and that memory.

First and foremost, those who, within these debates, were imagined as foreigners by the nationalist paradigm of identity were, by and large, born and brought up in France, and therefore, have gone through the same processes of acculturation as the dominant population. They are, therefore, to a large extent possessed of the same national memory as everyone else in France. Moreover, cultural representations of the past—such as those offered by heritage novels and films—open the door for identification with the national past on the part of those who have no direct connection with it. In this way, even someone who has not passed through such institutions as the French school system may assimilate into the national culture through the adoption of a certain set of "memories" created, for example, by watching heritage films.

Finally, multicultural novels and films affirm that those descended from immigration constitute a part of the French population born (for the most part), brought up, and educated in France. This affirmation of the fundamental Frenchness of those descended from immigration is grounded in a simultaneous acceptance and refusal of the model of *francité* imposed by the dominant culture. The acceptance of the dominant model is evident in the willingness of multicultural writers and filmmakers to emphasize the commonalties that exist between those descended from immigration and the larger French population. The refusal of the dominant model is found in the way in which these novels and films open up the space of *francité*, to include the experiences of immigrants and their children and grandchildren and their parents and even grandparents. Thus for writers and filmmakers descended from immigration, the act of writing or filming is the act of revising traditional models of French identity by communicating to the dominant culture the need for a hybrid "third space" while at the same time affirming that that space already exists.

In closing, I would suggest that the underlying commonalities in the assimilationist and multiculturalist models emphasized by the heritage and multicultural waves in cinema and literature have recently led to unexpected convergences of the two doctrines in contemporary French politics. I am thinking in particular of the recent condemnation of the policy of "integration" as failed and failing by French Minister of the Interior Nicholas Sarkozy and his subsequent calls for the creation and implementation of a French version of affirmative action.[30] Since affirmative action, by definition, consists of social and political measures taken to counteract the injustices of history, Sarkozy's calls may be read as a tacit form of official recognition of a common history uniting both French of European origin and those of postcolonial immigrant descent. Moreover, it may be read as an affirmation that a common memory of that history is still in play, and that the effects of this memory serve to reinforce and perpetuate a colonial mentality and a type of discrimination that is the legacy of the colonial period. If, indeed, Mr. Sarkozy's calls constitute the convergence of the two models of citizenship and identity, it will be interesting to see how debates about integration and identity in France evolve in the future.

Notes

1. For a more in-depth discussion of debates about immigration and integration, see Alec G. Hargreaves, *Immigration, "Race" and Ethnicity in Contemporary France* (London: Routledge, 1995) and Maxim Silverman, *Deconstructing the Nation: Immigration, Racism and Citizenship in Modern France* (London: Routledge, 1992).

2. See Riva Kastoryano, *Negotiating Identities: States and Immigration in France and Germany* (Princeton N.J.: Princeton University Press, 2002).

3. Pierre Nora, "Entre Histoire et mémoire," in *Les Lieux de mémoire*, ed. Pierre Nora (Paris: Gallimard, 1997), 23-43.

4. Nora, "Histoire et mémoire," 27.

5. Nora, "Histoire et mémoire," 31.

6. David A. Bell, "Remembrance of France Past," *New Republic*, 1 September 1997, 34.

7. This edition was published on 26 October 1985. It contains demographic "studies" and charts that "prove" that the French of European origin will be completely dis-

placed in France by those of immigrant origin. The issue's cover picture of the statue of Marianne wearing the Islamic headscarf is, in and of itself, evidence that this issue was meant more to alarm than educate.

8. See Panivong Norindr, "*La Plus Grande France*: French Cultural Identity and Nation Building under Mitterrand," in *Identity Papers: Contested Nationhood in Twentieth-Century France*, ed. Steve Ungar and Tom Conley (Minneapolis: University of Minnesota Press, 1996), 249-250.

9. See Hargreaves, *Immigration*, and Alain Gillette and Abdelmalek Sayed, *L'Immigration algérienne en France* (Paris: Éditions entente, 1976).

10. Silverman, *Deconstructing the Nation*, 257.

11. Gérard Noiriel, *Le Creuset français* (Paris: Seuil, 1988), 24-25.

12. See Alice Conklin, *Mission to Civilize: The Republican Idea of Empire in France and West Africa, 1895-1930* (Stanford, Calif.: Stanford University Press, 2000), 2-10.

13. Norindr, "*Plus Grande France*," 247.

14. Andrew Higson, who coined the term "heritage cinema," was defining a type of British film that began with *Chariots of Fire*, and afterwards evolved into a dominant trend in British cinema. The term was quickly applied to French films during and after the same period, because such French films exhibit many if not all of the characteristics Higson identified.

15. Andrew Higson, "Re-presenting the National Past: Nostalgia and Pastiche in the Heritage Film," in *Fires Were Started: British Cinema and Thatcherism*, ed. Lester Friedman (Minneapolis: University of Minnesota Press, 1993), 177.

16. Phil Powrie, *French Cinema in the 1980s: Nostalgia and the Crisis of Masculinity* (Oxford: Oxford University Press, 1997), 14.

17. Higson, "Re-presenting the National Past," 110.

18. Guy Austin, *Contemporary French Cinema: An Introduction* (Manchester, N.H.: Manchester University Press, 1996), 233.

19. Susan Hayward, *French National Cinema* (London: Routledge, 1993) 15.

20. Hayward, *French National Cinema*, 20.

21. Phil Powrie, "Configurations of Melodrama: Nostalgia and Hysteria in *Jean de Florette* and *Manon des sources*," in *French Studies* 66, no. 3 (July 1992): 297; Austin, *Contemporary French Cinema*, 158.

22. Shanny Peer, "Peasants in Paris: Representations of Rural France in the 1937 International Exposition," in *Identity Papers: Contested Nationhood in Twentieth-Century France*, ed. Steve Ungar and Tom Conley (Minneapolis: University of Minnesota Press, 1996), 44.

23. Paul Connerton, *How Societies Remember* (Cambridge: Cambridge University Press, 1989), 78.

24. Maureen Turim, *Flashbacks in Film: Memory and History* (New York: Routledge, 1989), 2.

25. Turim, *Flashbacks*, 2.

26. These writers enjoy a particular stature in France. Both Quignard and Rouaud have been awarded the Prix Goncourt, the most prestigious of French literary prizes. Jean Delay is a member of the French Academy, and Annie Ernaux is and has continued to be one of the best-selling French authors.

27. I have deliberately avoided the term "Beur" literature or film, because, despite the fact that many of the writers and filmmakers are "Beurs," the characteristics I have observed are evident in the works of writers and filmmakers of different backgrounds. For a more complete discussion of the characteristics of "Beur" writing, see Hargreaves, *Immigration* and Samia Mehrez, "Azouz Begag: *Un di zafas di bidoufile* or the *Beur* Writer: A Question of Territory," *Yale French Studies* 82, no. 1 (Spring 1993): 25-42.

28. Homi Bhabha, *The Location of Culture*, (London: Routledge, 1995), 19-39.

29. Noiriel, *Creuset*, 18.

30. See *Le Monde* 24 January 2004 and *Libération* 24 January 2004. As a "reward" for these and other criticisms of the Chirac government, Sarkozy was "promoted" to Minister of Finance.

13

The Algerian War Revisited

Susan Ireland

RECENT YEARS HAVE SEEN THE PUBLICATION of a series of texts that revisit the Algerian War in order to reexamine its place in French history and cultural memory. A foundational event for the Algerian nation, the 1954–1962 war also constitutes a traumatic event in France's past, a "drame de la mémoire collective française"[1](a crisis of French collective memory), whose repercussions have been compared to those of the Occupation of France by the Germans during World War II; hence the notion of an Algeria syndrome that mirrors the Vichy syndrome described by Henry Rousso.[2] Indeed, many of the metaphors used to describe the effects of the Algerian War designate it as a form of trauma while at the same time explicitly linking it to the question of memory. For Benjamin Stora, for example, the web of lies and repression surrounding "la mémoire algérienne" [the memory of Algeria] continues to "ronger comme un cancer, comme une gangrène, les fondements mêmes de la société française"[3] [eat away at the very foundations of French society like cancer, like gangrene]; Jocelyne Cesari uses a similar image of an unhealed wound: "La guerre d'Algérie . . . a ouvert une plaie dans l'identité nationale française. . . . Comme toute crise d'identité, elle a trait à la mémoire, au maintien de soi à travers le temps"[4] [The Algerian War . . . inflicted a wound on French national identity. . . . Like all identity crises, this one is related to memory, to the preservation of the self over time]. In the domain of literature, several recent works, which take up unresolved issues related to the war, suggest the need to heal this wound through the exploration of repressed memories. As such, they illustrate Stora's contention that, "Aucun peuple, aucune société, aucun individu ne saurait exister et définir son identité en état d'amnésie"[5]

(Peoples, societies, and individuals cannot exist and define their identity in a state of amnesia), and they underscore the importance of engaging in a more productive form of collective remembering, an anamnesis that can occur only when "the generation that lived through an event and the next generation come together to find a way to uncover and memorialize it."[6] Like the texts by French and Algerian authors in *L'Algérie des deux rives* (2003),[7] the three works to be examined in this chapter—Maïssa Bey's *Entendez-vous dans les montagnes...* (2002), Zahia Rahmani's *Moze* (2003), and Akli Tadjer's *Le Porteur de cartable* (2002)—illustrate the desire to move forward by refusing to "différer le travail collectif de mémoire et de toujours retarder l'occasion de la réconciliation"[8] (put off collective memory work and defer the possibility of reconciliation).

The emphasis on remembrance in these literary works reflects both the changing social and political climate and a renewed interest in the ways in which the war is remembered, a phenomenon Paul Silverstein calls the "fetish of memory."[9] Indeed, recent years have seen an outpouring of memory works (personal testimonies and fictional narratives) and of theoretical discussions of collective memory, all of which express the belief that the events of the past must be addressed in both France and Algeria and that "on ne peut pas partager l'avenir en niant le passé"[10] (we cannot share the future while denying the past). As many historians have observed, memories of the war on both sides of the Mediterranean were for many years marked by silence and repression, thus making it a "guerre sans nom" (nameless war) for the French and a "révolution sans visage" (faceless revolution) for the Algerians, the amnesia of the former mirroring the latter's obsession with commemoration.[11] Recently, however, a series of significant developments has helped prepare the way for a more open discussion of the war: the official recognition in 1999 that the "events" which took place in Algeria constituted a war, the opening of important military archives, the Papon trial (1998), the debate on torture surrounding the publication of Paul Aussaresses's controversial book,[12] the dedication of a national memorial to those who died in the war, and the designation of 5 December as "la journée nationale d'hommage aux morts pendant la guerre d'Algérie et les combats du Maroc et de la Tunisie"[13] (the national day for honoring those who died in the Algerian War and in the conflicts in Morocco and Tunisia), for example. At the same time, the desire of second-generation Algerians in France to recover their history, and the fact that the aftereffects of the war are still being felt in France in the form of racist incidents and the inflammatory discourse of the Front National, have kept the Algerian War in the limelight. The shift from repression to recognition regarding the events of 17 October 1961 is emblematic in this regard.[14] The official acknowledgment in 1999 that these events actually occurred is reflected in the appearance of a growing number of literary and historical works commemorating the event. While the titles of Anne Tristan's *Le Silence du fleuve*[15] and of the film *Une Journée portée disparue* draw attention to the initial covering up of the October massacre, Leïla Sebbar's *La Seine était rouge*,[16] as has been cogently demonstrated by Anne Donadey, "highlights the need for as many forms of testimony as possible if anamnesis is to take place."[17] In this work, Sebbar suggests how such a collective remembrance can occur by portraying the generation who lived through October 1961—including Algerian demonstrators, French police officers, and *harkis*—engaging in a dialogue with a group of young people of French, Algerian, and immigrant origin, who represent the next generation, each of them contributing something different to commemorating the event.

Like *La Seine était rouge, Le Porteur de cartable, Entendez-vous dans les montagnes . . .* , and *Moze* all illustrate the move toward reconciliation. Like Sebbar's text, these works explore the intersections of family stories and national history, depict more than one generation, and provide several different perspectives on the same events. In *Le Porteur de cartable*, for example, author of Algerian descent Akli Tadjer portrays the experiences of the *pieds-noirs* alongside those of Front de Libération Nationale (FLN) activists in order to underscore the need for mutual understanding. Using humor and a "second-generation" child's perspective, he foregrounds the parallel suffering of the two groups and the possibility of moving forward together. When two families, one *pied-noir* and the other Algerian, symbolically find themselves living next door to each other in a Paris apartment building at the end of the war, the friendship painfully but steadily formed between the two sons Omar and Raphaël suggests they are "deux faces de la même médaille"[18] (two sides of the same coin) and serves as an image of reconciliation.[19] Tadjer's sympathetic portrayal of both families creates a nuanced vision of the repercussions of the war: Omar's mother empathizes with the *pied-noir* family throughout the novel, and Tadjer uses the Algerian character Areski to explicitly acknowledge the pain caused by the uprooting of the *pied-noir* community—"Ça me fait toujours de la peine de voir des gens qui quittent leur pays. Parce que moi aussi j'ai quitté mon pays"[20] [It always upsets me to see people leaving their country. Because I too have left my country]. In similar fashion, Tadjer's depiction of a broad range of characters reinforces his balanced portrait of the diverse groups affected by the war, as does his inclusion of positive and negative figures and events on both the French and Algerian "sides": Mme Ceylac, Omar's beloved teacher who helps the two boys at school and whose brother is killed in Algeria, unscrupulous FLN militants such as Messaoud who manipulate the situation for personal gain and extort money from those who cannot afford it, the bitter rivalries between the various FLN factions, the OAS (Organisation d'Armée Secrète) bombing of a Parisian café frequented by North Africans, and *France-Soir*'s description of Omar's father as a "terrorist" because he catches and injures those who carried out the attack—to give but a few examples.

The parallel imprisonment of Omar's father in the La Santé prison and of Raphaël's mother in the neighboring Sainte Anne hospital, along with the psychosomatic illnesses experienced by the two children as a result of the war, highlights the themes of trauma and healing. This idea is humorously reinforced by the ending of the novel in which Omar and Raphaël set off together to take Mme Sanchez back to Algeria in an attempt to cure her debilitating depression, their journey paid for by money Omar has taken from FLN funds— "en [s]e disant qu'après tout l'argent de la révolution pouvait bien servir à rapatrier des Algérois chez eux"[21] [telling (him)self that money collected for the revolution could perfectly well be used to send some people back home to Algiers]. Although Omar's behavior toward Raphaël at first reflects the Manichaean view espoused by FLN activist Messaoud—"Les gentils c'est nous. Les méchants ce sont les roumis"[22] [We're the good guys. The French are the bad guys]—his friendship with Raphaël, which suggests a generational change, gradually brings him to understand the importance of acknowledging the experiences and suffering of others. Like Sebbar, then, Tadjer foregrounds the need to put an end to "Cette volonté de cloisonnement de la mémoire, ce refus absolu de reconnaissance des motifs de l'autre" [the desire to compartmentalize memories, the absolute refusal to recognize the motivations of others] that characterizes many earlier representations of the war.[23]

In *Entendez-vous dans les montagnes . . .* , Bey uses a train journey across France to suggest the same idea of a common voyage toward re-membering. The fellow travelers sharing a compartment in the train stand for three of the groups affected by the war and also represent three different generations: the daughter of an Algerian tortured and killed by the French, the French soldier (now a doctor) responsible for his death, and Marie, the granddaughter of a *pied-noir* family. As the narrator self-consciously remarks, "Et voilà! La boucle est bouclée! . . . Il ne manque plus qu'un harki"[24] [So! We've come full circle! . . . Now all we need is a *harki*]. Other metafictional comments comparing the scene in the train to a TV show designed to "lever le voile pour faire la lumière sur 'le passé douloureux de la France'"[25] [lift the veil in order to shed light on "*France's painful past*"] and to a play—"*Conversation dans un train*. Acte I. Les personnages sont en place"[26] [*Conversation in a Train*. Act I. The characters are in place]—further reinforce the notion of an allegorical *huis clos* performance to be played out in the train, complete with unity of time and place, a performance that confronts the painful realities of the war and recognizes that, "Personne n'est sorti indemne de cette guerre! Personne!"[27] [No one came out of this war unscathed! No one!]

Throughout the text, the weaving together of the doctor's and the narrator's memories and the alternation between past and present and France and Algeria, creates the impression of an intertwined history and a shared space of memory. In particular, the conversation that takes place between the doctor and the narrator underscores the progression from amnesia to recognition through the telling of two sides of the same story. The doctor's attempts to repress his experiences in Algeria and his involvement in the practice of torture link him to the theme of amnesia: "Comme tous les autres. D'abord aveugles et sourds, et depuis longtemps . . . muets . . . et même amnésiaques"[28] (Like all the others. Blind and deaf at first and, for a long time now . . . dumb . . . and even amnesic). Similarly, the narrator draws attention to the parallel silencing that has taken place in Algeria in the name of glorifying the revolution and creating national unity: "Chez nous, il y eut aussi . . . il y a encore des silences . . . il y a plein de blancs dans notre histoire"[29] (In my country too, there were . . . there are still silences . . . there are a lot of gaps in our history). The references to silencing also underscore the notion that unresolved issues cannot be avoided forever and suggest the familiar pattern of repression and resurgence characteristic of reactions to traumatic experiences: "pratiquer la culture du silence . . . pour se protéger. Peut-être . . . mais cela ne change rien à la souffrance des uns et des autres . . . cela finit tôt ou tard par remonter à la surface"[30] (creating a culture of silence . . . for self protection. Perhaps . . . but that doesn't change anyone's suffering in any way . . . it eventually resurfaces sooner or later).

Furthermore, the juxtaposition of the two sets of memories foregrounds the ways in which both characters are haunted by the past, thus highlighting the simultaneous recounting of two interrelated forms of trauma. The narrator's obsessive efforts to remember her father's face—"question qu'elle tente toujours de refouler"[31] (a question she always tries to repress)—and to imagine the faces of his torturers evoke the theme of repression and constitute her personal version of the "révolution sans visage"[32] (faceless revolution). Similarly, the man's current profession (doctor), which is explicitly linked to the theme of reparation, and the incorporation of his fragmented memories into the text in passages in italics, suggest his repression of the same events. In particular, his characterization of the past as a wound that has not properly healed recalls Stora's image of the gangrene resulting from forty years of silence, the festering wound the doctor describes standing for the continuing psychological and historical trauma that prevents the two sides ("les bords") from being reconciled:

> Comme si en passant le doigt ou en palpant une cicatrice ancienne dont les bords s'étaient refermés, croyait-on, on sentait un léger suintement, qui se transforme

peu à peu en une purulence qui finit par s'écouler de plus en plus abondamment,
sans qu'on puisse l'arrêter.[33]

As if when running your finger over or rubbing an old scar that had healed over,
or so you thought, you could feel it suppurating slightly, gradually filling with
pus and eventually oozing more and more without your being able to stop it.

The unfolding of the conversation emphasizes the importance of engaging
in a dialogue about the war, however difficult that may be. Recurrent references to the silences and furtive glances of the two main characters and their
acute sensitivity to each other's changing expressions and tone of voice foreground their initial reluctance to enter into a conversation and stress the halt-
ing, hesitant nature of their exchange. Likewise, the mounting tension and
growing sense of anguish, reflected in the frequent use of suspension marks
and incomplete sentences, highlight the interlocutors' realization that, "Il faut
continuer la conversation, et surtout, revenir au passé, coûte que coûte . . . là,
maintenant, il faut qu'il parle. Il faut qu'il aille jusqu'au bout"[34] [They must
continue the conversation, and above all, go back to the past, whatever the cost
. . . there, right now, he must talk. He must carry on to the bitter end], thus
creating an ironic parallel with the evocations of torture, whose objective is
also to "faire parler coûte que coûte"[35] [make people talk, whatever the cost].
At this point, the voyage into the past is presented as a joint enterprise with a
common destination, as the two characters help each other to continue, even
finishing each other's sentences. In this sense, the narrator's observation that,
"Ils ne sont pas encore arrivés à destination"[36] [They have not yet reached
their final destination], refers both to the train journey and to the conversation, which moves from a banal remark on the beauty of Algeria to an an-
guishing exchange on the subject of torture.

It is the presence of Marie, who represents a further generational shift and
the need to recover one's past, that enables the conversation to reach its conclusion. Her desire to move beyond the nostalgic visions embodied by her *pied-
noir* grandfather—"Il préfère nous raconter comment c'était avant. Avant les
événements, comme il dit"[37] [He prefers to tell us what it was like before. Before the events, as he calls them]—and to learn about the war that has shaped
her family's trajectory places her in the role of catalyst as the conversation
reaches its most difficult point. By directly broaching the subject of torture,
Marie brings to the fore the central theme that has been present since the beginning of the text in the separate memories of the other two characters, unspoken yet influencing all of their interactions.

The guilt and shame the doctor experiences when speaking of his involvement in torture make him an important symbol of the need to confront
painful issues related to the war on the individual and national levels. Indeed,

his final avowal and the narrator's reaction to it are portrayed as a form of catharsis. For the narrator, hearing the doctor's admission constitutes a difficult yet cathartic moment in that it enables her to confront "LA scène"[38] (THE scene), that of her father's torture: "même si une douloureuse palpitation la fait encore frémir, quelque chose s'est dénoué en elle. . . . [L]es bourreaux ont des visages d'homme"[39] [even though her painfully racing heart still makes her tremble, something inside her has been resolved. . . . [T]he executioners have human faces]. As the train enters the station at the end of the journey, the symbolic position of the two characters—"Face à face, l'homme et la femme ne bougent pas"[40] [Facing each other, the man and the woman do not move]—reinforces the notion of dialogue as a crucial stage of a difficult voyage that must be undertaken together and recalls Stora's recent observation that, "Les souffrances, d'une rive à l'autre de la Méditerranée commencent à se regarder en miroir"[41] [The sufferings on both sides of the Mediterranean begin to exchange looks as if in a mirror]. Such an exchange, Bey suggests, is essential to the process of healing, and by emphasizing the shared nature of the memories recounted, the conversation in the train underscores the notion of moving on together.[42]

The *harki* who is absent from Bey's novel appears at the center of Rahmani's *Moze*, which addresses what Mohand Hamoumou has called "un trou de mémoire franco-algérien"[43] [a gap in Franco-Algerian collective memory], "le tabou des tabous"[44] [the taboo of all taboos]—the situation of the *harkis*. At the end of an article published in 1990, Hamoumou concludes, "Nul doute qu'un jour un Algérien ou un Français osera écrire cette page de leur histoire commune"[45] [There is no doubt that one day an Algerian or a Frenchman will have the courage to write this page of their shared history]. Several recent works by the children of *harkis* have taken up this challenge, reflecting their determination to bring the situation of the *harkis* to the fore.[46] As Rahmani's protagonist puts it, "Ils l'auront quand même, le mot harki, à la bouche"[47] [whether they like it or not, they will have the word *harki* on their lips]. *Moze*, which is named after the narrator's father, is explicitly portrayed as Rahmani's contribution to putting an end to collective amnesia: "Par l'écriture je me défais de lui (Moze) et je vous le remets"[48] [Through my writing I release myself from him (Moze) and hand him over to you]. The image of handing Moze back, like the memories of torture that resurface in Bey's text, suggests the inevitable return of the repressed.

Composed of historical documents, prose narrative, minimalist dramatic dialogues, and poetic passages, Rahmani's text is at once a highly personal work of mourning and a powerful indictment of an international tragedy. In her "quête 'harkéologique'"[49] (harkiological quest)—to borrow an expression used by Dalila Kerchouche in *Mon Père, ce harki* (2003)—Rahmani, like

Kerchouche, explicitly writes as a "second-generation" daughter.[50] Her fragmented text, which evokes the effects of growing up in France as the child of a *harki*, returns insistently to the legacy of shame transmitted from one generation to the next: "J'ai honte. Honte de ma honte. Honte d'avoir honte"[51] [I'm ashamed. Ashamed of my shame. Ashamed of being ashamed]. Throughout the text, recurrent images of being marked or branded forcefully convey the pain caused by such an inheritance: "La faute de Moze, je veux dire qu'elle est ma chair et mon habit"[52] [Moze's misdeed forms my flesh and my clothes]; "je porte son matricule. Je suis la fille du harki numéroté"[53] [I wear his regimental number. I am the daughter of a serial-numbered *harki*]; "Je suis un enfant de salaud. Il faut que ça s'arrête les enfants de salaud"[54] [I am the child of a bastard. There must be no more bastard children].

Rahmani's emphasis on the urgency of moving from amnesia to reconciliation by facing the events of the past highlights the silence of all parties involved—France, Algeria, and the *harkis* themselves. As is suggested in a brief father-daughter exchange, Rahmani draws attention to the tragic consequences of the silence surrounding the fate of the *harkis*: "—J'ai étouffé mes mots. /—Tu en es mort!"[55] [I choked back my words. / You died because of it]. Likewise, the portrayal of Moze as a "mort-vivant"[56] (one of the living dead) reinforces the theme of his having been erased from collective memory. The date and nature of Moze's death serve as a further reminder of the need for recognition: after attending the official ceremony at the war memorial on 11 November 1991, he drowns himself in a local pond, the official commemoration of the "unidentified" soldier of other wars ironically highlighting the difference between the sense in which that soldier and Moze are "unknown": "Entouré des élus, lui, le revenant d'une guerre inconnue, lui, le soldat inconnu, a salué le monument absent d'une guerre qui a eu lieu. Moze a salué le monument aux morts absents d'une guerre qui l'a enfoui"[57] [Surrounded by the elected officials, Moze, the ghost from an unknown war, Moze, the unknown soldier, saluted the absent monument to a war that took place. Moze saluted the monument to the absent dead of a war that had buried him].

Like Bey, Rahmani foregrounds the need to confront traumatic events and engage in a dialogue so that mourning and re-membering can occur. The frequent recurrence of the verb "parler" (to talk) points to the importance of speaking out and being heard as part of the healing process: "Il faut parler, parler de ce qui a eu lieu! Parler avec ceux-là qui l'ont vécu. Parler avec eux pour taire la violence . . . parler pour que le visage existe, parler pour que les larmes viennent enfin"[58] [We must talk, talk about what happened! Talk with those who lived through it. Talk to them so that the violence will stop . . . talk so that their faces exist, talk so that tears will come at last]. Indeed, much of the text is composed of dialogue as Rahmani gives voice to many of those affected by or responsible for the situation of the *harkis*, including members of the Commission Nationale de Réparation[59] (National Reparation Commission), Moze himself, the French official investigating his death, Moze's wife, and his daughters who travel to Algeria to pursue the question of his being buried there. The inclusion of multiple perspectives thus suggests that, when it finally occurs, reconciliation will be the result of a collective endeavor in which every voice is heard.

Throughout these dialogues, recurrent references to issues such as betrayal, humiliation, and injustice foreground the narrator's condemnation of the way in which the *harkis* have been treated, and the personification of many of these concepts is used to convey their effects on the narrator and her father: "Tout hurle. Le Mal, la Justice, le Meurtre, la Vengeance, la Raison, le Tort, la Nation, le Peuple, l'Honneur, la Trahison, le Frère et le Pardon hurlent. Ces mots hurlent! . . . Et ces mots frappent"[60] [Everything screams. Evil, Justice, Murder, Vengeance, Right, Wrong, the Nation, the People, Honor, Treason, Brother and Pardon scream. These words scream! . . . And these words punch]. Rahmani's "j'accuse" (I accuse), with its echoes of Zola's famous words, succinctly conveys her indictment of France's role: "J'accuse le peuple français de m'avoir abandonné. J'accuse ce pays d'avoir tué mon père"[61] [I accuse the French people of abandoning me. I accuse this country of killing my father]. Likewise, she clearly designates the failure of the French to protect the *harkis* as a crime that should be acknowledged as such: "Dites-moi maintenant quel est le pire crime? Trahir son frère! C'est le crime de Moze. Mais trahir celui qui pour toi a trahi son frère, ça c'est un autre crime. N'est-ce pas le vôtre?"[62] [Tell me now, which is the worst crime? Betraying one's brother! That is Moze's crime. But betraying the man who betrayed his brother for you is a different crime. Is it not yours?]. Rahmani's impassioned call for justice again underscores the importance of facing the facts if wounds are to be healed, and she emphasizes the need for both France and Algeria to recognize their role in the massacre of the *harkis*, just as, in a painful dialogue with her mother, the narrator seeks on the individual level to ascertain whether her father was involved in the deaths of any Algerians while he worked for the French army.

In the middle of the text, a member of the Commission Nationale de Réparation (National Reparation Commission) raises the question, "Mais qui veut de la réconciliation? Toute cette histoire est trop sombre"[63] [But who wants reconciliation? This whole business is too murky]. Despite the polemical tone of certain passages, the end of *Moze* contains images that evoke the possibility of such a reconciliation and intimates that, for the daughter, returning to the past constitutes the only way of freeing herself from it. The short section entitled "Moze parle," which is set up as a dialogue between Moze and the narrator, begins with the words "Père je n'ai plus peur"[64] [Father, I am no longer afraid] and suggests that the daughter has been reconciled with her father. Indeed, her text itself constitutes a memorial to Moze that stands in sharp contrast to the earlier image of the Armistice Day commemoration, the epigraph to the final section and to the text as a whole foregrounding the theme of memory: "Je me souviens / Écris que tu te souviens. / Que tu t'en souviens"[65] [I remember / Write that you remember / That you remember these things]. The epilogue, with its subtitle "Moze le magicien," focuses on reconciliation in a broader sense and again opens with a reference to memory—"Au village on se souvient de Moze"[66] [In the village people remember Moze]. Here, the Frenchman Jean-Marie tells his friend Denis of the pleasure he derives from tending part of Moze's wife's garden and sharing its produce with her. The final images of growth and bearing fruit thus convey the narrator's hope for the future, an idea reinforced in the very last words of the text: "Je veux vivre jusqu'au jour où tu porteras des fruits. C'est ce que vient de dire la femme de Moze au petit pêcher rapporté d'Algérie qu'elle a planté cet automne"[67] [I want to live until the day you bear fruit. That's what Moze's wife just said to the little peach tree from Algeria she planted this autumn].

In an essay entitled "France-Algérie: Questions de mémoire," Thierry Fabre remarks:

Expurger les silences, fouiller les interdits, déverrouiller les discours établis qui maintiennent des vérités contraires et tenter enfin d'écrire ensemble notre histoire commune: c'est une ambition démesurée, sans doute, mais qui mérite d'être tentée. La mémoire collective a besoin de soubresauts pour être réactivée.[68]

Putting an end to silence, exploring taboos, destabilizing commonly accepted statements that support contradictory truths and trying together at last to write our shared history: this is undoubtedly highly ambitious, but is worth attempting. Collective memory needs a good kick-start to get it going again.

The works discussed in this chapter all participate in such an enterprise. Taken together, they point to the importance of revisiting the painful events of the past as a means of healing the wounds of history and of moving toward a shared re-vision of the war. As such, they attest to the significant role played by literary works in stimulating reflection on historical events and in reshaping individual and collective memories. How successful these texts will ultimately be in achieving the goal outlined by Fabre will depend, as Mireille Rosello and Mohand Hamoumou remind us, on the extent to which there exists a true desire for dialogue[69] and on whether the public in general is ready to listen.[70]

Notes

1. Benjamin Stora, Mehdi Lallaoui, and Anne Tristan, *17 octobre 1961, 17 illustrations.* (Bezons: Au nom de la mémoire, 2001), 29. These are Stora's words.

2. See Anne Donadey's "'Une Certaine Idée de la France': The Algeria Syndrome and Struggles over 'French' Identity" for a discussion of the Algeria syndrome (in Steven Ungar and Tom Conley, eds., *Identity Papers: Contested Nationhood in Twentieth-Century France* [Minneapolis: University of Minnesota Press, 1996], 215-232.) In *Le Syndrome de Vichy* (Paris: Seuil, 1990), Henry Rousso contends that the Vichy syndrome has four stages: interrupted mourning, repression, the return of the repressed, and obsession (Donadey, "Une Certaine Idée," 217-18); Donadey sees France as entering the third stage of the Algeria syndrome, "the shattering of established myths," at the beginning of the 1990s ("Une Certaine Idée," 218).

3. Benjamin Stora, *La Gangrène et l'oubli* (Paris: La Découverte, 1991), 8.

4. Jocelyne Cesari, *Faut-il avoir peur de l'islam?* (Paris: Presses de Sciences Po, 1997), 34.

5. Stora, *La Gangrène*, 319.

6. Anne Donadey, "Anamnesis and National Reconciliation: Re-membering October 17, 1961," in *Immigrant Identities in Contemporary France*, ed. Susan Ireland and Patrice J. Proulx. (Westport: Greenwood Press, 2001), 53.

7. Raymond Bozier, ed., *Algérie des deux rives 1954-1962* (Paris: Éditions Mille et une nuits, 2003).

8. Bozier, *L'Algérie des deux rives*, Foreword.

9. Paul Silverstein, "Franco-Algerian War and Remembrance Discourse, Nationalism and Post-Coloniality," in *Francophone Studies: Discourse and Identity*, ed. Kamal Salhi (Exeter: Elm Bank Publications, 2000), 149.

10. Stora, *La Gangrène*, 320.

11. Stora, *La Gangrène*, 8. See too the section of Silverstein's "Franco-Algerian War and Remembrance Discourse" entitled "Reified Narratives: France's Amnesia and Algeria's Mythification," 153-55.

12. Paul Aussaresses, *Services spéciaux: Algérie, 1955-1957* (Paris: Perrin, 2001).

13. Marie-Sandrine Sgherri, "Guerre d'Algérie: La Commémoration," *Le Point* 1618 (19 September 2003): 15.

14. On 17 October 1961, many Algerians were killed in Paris when a peaceful demonstration against the curfew imposed on them by Maurice Papon was brutally repressed; many of the dead were thrown into the Seine, and the event was subsequently covered up.

15. Anne Tristan, *Le Silence du fleuve* (Bezons: Au nom de la mémoire, 1991).

16. Leïla Sebbar, *La Seine était rouge* (Paris: Thierry Magnier, 1999).

17. Donadey, "Anamnesis," 51.

18. Akli Tadjer, *Le Porteur de cartable* (Paris: Jean-Claude Lattès, 2002), 262.

19. Omar shows Raphaël how to survive in France, while Raphaël teaches Omar about Algeria.

20. Tadjer, *Le Porteur*, 296.

21. Tadjer, *Le Porteur*, 306.

22. Tadjer, *Le Porteur*, 24.

23. Stora, *La Gangrène*, 252. Elsewhere, Stora describes this phenomenon as "la non-rencontre des mémoires" (the non-meeting of memories): "Le problème de tous les films qui ont été réalisés depuis la fin de la guerre d'Algérie, c'est qu'ils ont été faits pour des publics qui ne se mélangent jamais. On peut voir des films pour les pieds-noirs, des films pour les Algériens, ou pour les Harkis. Mais il n'y a pas de vision d'ensemble. De ce fait les mémoires ne se mélangent pas" (The problem with all the films made since the end of the Algerian War is that they were made for audiences that never mix with one another. One can see films for *pieds-noirs*, films for Algerians or for *harkis*. But there is no view of the whole. Because of this, their memories do not mix) (cited in Mireille Rosello, "Farança-Algéries ou Djazaïr-frances? Fractales et mésententes fructueuses," *MLN* 118, no. 4 (September 2003): 791-92).

24. Maïssa Bey, *Entendez-vous dans les montagnes* . . . (La Tour d'Aigues: L'Aube/ Éditions Barzakh, 2002), 40.

25. Bey, *Entendez-vous*, 40.

26. Bey, *Entendez-vous*, 40.

27. Bey, *Entendez-vous*, 65.

28. Bey, *Entendez-vous*, 69.

29. Bey, *Entendez-vous*, 60.

30. Bey, *Entendez-vous*, 58.

31. Bey, *Entendez-vous*, 17.

32. Stora, *La Gangrène*, 8.

33. Bey, *Entendez-vous*, 43.

34. Bey, *Entendez-vous*, 46.

35. Bey, *Entendez-vous*, 36.

36. Bey, *Entendez-vous*, 63.

37. Bey, *Entendez-vous*, 51. The grandfather thus illustrates Antoine Prost's contention that "*Pieds noirs* memory is built on the divide between before and after. What matters are the good memories of Algeria before the war" ("The Algerian War in French Collective Memory," in *War and Remembrance in the Twentieth Century*, ed. Jay Winter and Emmanuel Sivan [Cambridge: Cambridge University Press, 1999], 168).

38. Bey, *Entendez-vous*, 38.

39. Bey, *Entendez-vous*, 69-70.

40. Bey, *Entendez-vous*, 70.

41. Benjamin Stora, "La Guerre d'Algérie dans les mémoires françaises: Violence d'une mémoire de revanche," *L'Esprit créateur* 43, no. 1 (Spring 2003): 28.

42. The doctor's physical demeanor at the end of the conversation conveys this message: "Elle le regarde, elle l'observe, elle le détaille, attentivement, minutieusement. . . . Il a les yeux baissés, les main posées sur ses genoux. Il ne cherche pas à se dérober" (Bey, *Entendez-vous*, 70) [She looks at him, she observes him, she examines him attentively, in great detail. . . . His eyes are lowered, his hands rest on his knees. He does not try to hide from her gaze].

43. This is the title of an article by Mohand Hamoumou, "Les Harkis, un trou de mémoire franco-algérien," *Esprit* (May 1990): 25-45.

44. Zahia Rahmani, *Moze* (Paris: Sabine Wespieser, 2003), 26.

45. Hamoumou, "Les Harkis," 44.

46. These works include Mohand Hamoumou's own historical study, *Et ils sont devenus harkis* (Paris: Fayard, 1993), which examines the reasons for the silence surrounding the *harkis* on both side of the Mediterranean, and Dalila Kerchouche's *Mon Père, ce harki* (Paris: Seuil, 2003), the autobiographical account of her quest to understand her father's past.

47. Rahmani, *Moze*, 90.

48. Rahmani, *Moze*, 24.

49. Kerchouche, *Mon Père*, 187.

50. Kerchouche's text opens with the words, "Je suis une fille de harkis" (I am the daughter of a *harki*) (*Mon Père*, 13).

51. Rahmani, *Moze*, 179.

52. Rahmani, *Moze*, 24.

53. Rahmani, *Moze*, 120.

54. Rahmani, *Moze*, 79.

55. Rahmani, *Moze*, 179.

56. Rahmani, *Moze*, 19.

57. Rahmani, *Moze*, 129.

58. Rahmani, *Moze*, 136.

59. The commission's role, as described in the novel by one of its members, is to hear the narrator's testimony regarding her father in order to evaluate the harm done to him and to redress this injustice.

60. Rahmani, *Moze*, 79.

61. Rahmani, *Moze*, 125.

62. Rahmani, *Moze*, 140.

63. Rahmani, *Moze*, 90.

64. Rahmani, *Moze*, 175.

65. Rahmani, *Moze*, 175.

66. Rahmani, *Moze*, 183.

67. Rahmani, *Moze*, 188.

68. Thierry Fabre, "France-Algérie: Questions de mémoire," in *Le Maghreb, l'Europe et la France*, ed. Kacem Basfao and Jean-Robert Henry (Paris: Éditions du Centre National de la Recherche Scientifique, 1992), 354.

69. Rosello, "Farança-Algéries," 792.

70. Hamoumou, "Les Harkis," 44.

14

France and Algeria
Performing the "Impossible Memory" of a Shared Past

Janice Gross

A T THE END OF "CONFITURES ET BOBOS," Algerian playwright Aziz Chouaki comments on the effects of his *francarabe* youth spent in post-1962 Algeria as he issues a challenge to anthropologists:

> beaucoup d'Algériens, entre trente ans et plus dans ces années 2000, peuvent être considérés, moi inclus, avec toute la sérénité que ma conscience autorise, comme des pieds-noirs musulmans à part entière . . . Du boulot, pour l'anthropologie.[1]

> many Algerians thirty years and older in the year 2000, myself included, can be considered, with all of the impartiality that my conscience allows, Muslim *pieds-noirs* in the full sense of the word . . . Food for thought for anthropology.

Although jarring at first glance, the grafting of *musulman* (Muslim) onto the essentially French identity of the *pied-noir* settler of North Africa is a provocative oxymoron that illustrates the unstable nature of French-Algerian cultural memory as an incongruous assemblage of identity parts. While official historical memory would maintain a strict separation between the Algerian Muslims of the 1990s and the French *pieds-noirs* of the 1960s, Chouaki's linguistic invention is grounded in multiple levels of shared cultural experience of the two groups. For the one million *pieds-noirs* forced to abandon their home and identity in Algeria and flee threats from opposing terrorist groups in 1962, the choice between "la valise ou le cercueil"[2] (a suitcase or a casket) is strikingly similar to that of Muslim Algerians trapped between the violence of armed Islamists and a repressive military regime during the so-called Second Algerian War of the 1990s. Both groups turned to France for refuge, though it was a land most had never known, and which often had little desire to know them.[3]

In addition to facing rejection and physical threats from the forces of hatred within their respective societies, Muslim Algerians such as Chouaki, who fled to France in the 1990s, like the *pied-noir* refugees who left in 1962, were stripped of their memory rights and left with the mutilated memory of a "passé troué"[4] (a past with holes). In each instance, it was virtually impossible to "turn the page" of history, for it had been effectively ripped out of the book. For Algerian Muslims of Chouaki's generation, the erasure was that of official governmental policy that mandated a massive Arabization program in a desire to be rid of all things French. For the *pieds-noirs*, erasure was linked to France's need to cultivate national amnesia regarding all things Algerian. Yet, the most significant aspect of the Muslim connection to the *pieds-noirs* was the fact that both populations up to 1962 had lived side by side in Algeria, often as neighbors, and even as friends, thus creating a fabric of shared experience and authentic cultural memory. In *Ma mère l'Algérie*, the *pied-noir* writer Jean Pélégri recalls "cette histoire mal connue et souterraine . . . là où les rapports étaient quotidiens"[5] [this history not well known, below the surface . . . where relationships were everyday ones].

While French-Algerian memory has long reflected the contradictory character of multiple and intersecting identities,[6] Chouaki's linguistic recombination of the *pied-noir musulman* betokens the need to recover a zone of overlapping or "shared" memory by re-membering lost identity parts. As past identities shatter and become reshaped in the face of present realities, the naming process reveals the ongoing kaleidoscopic and contentious character of French Algerian identity.[7] For Michèle Baussant, the revival of this seemingly "impossible" shared memory of the *pied-noir* experience requires finding a way to "donner un sens à un univers d'absence"[8] (give meaning to an absent universe). Considered in this context, a number of authors, especially Algerians such as Chouaki, now living in France, turn to theatre as a site for reenacting a shared memory that official history has long suppressed. More than in other genres, theatre with its live actors can breathe new life into the process of witnessing, giving voice to shared experience in the past, and enabling outside observers to enter into the deep crevasses of memory. As described by Freddie Rokem in *Performing History*, "theatre very forcefully participates in the ongoing representations and debates about these pasts [of collective identities]."[9] Along with the representation of the past, theatre can open up a process of exchange with the past "to create an awareness of the complex interaction between the destructiveness and the failures of history" and the "efforts . . . to confront these painful failures."[10]

However, the path to such theatre is often rocky and precarious, as revealed in the recent planning for the Year of Algeria (*Djazaïr*) in 2003 which unleashed many unresolved and deep-seated identity struggles within Franco-French and Algero-Algerian layers. From a tumultuous planning process to boycotts and protests, voices from all persuasions weighed in on the official constructions of memory and commemoration related to the French-Algerian relationship. On one level, the voices of dissident Berbers in both Algeria and France called for recognition of "l'autre Algérie" (the other Algeria) in contrast to the officially sanctioned Arab-dominated Algeria ruled by the FLN-based government of President Bouteflika. Meanwhile in France, disaffected *pied-noir* and *harki* organizations joined forces to demand "la reconnaissance de l'ensemble des mémoires et de cultures"[11] [recognition of all memories and cultures], and to draft a letter to President Chirac calling for a Year of Algeria that would "faire progresser la vérité historique et inviter l'Algérie à renouer les liens entre elle et les Pieds-Noirs et les Harkis par des actes symboliques forts"[12] [move historical truth forward and encourage Algeria to renew its ties with the *pieds-noirs* and the *harkis* by means of strong symbolic actions]. When asked whether the events of 2003 might be an opportunity for French-Algerian reconciliation, Slimane Benaïssa, Algerian author, actor, and director living in France since 1993, disparaged the Bouteflika regime for its willingness to make peace with terrorists in Algeria while refusing to do the same with *harkis* and *pieds-noirs* in France. He went on to suggest that the programming itself might better have reflected a desire to confront ambiguities by performing a play by *pied-noir* Albert Camus or by the Berber writer Mouloud Mammeri, rather than the more canonical choice of the Arab Kateb Yacine.[13]

Quite apart from the identity politics of commemoration, a number of authors writing throughout the 1980s up to the present have turned to theater in order to challenge the destructive forces of unilateral and mutilated national memory. Benaïssa spoke of his fear of losing this fragile French-Algerian link when he arrived in France in the 1990s, while at the same time seeing the potential of being able to communicate with French and Algerian audiences simultaneously: "L'espace de mémoire commun à la France et à l'Algérie est plus grandiose qu'on ne le croit. Il est seulement dommage qu'il soit voué à l'oubli."[14] [The space of memory shared by France and Algeria is greater than one imagines. It's just a shame that it's being pushed into oblivion.] The desire to represent forgotten, suppressed, and politically volatile memory fragments involves a twofold practice that looks both to a reenactment of the past and to a healing process for the future. For Rokem, the practice of "performing history" serves to "overcome both the separation and exclusion from the past, striving to create a community where the events from this past will matter again."[15] The plays examined in this chapter—Aziz Chouaki's *Baya* (1989) and *Les Oranges*

(1998); Slimane Benaïssa's *Fils de l'amertume* (1996) and *Mémoires à la dérive* (2001); Fatima Gallaire's *Au loin les caroubiers* (1993); Richard Demarcy's *Les Mimosas d'Algérie* (1988)—reveal the power of theatre to open up new paths to shared collective memory between Algerian Muslims and the repatriated French, even to the point of representing the "mémoire impossible" (impossible memory) of the *pieds-noirs*. As a means of "performing a return of the repressed,"[16] the plays discussed here illustrate how theater can release as well as harness traumatic, volatile, and taboo memories while providing "restorative potentials"[17] for viewers and artists alike.

Written in the late 1980s and 1990s at a time of growing crisis in Algeria and tension within French-Algerian relations, each of these plays alludes to a space of shared memory where the documentary experience of a traumatic history is replayed through human exchanges that attempt to confront and reexamine the experience of the past. All plays in this study save one—Demarcy's *Les Mimosas d'Algérie*—were written by Algerians living in Paris. By exposing and dressing past wounds through the "telling" of long-repressed French-Algerian trauma, each play seeks to revive constructive memories of shared community that had been forced into oblivion by divisive and exclusionary politics on both sides. For the Algerian authors living in France, Chouaki, Benaïssa, and Gallaire, knew Algeria as children and young adults in the 1950s and 1960s. In the eyes of French author-director Demarcy, the urgency to write about Algeria in *Les Mimosas d'Algérie* (1988) evolved out of the urgency to revisit the past trauma of Algeria "comme un sujet nécessaire, possible, mais impossible tout en même temps"[18] [as a necessary subject, both possible and impossible at the same time], and to challenge France's readiness to "cultiver l'amnésie"[19] (cultivate amnesia). Demarcy's play was performed in France and in Algeria as part of the Year of Algeria program in 2003. By projecting the individual memory of the past through the lens of the present, each play revisits traumatic memories of the Algerian War for independence and, in some cases, the recurrent terror of the Second Algerian War of the 1990s.

Baya, the earliest play of the corpus, was written as a novel by Aziz Chouaki and published in Algeria in 1989 before the author moved to France in 1991. Constructed as a dramatic memory monologue in the voice of the middle-aged woman Baya, the text was discovered by French director Jean-Pierre Vincent and staged at the Théâtre des Amandiers at Nanterre in 1991. For Chouaki, Baya was a simple, uneducated middle-aged Algerian woman "contradictoire, sensible, et surtout libre dans sa tête"[20] [contradictory, sensitive, but especially free in her thoughts]. Performed initially in French and later translated into Arabic and staged in Algeria, the play presents the history of Algeria as a jumble of memory fragments recalled by Baya as she sorts through a box of old photographs. A fifty-eight-year-old in the 1980s, Baya

shuttles back and forth between past and present in fractured French, from
her marriage to Salah in 1952, her trip to Paris, her invitation to Marie's "l'a-
nis vers serre" (birthday) and her glee to discover that "Papa est d'accorps . . .
il dit que le Papa de Marie il est bien . . . il fait pas de la peaulitique" (sic).[21]
[Papa is a greed . . . he says Marie's daddy is okay . . . he isn't pull itical]. Her
unstructured remembrance takes place in the midst of housecleaning, as each
photo gives rise to an assortment of memories. Despite her effort to concentrate on the mindlessness of cleaning—"Le travail ça défoule, ça empêche de
penser"[22] [Work relieves tension, stops thinking]—she is nevertheless plunged
into a confusion of memories. According to Chouaki, his "multimedia" approach to recording Baya's random flow of fractured and jumbled thoughts
and images seeks to use a form of writing that mimics channel surfing and
computer processing in the delivery of rapid and disjointed chunks of information.[23]

One of the most vivid memory chunks for Baya is that of her friendship
with *pied-noir* girls, especially Marie Blanchot. In one memory flash, Baya is
catapulted into a horrific moment in 1962. She relives the mundane act of distributing different cuts of chicken to each family member, when she hears her
husband's almost casual announcement that Mr. Blanchot, Marie Blanchot's
father, "a été égorgé par erreur" (had his throat slit by mistake) in the confusion of reprisals.[24] Baya's once clear-cut sense of Algerian identity comes
crashing down in the same instant as she feels the plate slip from her hands.
Her emotional outrage toggles between the past horror and the present recall:
"Et moi, pourquoi ils m'ont pas égorgée avec? . . . briser ma vie comme l'assiette, là. Voilà, ma vie est comme l'assiette qui s'est brisée là. l'indépendance
. . ."[25] [So why not me too? slit my throat too? . . . shatter my life like the plate
down there. My life just like the plate all in pieces there. independence . . .]. In
the next instant, she sees her husband Salah eating, seemingly unfazed by the
horrible news, and she wonders "Bizarre Salah, ne ressent rien ou quoi?"[26]
[Strange Salah, doesn't feel anything or what?] In the next leap of memory, she
sees Salah handing her a letter sent from Marie in France. Baya rereads the letter that asks Baya to look in on Marie's elderly parents who had stubbornly insisted on staying in Algeria in 1962. The chapter ends with the jarring juxtaposition of Baya left alone with Marie's words echoing in her ears "Je sais que
tu aimes nos parents comme les tiens alors je peux te faire confiance."[27] [I
know that you love our parents as if they were your own, so I know I can trust
you.] For Baya, the world that once was, the world that had once made sense
to her, was brutally stripped away, scattered about as so many pieces of a dinner plate about to be served, as irretrievable as the lost memory of Algeria.

Not surprisingly, Chouaki's work invited criticism: "*Baya* a contribué à ma
réputation de salaud de la nation."[28] [*Baya* contributed to my reputation as a

bastard son of the nation.] Later, when director Ziani Chérif Ayad adapted the play into Arabic for the stage in Algiers, Chouaki explains: "Cela a provoqué une grosse bagarre, j'ai été taxé de nostalgique des Pieds-Noirs."[29] [That created a huge fight and I was accused of wanting to bring back the colonial era of the *pieds-noirs*.] For Chouaki, the simpleminded humanity of Baya was designed precisely to undermine the myth that "les pieds-noirs sont tous des salauds" (all *pieds-noirs* are bastards), and provide a counter-memory to the unilateral view of the officially sanctioned memory of Algeria. However truthful the portrayal of Algeria, Muslim Algerians of the diaspora were dismayed: "Ce que tu dis est vrai, mais ça ne se dit pas."[30] [What you say is true, but these things just aren't said.] In reopening this occluded memory path, Chouaki's work illustrates theatre's ability to recover and perform lost social memory and to unleash its repressed pain, shame, and anger in the face of official history.

In contrast to other plays examined in this chapter, *Baya* illustrates traumatic memory through the primary process of what LaCapra describes as "acting out." In *Writing History, Writing Trauma*, LaCapra considers the psychoanalytical model used in the treatment of historical trauma, and thus distinguishes between "acting out" memory which involves repetition and lack of distance, and "working through" memory with its emphasis on critical distancing and sharper delineation among past, present, and future.[31] For Baya, memory is primarily "acted out," as past trauma is constantly replayed and rewound, leaving the individual with the sense of seeming "to exist in the present as if one were still fully in the past, with no distance from it."[32] Yet, in spite of the traumatic memory that "dévore la tête" (devours her brain), she reminds herself that even though she's inclined to say "je m'en fous" (screw it all), she can't very well neglect her family and their needs.[33]

Baya's memory story magnifies the effects of repression of the multiethnic past of Algeria by projecting it through the eyes of one simpleminded woman. In the process, it presents a critique of Algeria's wholesale replacement of authentic lived memory with a monolithic construct of Arab-Muslim homogeneity, exposing a national identity crisis from which Algeria as a nation has yet to fully recover. Looking through the same lens of mutilated memory, Slimane Benaïssa wrote and performed *Les Fils de l'amertume* (*Sons of Bitterness*) in France in 1996 in an attempt to retrace the breakdown of memory that plunged Algeria into its inexplicable tragedy of identity.[34] For Algerian Benaïssa living in France as a "métis heureux" (contented hybrid), there was an urgent need to open up new paths of Franco-Algerian exchange, to write against what historian James D. Le Sueur had documented as a longstanding "politics of Othering" practiced both by France and Algeria.[35] When the character Youcef as a child recalls the fateful departure of the French in 1962, he queries his spiritual guide or sheikh:

—Sidi, pourquoi tous les Français partent?
—Comme ils sont venus un jour, ils partiront un jour. C'est ça l'indépendance.
—Alors, Sidi, l'indépendance c'est quand on reste tout seul?
—Et tous tes frères, ils ne te suffisent pas? . . .[36]

—Sidi, why are all the French leaving?
—Just as they came one day, they'll leave another day. That's what independence is.
—So independence is when you're all alone?
—And what about all your brothers? Aren't they enough for you? . . .

The explanation, however, does little to erase the child's pain at seeing his schoolmates leave never to return again, especially the lovely Gracia who "depuis un mois . . . ne vient plus à mes rendez-vous"[37] [for a month now she hasn't been coming to meet me . . .]. Just as for Baya, Youcef's memory was amputated and erased by the self-appointed guardians of national memory: the FLN (Front de libération nationale) and the FIS (Front Islamique du Salut). Censured for his memory of a pluralist Algeria (Francophone and Berber as well as Arab), the journalist Youcef is assassinated at the play's end by an Islamist terrorist who is also his cousin. Such acts of retaliation were common during Algeria's bloody civil war in the 1990s and a similar assassination occurred in France in 1993 when Jacques Roseau, head of the association *Le Recours* for repatriated *pieds-noirs*, was killed as a result of his effort to establish closer ties with Algerians, for which he had become regarded as a "pro-Arab traitor."[38]

Traveling deeper into the most taboo and unspeakable memory path, Benaïssa's play *Mémoires à la dérive* exposes the "shared memory" of torture. The play opens in a Pirandello-like scene with an author stalled in the act of trying to write his play. The Algerian character as author, son of a *maquisard* "martyr" of liberation, is caught in the grips of a memory paralysis with blocked access to truthful memory. He feels helpless and betrayed by a History that was aborted—"on ne peut rien faire d'une Histoire qui est avortée"[39] [we can't do anything with an aborted History]—aborted because "it is denied, repressed, rejected." In an attempt to liberate the author "from the weight of History,"[40] his actors handcuff him to a suitcase and force him to undergo a surreal form of psychoanalysis under the guidance of a French Breton psychiatrist (actor 1). Only when he is able to converse with his resuscitated father, played by actor 2, can the son peel away the surface layer of the glorious image of the valiant freedom fighter *maquisard*, and interrogate the shameful legacy of torture exacted by the Algerian *maquisards* against their own countrymen (*harkis*), a practice reproduced by the recent generation of Algerian *maquisards*: the Islamists. With memories cut loose and going every which way, as suggested in the title "à la dérive," the psychiatrist (speaking as actor 1) facilitates the encounter, but turns out to be none other than a former *appelé* or French recruit during the war in Algeria. Implicated in the father's torture and ultimate death, actor 1 plays out his repressed complicity in the unspeakable acts of torture and violence committed by both Algerians and French.

As Diana Taylor points out, "social memory is . . . constituted not only by what communities remember, but also by what they choose to forget."[41] In the sordid game of memory retrieval conceived of by Benaïssa, the "shared" memory of mutual inhumanity is one that both sides strive to suppress. However, in order to be freed from the past, the author must force each side to assume its rightful share of memory and responsibility if his play is to reach completion. In *Mémoires à la dérive*, the blurring between victim and executioner, Algerian and French, Christian and Muslim, forces the witnesses of history to confront their past through a simultaneous process of "distancing" and mutual "sharing." In her discussion of forgiveness, Julia Kristeva compares psychoanalysis to the dual purpose of writing as "a way of coming out of the trauma, of forgiving oneself or the other and translating it for someone else. This constitutes a distancing from the place of the crime through sharing."[42] In this sense, Benaïssa's French and Algerian characters come to assume shared responsibility for the past, thus allowing the play to come to an end through a process of distancing, which, in turn, releases the repressed trauma of torture from its tyranny through the confessional act of sharing it.

Chouaki's attempt to exorcise the trauma of Algeria's spiral of terror takes a different approach to shared memory in *Les Oranges*. In keeping with what Kateb Yacine proclaimed in 1962 to be "a multinational Algeria," one that "must not be mutilated,"[43] Chouaki's play *Les Oranges* (1998) pulls together memory threads in the mythical construct of "le Royaume des Oranges" (the Kingdom of Oranges). This saga of identity begins in 1830 when the emblematic orange is pierced by the first fateful bullet of French colonialism. As the present-day narrator extracts the bullet, the fruit exacts a solemn promise from the narrator: he must keep alive this essential memory and bury the bullet only when "tous les gens de cette terre d'Algérie s'aimeront comme s'aiment les oranges"[44] (all of the people of this land of Algeria will come to love each other as oranges do). In a postmodern context of exchange between the supernatural presence of the talking orange and the hip-hop culture of the youth of Algiers, Chouaki then introduces the irrefutable scientific evidence of a computerized soil sample which confirms the exact composition of Algerian identity:

> ... avec Djaffar, un copain chimiste, qui a un ordinateur. On a déduit que dans un mètre cube de terre d'Algérie, il y a du sang phénicien, berbère, carthaginois, romain, vandale, arabe, turc, français, maltais, espagnol, juif, italien, yougoslave, cubain, corse, vietnamien, angolais, russe, pied-noir, harki, beur. Voilà c'est ça, la grande famille des oranges.[45]

> ...with Djaffar, a chemist friend who has a computer. We deduced that in a cubic meter of Algerian soil, there is the blood of Phoenicians, Berbers, Carthaginians, Romans, Vandals, Arabs, Turks, French, Maltese, Spanish, Jewish, Italians, Slavs, Cubans, Corsicans, Vietnamese, Angolians, Russians, *pieds-noirs*, *harkis*, *beurs*. There you have it: the extended family of oranges.

From there, the sensual imagery of luscious fruits ushers in the communal act of sharing the fruit when Chouaki celebrates the contribution of *pied-noir* Albert Camus, not for his Nobel Prize, but for his way of cutting a watermelon:

> Mais je m'en fous de tout ça, de son *Étranger*, de son prix Nobel. Bien que ce soit. ... Non, ce qui me fascine le plus chez lui, Albert, c'est sa manière de découper la pastèque. Au lieu de découper des quartiers, comme tout le monde, lui, non, Albert. Il prend la pastèque à bras-le-corps et coupe de larges tranches rondes, comme ça chacun il a un peu de cœur.[46]

> I don't give a damn about his *Stranger* or his Nobel prize, however good it all is. ... No, what fascinates me about Albert is the way he cuts a watermelon. Instead of cutting it in quarters like everyone else, Albert, he holds it under his arm and slices it in large round slices; that way, everyone gets a little bit of the heart.

In keeping with Camus' vision of Algerian and French writers united across borders "comme des frères de soleil,"[47] the end of *Les Oranges* issues forth what Jacques Berque would have considered "un geyser, occulté de l'avenir"[48] (a geyser, bursting with the future). Despite its graphic depiction of the atrocities of Algerian history, the play clings to a hopeful memory for the future. Even when confronted with the image of a five-year-old child trying to glue his father's decapitated head back on, the narrator resumes his undying dream: "Des nuits et des nuits, j'ai rêvé d'un pays des oranges, où langues, religions, couleurs, goûts, feraient tous le même bouquet"[49] (Night after night I dreamed of a country of oranges, where languages, religions, colors, tastes, would all be part of the same bouquet). Rejecting the conclusion of a failed past, Chouaki paints a horizon of friendship and renewal between *pieds-noirs* and Algerians, so that in the end, even the "impossible return" of the *pieds-noirs* is realized:

La semaine prochaine, il y a Roger et sa femme, qui arrivent. Des anciens pieds-noirs du quartier. C'est la troisième fois qu'ils viennent. Déjà c'est la bagarre pour les inviter, tout le monde veut les sortir.[50]

Next week, Roger and his wife arrive. Former *pieds-noirs* from the neighborhood. It'll be their third visit. Everyone's already fighting over who'll get to have them over; everybody wants to take them out on the town.

What Chouaki alludes to as a fantasized return visit of *pieds-noirs* to Algeria in *Les Oranges*, is, in fact, the focal point of exchange in *Au loin les caroubiers* by Fatima Gallaire. In this play, a French couple and their grown children, invited by their former neighbors from Algiers to make a return visit to Algeria, come to celebrate their reunion and the anniversary of fifteen years of Algerian Independence. The idea for the play took shape when *pied-noir* director Jean-Christian Grinevald commissioned Gallaire to write a play about Algeria entitled *Sans une goutte de sang* (*Without a Single Drop of Blood*).[51] For Gallaire, living in France and "continuant, loin d'Algérie, à souffrir pour l'Algérie"[52] [continuing, far away from Algeria, to feel the pain of Algeria], the play also provided an opportunity to replace the tragic proportions of history and rupture with the simple shared memory of daily life as experienced by Arab and French families and their children. In gleeful anticipation of seeing their long-lost neighbors again, the Algerian mother, Tama, recalls the fateful moment of separation: "Nos amis. Ceux qui ont été si proches de notre cœur, si proches qu'ils l'ont emporté avec eux en partant . . . adorateurs de Jésus et de Moïse, oui, nos amis . . . les amis d'une vie. Ils vont revenir."[53] [Our friends, so dear to our hearts that when they left they took our hearts away with them . . . worshipers of Jesus and Moses, yes, our friends . . . the friends of a lifetime. They're coming back.]

For Gallaire, however, writing this play carried with it an enormous sense of responsibility; her approach to "this tragedy of history" was to construct it using music and the delicacy of a language similar to that of Chekhov with "une écriture en filigrane d'or qui ne blesserait personne"[54] (a golden filigreed language that would hurt no one). Nevertheless, to obscure the untold pain and forgotten horror of the past would be to abdicate responsibility in disclosing the full story of Algeria. So even in the face of a jubilant reunion of the families as the Algerian mother Tama lovingly embraces Chris, her "French son,"[55] that is, the son of her former *pied-noir* neighbors, the page cannot be turned without event. At the moment when Enrico, a friend of Chris, begins a song in Arabic, a minor character, Fred, barges in and launches into accusations aimed at the French father formerly known as "El Commissar." Witness to the joyful reunion between the two families, Fred, a French Algerian who stayed behind, finds it impossible to restrain his gangrenous memory of Algeria's wartime past. Despite attempts by the others to recall a more positive tone in recognition of Algerian liberation no matter the cost, Fred remains stalled in his mutilated memory. Ultimately, Fred forces both families, their children, and their children's friends to stare into the sordid recesses of his own personal and long-repressed crisis of memory.

In the repetitious act of reliving the anguish of his past, Fred's destructive "acting out" ultimately leads to his own confession of guilt: he was the anonymous "taupe" or secret informer who had turned over the names of local youth to the ruthless secret forces, including Kader, the son of Tama, who underwent the unspeakable horrors of the "interrogation." Filled with self-loathing, the self-exposed traitor goes into a fit begging his judges and victims for physical punishment and torment, though they refuse to engage in such a despicable form of punitive "justice." In the end, the Algerian and French fathers help the pathetic Fred back to his feet and accompany him home before resuming the festivities of renewal:

> Hé les amis, on ramène Fred chez lui. Nous reviendrons de suite. Laziza, refais du café. Les garçons à vos guitares. Nous allons fêter dignement ce jour de fête, ce jour de retrouvailles, ce jour d'indépendance![56]

> All right, now, friends, we're taking Fred back home. We'll come right back. Laziza, make up some more coffee. Boys, get your guitars ready. We'll have a proper celebration on this happy day of reunion, this day of independence!

Published in the early 1990s, *Au loin les caroubiers* provides a way to experience life beyond the destructive effects of the Algerian War and to draw upon personal lived experience from a vantage point of fifteen years. Written in a moment of renewed hope for Algerians and before the growing tide of armed conflict between the government forces and Islamists, the play rehearses a dual process of renewal and reckoning. Both generations, parents and children alike, prove resilient to the destructive forces of the past, and draw strength from their shared memory and common ancestry as "Mediterranean" peoples in the broadest sense. The play joins together generations of varied backgrounds, including Chris's young musician friend Enrico, who calls himself Arab-Jewish, and who playfully describes the tumultuous nature of "Mediterraneans" with their penchant for extremes, "C'est toujours comme ça chez nous les Méditerranées. On mélange tout, le rire et le pleur, le deuil et la fête, la dispute et l'amitié . . ."[57] [It's always like that for us Mediterraneans. We mix everything together: laughter and tears, mourning and celebration, arguments and friendship . . .] In an odd mixture of painful memory and present joy, the play manages to face squarely the bitter realities of the past in its willingness to "crev[er] l'abcès" (lance the abscess) and speak freely of Kader's torture in "la baignoire et l'électricité dans les couilles"[58] [in the bathtub with electric shocks to the testicles], without sacrificing the desire to imagine a new future. Forgiveness and pardon are readily granted by the French and Algerian families who usher Fred back to his isolated corner of amputated memory to lick his wounds. Even though the *caroubiers* (carob trees) in the title have been felled with Chekhovian inevitability, the cherished and tender memories of the past still reverberate eerily with an unquenchable longing for reconnection as the play closes with the same melodic lute music as at the beginning. As in the other plays, we see once again an example of what historian Philip Naylor called the "astounding bilateral resilience" of the French-Algerian relationship with its capacity to recover, despite "recurrent psychodramas [. . .] and other less spectacular crises."[59]

The final play under study here, *Les Mimosas d'Algérie* by French author Richard Demarcy, illustrates the healing power of communication and witnessing across generations situated within the context of French-French relations during the war. After much searching, Demarcy finally came upon *the* subject that made it possible for him to create a play about the Algerian war when he read Jean-Luc Einaudi's documentary work *Pour exemple—L'Affaire Fernand Iveton* in 1988. Based on the incident of a communist factory worker condemned to the guillotine for acting as a helpmate to fellow Algerian workers, Demarcy reconstructs the memory of French life both for a child and an adult in Algeria between 1954 and 1962. Demarcy's play retraces the memory pathway of a granddaughter who returns to Algeria from France after over thirty years of separation to visit her grandmother. Determined to journey deep into the recesses of her unexplored past, Christiane resolves to discover the truth about the silence surrounding the mystery of her father's death in Algeria in 1957. Demarcy's story revisits the repressed past of France's brutality against those citizens judged to be acting as traitors in support of the Algerian independence movement. As in the case of Iveton, the shocking death by guillotine was designed to deter other would-be sympathizers.

The play performs the tender yet painful extraction of memory from an isolated aging woman who stayed behind to live out the only life she had ever known in Algeria. Her repressed memory is reactivated when the granddaughter seeks to understand why she had always felt like "une enfant coupable sans savoir de quoi"[60] [a guilty child who didn't know what she was guilty of]. The delicate back and forth movement between the two characters recreates the intricate process of witnessing accomplished largely due to the granddaughter's skillful and supportive insistence. When the adult Christiane demands to know the truth of her father's death, no matter how painful, the old woman recoils at the thought of "telling": "Non, non, je veux oublier. Tais-toi, tu me fais souffrir. Tu es revenue pour me faire souffrir"[61] [No, no, I want to forget. Be quiet. You're making me suffer. You've come back just to make me suffer]. Conversely, for the granddaughter, the pain of the grandmother's "not telling" is unbearable. Both are held hostage to an unexplored memory which left both women feeling isolated and disconnected both from the past and the present. If left in this unarticulated state, memory could cause even more suffering in what Dori Laub described as the "perpetuation of its tyranny."[62] Thus, Christiane insists, "Si, parlons, parlons doucement de tout, même de l'horreur, maman. . . . Il faut, apprivoiser notre douleur, doucement"[63] [But yes, let's talk, let's talk tenderly about everything, even the horror, grandma. . . . We have to bring our sorrow under control, tenderly]. In preparation for the ceremonial telling, the grandmother collects a bouquet of mimosas and places it on the dinner table where she has set three places signaling the ever-present absence of her son. Culling through a box of newspaper clippings, the old woman recounts the events. Weakening near the end, she asks Christiane to read the final account of her father's gruesome death by guillotine.

With the newfound knowledge that her father was not the traitor she had imagined, the daughter reclaims the lost memory of her father as a hero, as one of the few "à avoir eu le courage, un des seuls à avoir compris vers où allait l'histoire, un des rares pieds-noirs ici, fraternel d'abord"[64] [to have had the courage, one of the few to have understood where history was headed, one of the exceptional *pieds-noirs* to be fraternal above all else]. With pride in her father's humanity and courage, the daughter solidifies her memory in a final material gesture that puts order into the jumbled pieces of her family's past. Asking her grandmother for glue so that she can put back together the pieces of a photo of her father, she assumes rightful ownership of an image she had torn up long ago in a fit of anger and resentment.

In a dual process of "acting out" and "working through" the trauma of the past, the play depicts two parallel performative acts. In the case of the grandmother, the process is one of witnessing, with the past replayed in what Taylor terms *living through,* a process described by Felman and Laub as "repossessing one's life story."[65] Providing the grandmother with a critical distance and a compelling need to share, the granddaughter enables both women to come together in a "'claiming' experience,"[66] and to do so in such a way that "the events of this past will matter again."[67] After spending the entire night in a vigil of mourning over their "dead one," the two women recover the delicate beauty of the "mimosas" in the title. The ultimate "restorative potential" of this journey into the past ends in the young woman's resolve to bring her own children and husband back to share in her reconnection to her past in Algeria. More importantly, however, the play transmits a significant social memory that history has largely neglected or suppressed: the memory of solidarity between Algerians and certain *pieds-noirs* in the struggle for independence.

Featured as part of the Year of Algeria, the play was performed both in France and in Algeria to enthusiastic audiences. In describing his belief that "each society must do memory work," Demarcy considers this mutual search for a truthful past to be "une cérémonie heureuse" (a joyful ceremony), not designed to arouse anger or hate, but rather to instill a sense of peace.[68]

By situating both the trauma and the intermittent joy of the French-Algerian past in relation to the present, each play retrieves memory in a constructive way so as to reassign new meaning to once unexamined, repressed, or otherwise mutilated memories. In this way, "the past is replayed in the present—both as a symptom of distress . . . and as part of the healing process."[69] The fact that all but Demarcy's play were written by Algerian exiles, themselves casualties of Algeria's ongoing crisis of national identity, suggests a desire to resuscitate a neglected layer of shared cultural memory born of a multiethnic Algerian community decimated by the draconian politics of Arabization and the more recent tyranny of radical Islamist groups. In contrast with the stagnant memory of "nostalgérie" and a defunct utopian past, these plays seek to revive the Camusian dream of communality and interconnectedness. As members of a generation old enough to have known the trauma of the past, yet desirous of healing and reconciliation, these authors seek to reinfuse painful memories with vital elements for a renewed future of French-Algerian shared experience. As the last generation to have experienced this shared identity, Benaïssa, Chouaki, and Gallaire now assume the responsibility of bearing witness, not only to the initial trauma of the war and its aftermath, but more importantly to the ongoing trauma of exile, of loss, of forced separation, and of dashed hopes for a democratic and pluralist Algeria. Although the dream of a thriving and free Algeria held by many Algerians in 1962 goes unfulfilled, it may still be possible, as these and other creative works illustrate, to recall in some measure the human dimensions of a shared hope for the future. In "Le Rêve algérien" ("The Algerian Dream"), filmmaker Jean-Pierre Tlemcen replays the dream of French-Algerian solidarity in a documentary that retraces the dream as lived by *pied-noir* Henri Alleg, whose life was spent as an activist for Algerian independence.[70] From his indictment of French torture in the famous work *La Question* to his decision to remain in Algeria from independence in 1962 until the coup d'état of 1965, Alleg, at age 82, is living proof of another significant but neglected link in the memory of a shared past.

What then is the hope for the future of shared French-Algerian memory? For historian Benjamin Stora and others, it may reside only with the current generation, free of responsibility for the past, those now able to finally "turn the page," and read it only as "a page of their history" without the "noise" from the past.[71] Yet, for the authors examined in this study, theatre exists as a unique site where even "un passé sans devenir" (a stalled past)[72] can come to life again, and parts of a "page déchirée" (torn out page) from the history books can be read anew. For both the French *pieds-noirs* and Chouaki's *pieds-noirs musulmans*, the collective memory of a shared past, albeit full of holes ("ce passé troué"), when combined with the distancing effect of "exile," might provide a sharpened vision of French-Algerian memory with its recognition of the other. In *Reflections on Exile*, Edward Said describes this unique capacity for memory to affect the future: "Since almost by definition exile and memory go together, it is what one remembers of the past and how one remembers it that determine how one sees the future."[73] Similarly, Naylor points to the value of the shared history and heritage of hybrid communities that join France and Algeria. He applauds their insistence on "claiming an identity, becoming visible," for, in his estimation, these groups hold "great untapped potential to help Algeria and France resolve their . . . postcolonial transformation of identities."[74] Thus, in different ways, each play seeks to reinfuse memory with Rokem's "restorative potentials" in the hope of moving toward a more constructive vision for what Berque calls "mémoire de demain" (memory for tomorrow) "d'un avenir encore refoulé"[75] (of a future still repressed).

Notes

1. Aziz Chouaki, "Confitures et bobos," in *Une enfance outremer*, ed. Leïla Sebbar (Paris: Éditions du Seuil, 2001), 72. Beginning with the title, Chouaki's playful language rebounds from "bobos" as the scrapes of childhood to "bobos" as trendy bourgeois bohemians. With "à part entière" it revives de Gaulle's famous phrase during the Algerian War emphasizing the uniformity of French identity for all: "il n'y aura que des Français à part entière, avec les mêmes droits et les mêmes devoirs" (there will only be French people in the full sense of the word, with the same rights and responsibilities).

2. Alain-Gérard Slama, "L'Exode des pieds-noirs," *Les Collections de l'Histoire* 15, (2002): 86.

3. Hostility toward the *pieds-noirs* was severe, as remarks by the mayor of Marseilles and others indicated in 1962. See Alain-Gérard Slama, *La Guerre d'Algérie, histoire d'une déchirure* (Paris: Découvertes Gallimard, 1996), 122.

4. Michèle Baussant, *Pieds-noirs, mémoires d'exils* (Paris: Stock, 2002), 7.

5. Jean Pélégri, *Ma mère l'Algérie* (Arles: Actes Sud, 1990), 33.

6. Earlier labels expressed oppositional relationships during the war: *harkis* (Muslim soldiers who fought for a French Algeria), *porteurs de valise* (French Algerians who supported Algerian freedom fighters), or *Francaouis* (*pied-noir* term for the French in France). In post-1962, naming reflected new generational identities for their offspring in France, such as *beur* (*verlan* or back formation slang for *arabe*) or the more politically motivated *passerelles* (footbridges) claimed by the children of the *harkis*.

7. Mireille Rosello describes the dilemma of naming in "Farança-Algéries ou Djazaïr-frances? Fractales et mésententes fructueuses," *MLN* 118, no. 4 (2003): 804, and affirms

the need to "compose," and to recognize the unending process of discovering "des positions de 'sujets' encore en devenir" (subject positions still in the making).

8. Baussant, *Pieds-noirs*, 253.

9. Freddie Rokem, *Performing History* (Iowa City: University of Iowa Press, 2000), 3.

10. Rokem, *Performing History*, 3.

11. "L'Année France-Algérie 2003," www.piedsnoirs-aujourd'hui.com/avis0037.html (3 April 2003).

12. Gilles Bonnier, "Collectif 'L'Année de quelle Algérie?'" 2003, www.bartolini.fr/bone/titre_rubrique/annee_2003/collectif.html (13 November 2004).

13. Slimane Benaïssa, Interview with Thierry Guichard, "L'Écrivain comme un juge de paix," *La Matricule des Anges* 44, (July 2003):18.

14. Mona Chollet, "Slimane Benaïssa, dramaturge algérien," *Périphéries*, January 1998, www.peripheries.net/g-bena.htm (1 April 2004).

15. Rokem, *Performing History*, xii.

16. Rokem, *Performing History*, xi.

17. Rokem, *Performing History*, 3.

18. Richard Demarcy, "Mémoire vivante," Introduction to *Les Mimosas d'Algérie* in *Acteurs* 96-97 (1991), 76.

19. Demarcy, "Mémoire vivante," 77.

20. "Aziz Chouaki: Humour et poésie: Entretien avec l'auteur," in *L'Étoile d'Alger*, in *Algérie Littéraire/Action* (October 1997): 112.

21. Aziz Chouaki, *Baya* (Alger: Laphomic, 1989), 106.

22. Chouaki, *Baya*, 78.

23. Chouaki, *L'Étoile*, 112.

24. Chouaki, *Baya*, 79.

25. Chouaki, *Baya*, 79.

26. Chouaki, *Baya*, 79.

27. Chouaki, *Baya*, 81.

28. "Aziz Chouaki: 'L'Humour c'est le maquis suprême. Entretien avec Maïa Bouteillet,'" *UBU* Spécial Théâtres d'Algérie 27/28 (2003): 49.

29. Chouaki, "L'Humour c'est le maquis," 49.

30. Chouaki, "L'Humour c'est le maquis," 49.

31. Dominick LaCapra, *Writing History, Writing Trauma*. (Baltimore: The Johns Hopkins University Press, 2001), 142-43.

32. LaCapra, *Writing History*, 143.

33. Chouaki, *Baya*, 149.

34. See Janice B. Gross, "The Tragedy of Algeria: Slimane Benaïssa's Drama of Terrorism," *Theatre Journal* 54 (2002): 269-387.

35. See chapter "The Politics of Othering," in James D. Le Sueur's *Uncivil War: Intellectuals and Identity Politics During the Decolonization of Algeria* (Philadelphia: University of Pennsylvania Press, 2001), 214-255. Quoting Jacques Berque, Le Sueur traces the destructive politics of attacking the "Other." When France kept the Algerian at a distance as the "Other," "it jeopardized its own future" (237), just as Algeria's adoption of Othering reached unprecedented levels of violence as "the hallmark of an ongoing civil war." (255)

36. Slimane Benaïssa, *Les Fils de l'amertume* (Carnières: Éditions Lansman, 1997), 24-5.

37. Benaïssa, *Fils*, 25.

38. Benjamin Stora, "Préface à l'édition de 1998," in *La Gangrène et l'oubli* (Paris: La Découverte, 1998), ii.

39. Slimane Benaïssa, *Prophètes sans dieu* suivi de *Mémoires à la dérive* (première version), (Carnières: Éditions Lansman, 2001), 55.

40. Benaïssa, *Mémoires à la dérive*, 55.

41. Diana Taylor, "Yuyachkani: Remembering Community," in *Performing Democracy*, ed. Susan C. Haedicke and Tobin Nellhaus (Ann Arbor: University of Michigan Press, 2001), 312.

42. Julia Kristeva, "Forgiveness: An Interview," Trans. Alison Rice, *PMLA* 117.2 (2002): 287.

43. Kateb Yacine, *Le Poète comme un boxeur* (Paris: Seuil, 1994), 52.

44. Aziz Chouaki, *El Maestro* suivi de *Les Oranges* (Paris: Éditions THEATRALES, 2000), 31.

45. Chouaki, *Les Oranges*, 49.

46. Chouaki, *Les Oranges*, 39.

47. Text addressed to Emmanuel Roblès as cited by Jean-Jacques Gonzales, "Une utopie méditerranéenne, Albert Camus et l'Algérie en guerre," in *La Guerre d'Algérie, 1954-2004, la fin de l'amnésie*, ed. Benjamin Stora and Mohammed Harbi (Paris: Robert Laffont, 2004), 597-620.

48. Jacques Berque, *Il reste un avenir* (Paris: Arléa, 2002), 86.

49. Chouaki, *Les Oranges*, 66.

50. Chouaki, *Les Oranges*, 69.

51. Fatima Gallaire, *Au loin, les caroubiers* suivi de *Rimm, la gazelle*. (Paris: Éditions des Quatre-Vents, 1993), 3.

52. Gallaire, *Au loin*, 3.

53. Gallaire, *Au loin*, 8.

54. Gallaire, *Au loin*, 3.

55. Gallaire, *Au loin*, 22.

56. Gallaire, *Au loin*, 47.

57. Gallaire, *Au loin*, 36.

58. Gallaire, *Au loin*, 45.

59. Phillip C. Naylor, *France and Algeria: A History of Decolonization and Transformation* (Gainesville: University Press of Florida, 2000), 288.

60. Richard Demarcy, *Les Mimosas d'Algérie*, Acteurs 96-97 (1991): 87.

61. Demarcy, *Les Mimosas*, 85.

62. Dori Laub, "Truth and Testimony: The Process and the Struggle," in *Trauma, Explorations in Memory*, ed. Cathy Caruth (Baltimore: The Johns Hopkins University Press, 1995), 64.

63. Demarcy, *Les Mimosas*, 84.

64. Demarcy, *Les Mimosas*, 87.

65. Taylor, "Remembering Community," 322.

66. Taylor refers to Caruth and Laub in "Remembering Community," 323.

67. Rokem, *Performing History*, xii.

68. Richard Demarcy, "Faire de l'histoire une fiction," www.Djazair2003.org/ceuxquifont.php?art=26 (4 August 2003).

69. Taylor, "Remembering Community," 322.

70. Shéhérazade Hadid, "Humble parmi les humbles," *JA/L'Intelligent* 2239 (December 2003): 83.

71. Benjamin Stora, "Le Retour de la mémoire," *Les Collections de l'Histoire* 15 (2002): 107.

72. Baussant, *Pieds-noirs*, 6.

73. Edward Said, *Reflections on Exile and Other Essays* (Cambridge: Harvard University Press, 2002), xxxv.

74. Naylor, *France and Algeria*, 265.

75. Berque, *Il reste*, 86.

Index

About the Contributors

Joshua Cole is Associate Professor of History at the University of Michigan. He is the author of *The Power of Large Numbers: Population, Politics, and Gender in Nineteenth-Century France* (Cornell University Press, 2000) and a contributing author for *Capital Cities at War: London, Paris, Berlin, 1914-1919* (Cambridge University Press, 1997). He is currently working on the history and memory of several episodes of extreme violence that took place within the French imperial sphere in the post–World War II period.

Jean-Luc Desalvo is Associate Professor of French at San José State University in California. His areas of interest are nineteenth- and twentieth-century French literature and culture. His area of expertise is in Francophone (African, Caribbean, Canadian, and Vietnamese) literature and culture. He has published numerous articles and book chapters on contemporary Acadian literature and cultural issues in the works of Antonine Maillet and Claude LeBouthillier. He is the author of *Le Topos du mundus inversus dans l'œuvre d'Antonine Maillet* (International Scholars Publications, 1999), which represents the most comprehensive study to date of Maillet's literary corpus.

Sylvie Durmelat is Associate Professor in the Department of French at Georgetown University. Her areas of research include urban and migrant cultural productions in hexagonal France and Caribbean and North African literatures. She has published chapters and articles on literatures of immigration and film. Her book, *Fictions de l'intégration: Du mot beur à la politique de la mémoire*, is due out with L'Harmattan in 2005.

Janice Gross is Seth Richards Professor in Modern Languages at Grinnell College. Her recent publications are based on extensive interviews with Algerian playwrights in Paris and examine how theatre is used to perform the problematic nature of violence, terrorism, identity, exile, memory, and Islam. She is translator (with Daniel Gross) of Slimane Benaïssa's novel about 9/11 and the making of an Islamic terrorist, *The Last Night of a Damned Soul* (Grove Press, 2004).

Alec G. Hargreaves is Ada Belle Winthrop-King Professor of French and Director of the Winthrop-King Institute for Contemporary French and Francophone Studies at Florida State University. A specialist on postcolonial minorities in France, he has authored and edited numerous publications including *Voices from the North African Immigrant Community in France: Immigration and Identity in Beur Fiction* (Oxford/New York: Berg, 1991; 2nd edition 1997), *Immigration, 'Race' and Ethnicity in Contemporary France* (London/New York: Routledge, 1995), *Post-Colonial Cultures in France* (London/New York: Routledge: 1997), co-edited with Mark McKinney, and *Minorités postcoloniales anglophones et francophones: Études culturelles comparées* (Paris: L'Harmattan, 2004).

Susan Ireland is a Professor of French at Grinnell College. Her research interests include contemporary French fiction, Quebec women writers, the Algerian novel, and the literature of immigration in France and Quebec. She has published articles in these areas and with Patrice Proulx has edited *Immigrant Narratives in Contemporary France* (Greenwood, 2001) and *Textualizing the Immigrant Experience in Contemporary Quebec*. She is also an editor of *The Feminist Encyclopedia of French Literature* (Greenwood, 1999).

Hee Ko is a graduate student in history at the University of California at Berkeley. Her research and teaching interests include colonial theory and human rights history. She is completing her doctoral thesis on "Colonial Nostalgia and Islamic Nightmares: Memories of the Algerian War, the Rise of the Extreme Right, and the Remaking of French National Identity."

Alison Murray Levine is Visiting Assistant Professor of French at Colby College. Her publications in twentieth-century French cultural history and colonial history have focused on colonial tourism, colonial cinema, teaching colonial history through film, and the social uses of documentary film during the interwar years. In the field of contemporary French film, she has written on colonial nostalgia in contemporary cinema, film adaptations of literary texts, and 1990s social cinema. She is completing a manuscript entitled *Framing the Nation: Documentary Film in Interwar France* that chronicles the development of documentary film as a mass medium that was used to advance specific social agendas both in the French regions and in the French colonies.

Florence Martin is a Professor of French in the Department of Modern Languages and Literatures at Goucher College. She is on the advisory board of *Studies in French Cinema*. Her current areas of research and teaching are Twentieth-Century French and Francophone literature and cinema. Her publications include articles in such journals as *Studies in French Cinema, French Review, Études Francophones, CELFAN*, and book chapters published in England, France, and the United States. She is the author of *Bessie Smith* (Paris: Éditions du Limon, 1994) and the coauthor with Dr. Isabelle Favre of *De la Guyane à la Diaspora Africaine: Écrits du Silence* (Paris: Karthala, 2002). She is currently working on a book-length manuscript to be published in English on Francophone women filmmakers.

Nick Nesbitt is an Associate Professor of French at Miami University (Ohio). He has published extensively on Francophone literature and postcolonial and critical theory. He is the author of *Voicing Memory: History and Subjectivity in French Caribbean Literature* (University of Virginia Press, 2003). He is currently completing a book entitled *Universal Emancipation: The Haitian Revolution and the Singularization of the Enlightenment*.

Dayna Oscherwitz is Assistant Professor of French and Francophone Studies in the Department of Foreign Languages and Literatures, Southern Methodist University, in Dallas, Texas. Her areas of research include French cinema, African cinema, the Francophone novel, and contemporary French civilization with an emphasis on the way in which the colonial past has shaped and continues to shape contemporary France. She has published articles on Francophone writers such as Calixthe Beyala, Gisèle Pineau, and Patrick Chamoiseau. She is coauthor of *The Historical Dictionary of French Cinema* (Scarecrow Press, 2005). She is currently completing a manuscript entitled *On Common Ground: History, Memory and the Idea of Nation in (Post)Colonial France*.

Catherine Reinhardt is lecturer and coordinator of the teacher credential program in Modern Languages at California State University, Fullerton. She is author of the forthcoming volume *Claims to Memory: Beyond Slavery and Emancipation in the French Caribbean* (Oxford: Berghahn Books, 2005) and has published widely on race, slavery, and memory.

Mireille Rosello teaches French and Comparative Literatures at Northwestern University. Her main research interests are Francophone literatures and cultures (especially Caribbean, North African, and diasporic voices), gender constructions and visual narratives. She has written on surrealism (*L'Humour noir selon André Breton*, Corti, 1987), on French novelist Michel Tournier (*L'In-différence chez Michel Tournier*, Corti, 1990), on Caribbean literature (*Littérature et identité créole aux Antilles*, Karthala, 1992). Her latest publications are *Infiltrating Culture: Power and Identity in Contemporary Women's Writing* (Manchester University Press, 1996), *Declining The Stereotype: Representation and Ethnicity in French Cultures* (University Press of New England, 1998) and *Postcolonial Hospitality: The Immigrant as Guest* (Stanford, 2002). Her new *France-Maghreb: Performative Encounters* is forthcoming (University of Florida Press).

Nicole J. Simek is a graduate student at Princeton University. Her research focuses on French West Indian literature, and she is currently completing a dissertation entitled "Altered Exemplarity: Critique and Commitment in Maryse Condé's Novels." In addition to forthcoming articles on Caribbean women's autobiography and French dramatist Philippe Minyana, she has published work on Baudelaire, Boileau, and female friendship.

Marie-Pierre Ulloa is completing a doctoral thesis on French Cultural History (1945-1970) in the Department of History at the Institut d'Études Politiques de Paris. She is a visiting scholar at Stanford University. Her areas of research include cultural issues in France after World War II, decolonization, and film studies. She is the author of *Francis Jeanson, un intellectuel en dissidence. De la Résistance à la guerre d'Algérie* (Paris: Berg International, 2001). She also works for the San Francisco Arab Film Festival, where she is in charge of the selection of movies from France and the Maghreb.